Digital Forensics for Legal Professionals

Digital Forensics for Legal Professionals

Understanding Digital Evidence From the Warrant to the Courtroom

Larry E. Daniel
Lars E. Daniel

Robert Maxwell, Technical Editor
Sue Spielman, Technical Editor

AMSTERDAM • BOSTON • HEIDELBERG • LONDON
NEW YORK • OXFORD • PARIS • SAN DIEGO
SAN FRANCISCO • SINGAPORE • SYDNEY • TOKYO

ELSEVIER

Syngress is an imprint of Elsevier

SYNGRESS

Acquiring Editor: Chris Katsaropoulos
Development Editor: Heather Scherer
Project Manager: Danielle S. Miller
Designer: Alisa Andreola

Syngress is an imprint of Elsevier
225 Wyman Street, Waltham, MA 02451, USA

Library of Congress Cataloging-in-Publication Data
Daniel, Larry (Larry E.)
  Digital forensics for legal professionals : understanding digital evidence from the warrant to the courtroom / Larry Daniel and Lars Daniel.
    p. cm.
  ISBN 978-1-59749-643-8
  1. Electronic discovery (Law)–United States 2. Evidence, Documentary–United States. 3. Electronic records–Law and legislation–United States. 4. Computer files–Law and legislation–United States.
    I. Daniel, Lars (Lars E.) II. Title.
  KF8902.E42.D36 2011
    347.73'64—dc23

                                                                                    2011028669

British Library Cataloguing-in-Publication Data
A catalogue record for this book is available from the British Library

ISBN: 978-1-59749-643-8

Printed in the United States of America
11 12 13 14 15   10 9 8 7 6 5 4 3 2 1

For information on all Syngress publications visit our website at www.syngress.com

Contents

SECTION 2   EXPERTS

Preface

There is a tremendous knowledge gap in our legal system today when it comes to matters involving digital evidence. In our years of experience in working with attorneys as digital forensics experts, common questions arise again and again: What do I ask for? Is the evidence relevant? What does this item in the forensic report mean? What should I ask the other expert? What should I ask you? Can you explain that to a jury?

While computers and digital devices work on the binary system of simple on or off or yes or no, digital evidence cannot be interpreted in such a simplistic manner. One of the greatest mistakes that can be made is to look at any digital evidence in isolation without properly considering all of the processes, inputs, and outputs that can impact the interpretation. If the only answer to a piece of digital evidence were, "It's there or it isn't," there would be little need for experts in the field to do any more than act as data recovery technicians. No bit of digital evidence is truly isolated in such an absolute fashion; it requires that the evidence be interpreted in light of all of the processes, inputs, and quirks of the various computer operating systems and software, as well as the interaction of people with the machines.

In many cases, this knowledge gap has put attorneys in the position of not knowing that digital evidence could make a difference in their cases, or has even caused a tendency to avoid dealing with digital evidence altogether.

This book is our contribution to filling that knowledge gap so that people who are in the legal system can have a better chance to understand the evidence that is involved and presented in cases and in courts.

INTENDED AUDIENCE

This book is intended for anyone who works with digital evidence in legal matters. While it was specifically written for attorneys and judges, this book can benefit law students, digital forensics students, and criminal justice students as well. Also, anyone who is responsible for managing the IT department for corporations and law firms can use this book to gain an understanding of the many issues to be considered when dealing with digital evidence.

And for those in management, and human resources, this book can provide an overview of the types of evidence that can be present on employees' computers, and how and why computer and cell phone evidence should be preserved in case of future litigation.

ORGANIZATION OF THIS BOOK

This book consists of four main sections, which are as follows:

- Section I: Overview of Digital Forensics
- Section II: Experts
- Section III: Motions and Discovery
- Section IV: Common Types of Digital Evidence

Section I: Overview of Digital Forensics

Chapter 1: Digital evidence is everywhere and permeates every aspect of the average citizen's life. No matter what you are doing these days, a digital footprint is probably being created that contains some type of digital evidence that can be recovered. Sending an e-mail, writing a document, taking a picture with your digital camera, surfing the web—all of these activities create digital evidence. This chapter will give an overview of what digital evidence is, how it is created, and where it is stored.

Chapter 2: In this chapter, we discuss a short history of personal computers, computer forensics, and the basic tenets of digital forensics. Digital forensics includes the acquisition, preservation, analysis, and presentation of electronic evidence, no matter where it may come from. This chapter gives a brief overview of the four areas of digital forensics and explains the importance of each.

Chapter 3: Originally the field of digital forensics only included computers, primarily personal computers. Over the last 20 years or so, as computers have become connected through small local networks and ultimately through the largest network of them all, the Internet, the term computer forensics has become too limited to encompass the entire field. In this chapter we provide an overview of the various subdisciplines in digital forensics.

Chapter 4: Digital forensics is a relatively new field compared to traditional forensic sciences. Digital forensics began as computer forensics in the early 1990s and has expanded with the introduction of new technology such as cellular phones, digital cameras, global positioning devices, and the explosive growth of Internet usage. With that comes the issue of whether or not there are established best practices and who is following them. What best practices should digital forensics examiners be following, why, and what are they really doing?

Chapter 5: In the realm of digital forensics, there are a variety of tools in use today. There are tools for acquiring digital evidence and tools for analyzing digital evidence. There are three types of digital forensics software in use today: commercial tools, open source (free) tools, and tools developed for and available only to law enforcement agencies. In this chapter we take a look at the different types of tools and who uses them. We will also review the requirements for a tool to be "forensically sound."

Chapter 6: Digital forensics evidence is used in many ways in legal matters not only as part of civil and criminal trials, but also during the pre-trial and post-trial phases. Sometimes a forensic examination can result in charges being dropped, sentences being reduced, and civil matters being settled, all without ever going to trial. The other side of the coin is that the result of a forensic examination may help a defendant to understand that going to court is too risky versus taking a plea bargain. In this chapter we will look at how some of these roles are played out through case examples and example trial questions.

Section II: Experts

Chapter 7: When digital evidence is part of a case, it can be dangerous to proceed without an expert. Experts worth their salt are needed to help you get the evidence, find the information you need, and then analyze that information to find data that is useful to your case. Experts can act as an equalizer, and this is especially true when the opposing side has an expert themselves. To proceed in a case where the other side has an expert and you do not can lead to undesirable results in litigation. A qualified digital forensics expert can guide you through the intricacies of digital evidence in a way that makes sense in your case. This chapter will explain why you need to employ an expert when you are dealing with electronic evidence and why employing an expert is a time-sensitive task.

Chapter 8: With the ready access to computer technology and the explosion of people who support that technology, a gap has formed between those that know and those that do not. Because computer and digital technology has grown so rapidly in just a matter of a few years and become an integral part of our society, we have a technology generation gap. Those who were not raised with computers tend to be left behind in the understanding of how these devices work. The problem is that people who know something about computers appear to know more than they actually do. The ability to fix your computer, help you get you hooked up to the Internet, or even restore your crashed computer has no bearing on forensically examining a computer. In this chapter we explain the differences between digital forensics experts and computer experts.

Chapter 9: This chapter covers how to go about locating and prequalifying an expert. Also included are recommended selection criteria as well as an explanation of the currently available certifications and what they mean. Additionally, we will give you the information you need to avoid getting burned by an expert with a "reputation."

Chapter 10: Depending on the type of service you need in a particular case, an expert should be expected to assist you with all of the steps regarding digital evidence. Many attorneys and commercial clients are dealing with digital evidence for the very first time, and there is a significant knowledge gap as to the handling of cases involving digital evidence. It is the expert's role to bridge this gap by assisting the attorney in identifying and obtaining evidence through discovery, reviewing expert reports and providing an assessment of the case, making sure that any evidence is properly collected and handled in a forensically sound manner, educating the attorney about the specific evidence in the case, and assisting the attorney with trial preparation. This chapter will explain what this process looks like and how it should proceed.

Chapter 11: Digital forensics experts are products of their background, education, and experience. For this reason, different types of examiners take different approaches to the same problems. This can result in a wide disparity in the quality and efficacy of the results of their work in a case. These differences show themselves not only in the examiners' approach to an examination of the actual evidence but their approach to the entire case.

Chapter 12: An expert must be technically proficient in digital forensics—this is a given. However, the other skills needed to see a case to the end are often overlooked. In this chapter we will explain the challenges an attorney will face in employing and using a digital forensics expert, as well as how to spot problems early before you put the expert on the stand.

Chapter 13: Qualifying an examiner as an expert in court appears to be a very straightforward process on the surface. However, making sure you know what the minimum qualifications should be for a computer forensics expert or other type of digital forensics expert is important for two reasons: One, can the examiner you have engaged qualify as an expert? And two, does the expert on the other side have the necessary qualifications to testify as an expert? It happens too often that someone will try to pass themselves off as a forensics expert when in fact they have no training or experience in the field. Persons with computer experience alone, no matter how extensive, are not forensic experts and should not be allowed to qualify as such.

Section III: Motions and Discovery

Chapter 14: With the ubiquitous nature of digital evidence, it may seem as if finding and recovering digital evidence is a simple task. It is not. There are legal and technical barriers to obtaining digital evidence that must be overcome in every instance involving electronic data. Depending on the type and location of the evidence, if one can even make that determination, there are legal hurdles to cross before you can obtain that evidence, whether it is protected in some way by the Stored Communications Act (SCA), Electronic Communications Privacy Act (ECPA), HIPAA, Fourth Amendment protections against unlawful search and seizure, or expectations of privacy in the workplace.

Chapter 15: We will show how to analyze initial discovery documents to determine what digital evidence should be available to be discovered, as well as the language needed to get everything that is relevant for examination by an expert. We will also show you what to ask in order to get evidence that was collected but not examined or copied due to technical limitations of law enforcement agencies. We will also cover some not-so-obvious items that are helpful to get during the discovery process.

Chapter 16: Methods for getting the evidence in civil cases are different than those in criminal cases because civil cases are governed by different rules. In this chapter we briefly discuss the rules governing civil discovery. We also begin laying out the process for determining what to ask for and where it might be and take a walk-through approach of the method by using a case scenario. Also included are simple examples of civil discovery orders for electronic evidence.

Chapter 17: In this chapter we cover the language needed to get discovery of computer and storage media. We include here examples of language you can use for simple discovery orders, restraining orders, and a consent to search form. These are only examples and should be modified to suit your individual case.

Chapter 18: Whenever you must deal with video evidence, in any format, you will want to attempt to have the evidence properly preserved by specifying early on that the evidence is not to be viewed on the original media. Taking immediate steps to issue a preservation order for the evidence and specifying that the evidence is to be properly handled, preserved, and copied are critical elements in having evidence that can be used in litigation.

Chapter 19: In order to have the best results possible in any enhancement or forensics work performed against an audio recording, it needs to be treated with care during the processes of collection, preservation, and copying. Also, simply getting a copy of the recording without specifying the output format and copy process may not be the best option, as there are numerous factors with audio recordings that can cause deterioration in the audio quality.

Chapter 20: Social media evidence is a factor in more and more cases, both civil and criminal. Getting this type of evidence poses a challenge both from the standpoint of properly asking for the evidence but also in the ability to get the evidence due to both technical and legal barriers. In this chapter we will look at some of the methods for crafting subpoenas to obtain social media evidence from service providers.

Chapter 21: Cases involving contraband, specifically child pornography, require that you follow specific rules to make sure that you get what you need in the case and also can get access to the evidence to be examined by a digital forensics examiner. In this chapter we will discuss how to go about handling discovery in a child pornography case.

Chapter 22: In this chapter we will look at various types of record requests and include the technical language for those requests. We have included links to web sites where you can locate the custodian of records for nearly all of the Internet service providers. We show you how to find the custodian of records for a web address by following a step-by-step process you can perform using your Internet-connected computer, and we also show how to obtain subscriber information for web-based e-mail accounts.

Chapter 23: Evidence in cases involving Global Positioning Systems (GPS) can be a vital factor. Gathering that evidence can be a challenge as the data or evidence being sought can reside in several places: on physical devices, at third-party service providers, and as backups or data downloads. In this chapter we will look at where the data might be found and the motion language to use to make sure you get all of the evidence for analysis by your GPS expert.

Chapter 24: Call detail records are used in many criminal cases to attempt to determine where a subject was from the cell tower location information. Getting the right records can make a difference in being able to properly analyze and interpret this type of evidence. This chapter covers what to ask for and how to ask for it to make sure you get everything possible.

Chapter 25: Anyone who deals with indigent clients knows that request-ing funding is a basic part of getting an expert engaged. In this chapter we pro-vide some sample language for an Ex Parte Order for Expert Funds as well as some information regarding dealing with extraordinary expense requests by covering some of the questions that a judge may want clarified in a case where you may need to engage a nonlocal expert, and the answers to those questions.

Section IV: Common Types of Digital Evidence

Chapter 26: Hash values play an important role in digital forensics, especially in verifying that a forensic image of digital evidence is exactly the same as the origi-nal; a digital fingerprint if you will. When asked on the witness stand, any examiner should be able to show that he or she took the proper steps to verify the evidence collected using hash values for verification of the forensic copy against the original evidence.

But to ignore the benefit of hash values in a case beyond simply verifying evi-dence does them a great disservice. If a particular file is of interest in your case, hash values can be used to find that file buried just about anywhere in a compu-ter, even if the name of the file has been changed. Hash values can be used to link one device to another, such as a USB thumb drive to a computer, which can be particularly useful in cases that involve data theft or the distribution of contraband. Likewise, hash values can be used to help prove that something does not exist on a computer or other digital device. A good examiner knows the importance of hash values and how to use them. In this chapter we will highlight some of the more common uses of hash values and how you can put them to work in a case, and we will share some examples of how we have used them ourselves.

Chapter 27: Metadata can be a veritable gold mine of useful information in a case. The prefix meta in English is used to express the idea that some information is about its own category. Hence the meaning of metadata is "data about data," just as metacognition means "knowing about knowing." While this might seem somewhat cryptic, when you get down to the nuts and bolts, metadata is not hard to understand. Metadata is found inside a file, kind of behind the scenes where an ordinary com-puter user will not see it. It stores useful information that the operating system uses to make a computer user's experience easier and more enjoyable. The information stored within metadata can be used to build timelines, establish alibis, and so much more. In the hands of a skilled digital forensics expert, metadata can shed light on a particular issue in a case, or be the turning point altogether. In our experience as examiners, we have seen tiny snippets of metadata change how entire sequences of events were interpreted.

Chapter 28: When you open a folder like your My Pictures folder, you can view the files in a thumbnail format, like a bunch of small pictures. These small pictures or thumbnails are stored in a special file called a thumbnail cache database. These thumbnail databases can be read using special software and used as evidence in both civil and criminal cases.

Thumbnail caches are used in a wide variety of cases, mostly to attempt to establish whether or not an image file existed on the computer at some point in the past, even if that purpose is to corroborate some other piece of digital evidence.

Chapter 29: One of the foundations of digital forensics is data recovery. Luckily for digital forensics examiners, truly deleting data on digital devices, especially computers, is quite hard to do. This chapter explains the ins and outs of how a computer works when it deletes data, and the different ways it does so. Usually in digital forensics, it is not a matter of whether data still exists or is really gone. The black and white are thin lines bordering the chasm of grey when it comes to deleted data. Usually it is just a matter of to what degree the data has actually been deleted. This chapter will explain the different levels of deletion, such as the Recycle Bin and unallocated space, and how this data is recovered and used.

Chapter 30: Computer time stamps play a role in many cases, both civil and criminal. Computer time artifacts are undoubtedly one of the most important forms of digital evidence. They play a critical role when establishing a timeline for a body of evidence for any case where time is important. If the case involves an alibi, computer time artifacts can be used as part of a body of evidence to negate or validate the alibi claims. If the case involves data theft, computer time artifacts can be used to help determine when the alleged theft occurred.

The purpose of this chapter is to familiarize you with the complexity of interpreting the date and time stamps recorded by computer operating systems and applications. To completely cover the subject of computer time stamps would require an entire technical book.

Chapter 31: As you surf the Internet, the web browser you are using saves information to your computer in temporary storage. This process of saving web pages and documents in temporary storage is called Internet browser caching or web caching. The purpose of web caching is to improve the experience of the computer user as he or she browses the Internet. In this chapter we cover what web caching is and how it is used as evidence.

Chapter 32: A shortcut or link file is a pointer to a file in a different location, which is called the target file. Link files are used liberally by the Windows operating system, and they can be created in numerous ways. A user can create a link file intentionally, for example, by placing a shortcut on the desktop, or they can also be created by Windows, without the user's knowledge. The overall purpose of a link file is to enhance the user's experience as he or she navigates a computer. A link file can help you find documents you recently opened or quickly open a program on a computer via an icon placed on the Windows desktop. Digital forensic examiners certainly appreciate the convenience link files lend to the experience of using a computer, but they appreciate much more the trail of digital bread crumbs that link files leave sprinkled about. Link files can be used in a case in many ways, such as helping establish timelines, proving or disproving the existence of a file on a computer, and showing the transfer of a file from one device to another.

Chapter 33: Call detail records are coming into play more often in cases every day. The purpose of the call detail records is to attempt to place the cell phone user in a geographical location based on the tower used by the cell phone to send or receive a phone call, text message, or Internet data connection. This kind of evidence is fraught with potential misunderstanding by courts and juries alike and should be treated accordingly. This chapter gives an overview of cellular systems and looks at how the evidence is viewed in many cases.

Chapter 34: E-mail is probably one of the most prolific forms of evidence available today. It seems that everyone has an e-mail account, from children to octogenarians. With the availability of free e-mail accounts that can be set up in a matter of minutes, the number of e-mail accounts exploded in the late 1990s.

This chapter examines e-mail as evidence and how and where it is stored. Also included in this chapter are some case studies of e-mail used as evidence in actual criminal and civil cases.

Chapter 35: The widespread use of social media outlets such as Facebook, Twitter, MySpace, and LinkedIn ultimately means that evidence is continually being created, and is often available right in the public domain. The usage of social media does not require that someone be tethered to a computer anymore. Almost all social media outlets can be accessed using phones, iPads, and other mobile devices. And all of these can leave some type of evidence on a computer, a phone, or at a third-party service provider that can be collected for use in a criminal or civil case.

Chapter 36: There is no "server" needed for peer-to-peer file sharing. Every computer connected to the network is both a server and a workstation. As of this writing, one of the largest of the file-sharing companies, LimeWire, has been ordered to cease operations. However, the file-sharing community is still alive and well thanks to the many other providers of this type of software and services, such as FrostWire, BearShare, BitTorrent, and dozens of others. This chapter covers how the file-sharing system works and how evidence is obtained and used in cases.

Chapter 37: Cell phones can store more data and perform more functions than ever before. Today's smart phones can perform functionalities that were only possible with a computer a handful of years ago. Ultimately, this increase in complexity means that people tend to use their cell phones for more and more functions. In turn, the more functions someone can perform with a phone, the more data that phone stores, and that makes cell phones a tremendous source of potential evidence in all kinds of cases. This chapter covers the evidence available from cell phones, along with the proper methods for collecting and preserving cell phone evidence.

Chapter 38: Video and image evidence must be handled with great care, and any examinations or enhancements performed must be thoroughly documented. If the evidence is not received in the most viable format and preserved correctly, or if the examiner does not perform the forensic examination properly, it is possible to jeopardize the evidence by creating new evidence through the addition of image artifacts. In this chapter, we look at some of the ways that video and photo evidence is used in cases, and also at how evidence should be properly handled and enhanced. This chapter also shows some of the documentary methods that should be included with any enhancement to show exactly what was done in the enhancement process.

Chapter 39: The sole purpose of database systems is to allow for fast and accurate storage and retrieval of records. Data is the lifeblood of businesses from the smallest home business to global mega-corporations. This chapter explores how data is stored, how it is retrieved, and how it can be a factor in electronic evidence. We will also look at the challenges involved in getting data as evidence and at metadata, or data about the data, and its value as evidence.

Chapter 40: You have probably heard the phrase, "follow the money." This is true in all kinds of cases, from domestic disputes to Ponzi schemes and murder cases. Since so many people and businesses manage their money electronically today, there is a wealth of potential electronic evidence available residing anywhere from the Internet cache on a computer, to an e-mail attachment, inside an accounting program database, and even on a person's phone.

Chapter 41: Online gaming today is now the most popular form of gaming in the world. With the advent of high-speed Internet, it became possible for online gaming to really take off as a genre, and today tens of millions of people play games such as World of Warcraft, Everquest 2, The Sims Online, and Second Life. Console gaming units like the Xbox and PlayStation platforms now have online capability so that people can play together online. Where games like this exist, evidence also exists that can be used in investigations and legal actions.

Chapter 42: Global positioning systems, or GPS units, have become commonplace in modern society. As is true with any device that can record and store data, these devices can become a source of evidence in civil and criminal cases. In using GPS data as evidence, it is important to understand what impacts the accuracy of the data these devices produce as well as the potential for errors in analyzing the data. The first part of this chapter provides some background on how global positioning systems work, and how they store data that can become evidence in a case.

Acknowledgments

We want to thank Angelina Ward at Syngress for her encouragement to turn our idea into a book. Also, the assistance of many people at Syngress has been invaluable during the process of writing the book; we thank Heather Scherer who has kept us on track and assisted in the editing of the book, and our technical editors Robert Maxwell and Sue Speilman for making such insightful comments during the writing process that helped us to clarify many points throughout the book.

- Attorney James G. Connell, III for his invaluable insight and assistance in the section on Motions and Orders.
- Our friend and trainer, telecommunications expert Ben Levitan, for his help and critical review of the chapters on cell tower technology and call detail records.
- Attorney Parrish Hayes Daughtry for her encouragement and early review of some critical chapters.

Dedication

For my wife Erna, who has provided me with unwavering support and encouragement for the last 30 years. No matter how silly my ideas or risky my endeavors, she has been my anchor and safe harbor. She is the love of my life.

For my sons, Geoffrey and Lars; while they have taken different paths in life, they are both fine men in their own right, of whom I am forever proud.

Larry

God has poured out abundant grace on my life. Apart from God saving me through the atoning work of Jesus Christ on the cross, rescuing me from sin and death, this is nowhere more evident than in the instruction and love my parents have shown me.

For my mother; you have been a pillar of support and refuge of care. You have always been there when I needed you, ready with an encouraging word and sage guidance as I weather the storms of life.

For my father; you have taught me what it means to be a man. Your example of sacrifice, diligence, and indefatigable labor for the sake of our family has left an indelible mark on me. If I grow to become half the man you are, I will consider my life well lived.

Soli Deo Gloria
Lars

About the Authors

Larry E. Daniel is a Digital Forensics Certified Practitioner (DFCP), an EnCase Certified Examiner (EnCE), and a Blackthorn 2 Certified GPS Examiner (BCE). As a digital forensics consultant working with clients throughout the U.S. and handling all types of civil and criminal cases since 2001, Larry has completed over four hundred cases. He has qualified and testified as a computer forensics expert witness, a cell phone forensics expert witness, and a cell tower technology expert witness. Larry is a member of the American College of Forensic Examiners, an associate member of the National Association of Criminal Defense Lawyers, and a member of the American Society of Digital Forensics and eDiscovery. Larry has spoken at SANS, Techno-Forensics, Computer Enterprise Investigations Conference, Department of Defense Cybercrime Conference, and the NACDL National Conference, and has provided Continuing Legal Education training classes at bar associations and national- and state-level attorney conferences in Alabama, North Carolina, Tennessee, Virginia, California, Washington, Nevada, Illinois, and Louisiana.

    Lars E. Daniel is an EnCase Certified Examiner (EnCE) examiner and forensic artist. Lars performs computer and cell phone forensics, video and photo forensics, and audio forensics. Lars earned a bachelor's degree from the University of North Carolina with a concentration in Media Integration, and is a Photoshop expert. He has attended over two hundred hours of forensic training in computer and cell phone forensics and has qualified and testified as an expert witness. Lars has provided photo forensics, video forensics, audio forensics, and composite art services to law enforcement, criminal defense attorneys, and for the Vidocq Society. He has presented at dozens of CLE training events and conferences including the Computer Enterprise Investigations Conference.

About the Tech Editors

Robert Maxwell is the Lead Incident Handler for University of Maryland College Park, and the Founder and Managing Director of the Digital Forensics Lab at UMD, focused on education and curriculum development. He also coaches UMD's competitive CyberSecurity team, and is a Senior Contributor to Byte magazine. He lives with his wife and two children in bucolic Damascus, Maryland.

Sue Spielman serves as a consultant, technical, and testifying expert witness in legal matters pertaining to enterprise software and mobile development, object-oriented coding, domestic and international patents, IP, invalidity, and web application design/development and deployment. She is the President and Senior Consulting Engineer of Switchback Software LLC and can be reached at sspielman@switchbacksoftware.com.

What Is Digital Forensics?

Digital Evidence Is Everywhere

INTRODUCTION

Digital evidence permeates every aspect of the average person's life in today's society. No matter what you are doing these days, a digital footprint is probably being created that contains some type of digital evidence that can be recovered. Sending an e-mail, writing a document, taking a picture with your digital camera, surfing the web, driving in your car with the GPS on—all of these activities create digital evidence.

1.1 WHAT IS DIGITAL FORENSICS?

The term *forensics* can be defined as the application of science to a matter of law. The most accepted definition of digital forensics comes from the definition of computer forensics: computer forensics is the collection, preservation, analysis, and presentation of electronic evidence for use in a legal matter using forensically sound and generally accepted processes, tools, and practices.

Specifically, digital forensics is the application of computer technology to a matter of law where the evidence includes both items that are created by people and items that are created by technology as the result of interaction with a person. For instance, data created by a machine process requires that the machine be programmed to create data, and the machine must also be turned on by a person or even by an automatic process that is ultimately started by a person.

Data created as the result of an action performed by a person or user would result in data being recorded both manually and automatically.

The difference in those two types of data from an evidentiary standpoint is that when a computer or other device records data automatically through some process that is designed to be completed independent of user interaction, it is creating machine data; when data is stored or recorded in response to a user's actions, it is creating personal data.

Personal data should ultimately be attributable to an individual; however, making that attribution can be difficult due to the presence or absence of individualized user accounts, security to protect those user accounts, and the actual placement of a person at the same location and time when the data is created.

1.2 WHAT IS DIGITAL EVIDENCE?

Digital evidence begins as electronic data, either in the form of a transaction, a document, or some type of media such as an audio or video recording. Transactions include financial transactions created during the process of making a purchase, paying a bill, withdrawing cash, and even writing a check. While writing a check might seem to be an old-fashioned method that is not digital or electronic in nature, the processing of that written check is electronic and is stored at your bank or credit card company. Nearly every kind of transaction today is eventually digitized at some point and becomes digital evidence: doctor visits, construction projects, getting prescriptions filled, registering a child at daycare, and even taking the pet in for a rabies shot.

In today's connected world, it is nearly impossible to be completely "off the net" such that your activities do not create some form of electronic record.

The explosion of social media sites has created a whole new area of electronic evidence that is both pervasive and persistent. People today are sharing their everyday activities, their thoughts, their personal photos, and even their locations via social media such as Twitter, Facebook, and MySpace. Add to this the explosion of the blogosphere, where individuals act as citizen journalists and self-publish blog posts on the Internet ranging from their political views to their personal family blogs with pictures of their kids and pets.

In order for electronic data to become digital evidence, it must be stored somewhere that is ultimately accessible in some fashion; and it must also be recoverable by a forensic examiner. One of the great challenges today is not whether digital evidence may exist, but where the evidence is stored, getting access to that storage, and finally, recovering and processing that digital evidence for relevance in light of a civil or criminal action.

The potential storage options for electronic evidence are expanding every day, from data stored on cell phones and pad computers to storage in the "cloud" where a third-party service provides hard drive space on the Internet for people and businesses to store data.

More and more everyday computing processes are moving to the Internet where companies offer software as a service. Software as a service means that the customer no longer has to purchase and install software on their computer. Some examples of software as a service range from accounting programs like QuickBooks Online, Salesforce.com, or a sales management application to online games that are entirely played via the Internet with no required software installation on the local computer.

1.3 **HOW DIGITAL EVIDENCE IS CREATED AND STORED**

Whenever someone creates an e-mail, writes a document using Notepad or a word processing program, takes a ride in their car with the global positioning unit (GPS) turned on, or pays a bill online, they create digital evidence. Operating your computer, surfing the Internet, or making a phone call on your cell phone—all of these create digital evidence. Digital cameras, digital video cameras, web cams, and digital audio recorders all create digital evidence.

Those are the more well-known forms of digital evidence. However, it is easy to overlook the many ways in which we create digital evidence, many times without realizing we are doing so. If you play games online with other players, view videos from the Internet, shop at one of the thousands of online stores, create a shipping label through UPS, or even send a greeting card through Hallmark's online site, you are creating digital evidence. And don't forget about the copy machine at work. Chances are if it is a fairly new copier, scanner, and fax unit, it has a hard drive in it as well that stores data. That security camera you see yourself on at the local convenience store is making a digital record of your visit, as is the financial institution that processes the credit or debit card you just used to buy that pack of gum.

These days it is just about impossible to get through a day without creating some form of digital footprint. Even if you are completely "off the grid" and don't use a computer or cell phone, running a red light where there is a traffic enforcement camera can capture your license plate, noting your location, and of course, sending you a ticket in the mail and creating a digital record with all of that information. Figure 1.1 shows some of the many ways digital footprints are created.

In the beginning the only storage device available for personal computers was the floppy disk or audio cassette tape. When you wanted to share a file or document with someone, you had to save it to a floppy disk or cassette tape. Then you would mail the diskette or use the old "sneaker net" and jog yourself and the diskette over to the person who needed the file.

Today the storage technology available for the average computer user has evolved into multiple storage options including the floppy disk and hard drives. The floppy disk is beginning to disappear as a primary form of storage in favor of USB (Universal Serial Bus) thumb drives, portable hard disks, and online storage.

As a result of this incredible growth in storage options, today digital evidence can be found on everything from floppy disks to media cards, solid-state memory sticks, solid-state hard drives, cell phones, network attached storage devices, game consoles, media players, hard drives, and the "Internet cloud." The Internet cloud is a collection of companies that provide data storage and applications entirely based on having huge banks of servers and data stores, allowing businesses to access a large network and computer infrastructure without having to make large

FIGURE 1.1

Digital footprints are created all the time, whether you want them to be or not

investments in hardware and software. This allows businesses and individuals to have these resources available on a monthly or usage fee basis. The attraction of cloud-based storage and services is that the hardware and software needed are maintained and updated by the service provider and not by the individual or business. This is very attractive when a business does not want to make huge capital investments in buying hardware and software that must be maintained, secured, and updated on a regular basis.

The high-density 3.5-inch floppy disk could store 1.44 megabytes of data. Today, a user can attach a multiterabyte hard drive to a computer simply by plugging the device into an available USB port. Figure 1.2 illustrates the growth in storage capacity sizes over time.

As more and more people take advantage of remote storage for backups using online backup services such as Carbonite, Mozy Pro, and other solutions offered to store data on the Internet via cloud storage, it is becoming more of a challenge to track down where all the data might reside in a forensic case.

And speaking of the "cloud," there are now many applications and storage options available through such services as Google Apps, Google Docs, Microsoft's Windows Live Skydrive, Apple's Mobile Me, Dropbox, and many other Internet-based hard drive storage and data-sharing sites.

The most commonly used application for users who want to connect with one another is e-mail. E-mail is also one of the most commonly sought forms of digital evidence in all types of cases, civil, criminal, or domestic. In the early days of networked computing, e-mail was primarily a function of corporate networks that had some form of e-mail server such as Novell's GroupWise, Lotus Notes, or Microsoft Exchange as well as various other types of server-based e-mail systems.

A 1 Terabyte hard drive
is equal to
728,178 Floppy Disks

FIGURE 1.2

Growth in data storage capacity has been exponential since the introduction of the personal computer

There were e-mail programs that predated these applications; however, they are not of interest in this book because they are either not publicly accessible or they are no longer in service anywhere. While we could spend a lot of time covering all of the e-mail applications that have come and gone, detailing a complete history is not the purpose of the book. Our concern here is identifying digital evidence that you might encounter in legal actions today. E-mail can be stored on mail servers in large databases, on personal computers in the form of personal folder files, offline folder files, or e-mail databases created by the e-mail client being used.

In addition to corporate e-mail systems, there are now dozens of free public e-mail providers available to anyone with access to the Internet. Services such as Yahoo Mail, Microsoft's Hotmail and Live Mail, America Online's AOL Mail, Gmail, and dozens of others have made e-mail available to the masses. These accounts are typically free to use, require no real authentication of the user's identity, and are widely used for both benign and nefarious purposes.

E-mail services like those previously mentioned are entirely browser-based, where the user reads and sends their e-mail via Internet Explorer, Firefox, Google Chrome, or Safari, to name a few. E-mails from these browser-based services can many times be found in the Internet cache on the computer. (See the section "How Internet Browser (Web) Caching Works" in Chapter 31). Online-only e-mail can also be recovered from the company that provides the free e-mail service such as Yahoo, Microsoft, Google, and America Online (AOL).

More recently, as the social media phenomenon has exploded with applications such as MySpace, Facebook, Twitter, and LinkedIn, a new area of digital evidence has emerged dealing with these online applications. Not only can users create and post their own personal user profiles via these applications, but nearly all of them support both their own e-mail and chat functionalities.

Internet chat rooms are popular not only with people discussing hobbies, but also with people who are into the swinging lifestyle, child predators, cyber bullies, and people who are conducting illicit affairs. These same chat rooms are frequented by law enforcement personnel conducting online investigations into child predator activities, where they pose as underage children and make arrangements to "meet" the child predator in a sting operation. You can see how this works by watching the popular "To Catch a Predator" series on MSNBC. These chat room types of applications have been around since the early 1990s in the form of Internet Relay Chat servers. America Online, CompuServe, and Prodigy also provided their users with chat services early on in their incarnation. Today, services like Yahoo Chat, MSN Chat, AOL Chat, mIRC, Facebook Chat, and dozens of others offer millions of users the ability to chat with one another, both one-on-one via a friends list or in public and private rooms created by the users themselves.

Internet chats can be hard to recover since many of the programs people use to chat with others do not store a log of the chats on their local computer by default. In some instances, chat logs are stored by the chat service provider and can be recovered via subpoena. Even though the chat program may not automatically be storing logs of the chats, many times fragments of the chats can still be recovered from the user's hard drive.

Peer-to-peer file sharing has grown immensely in the last decade through the introduction of Napster, followed by Kazaa and LimeWire and finally BitTorrent. These applications create a way for personal computer users to form networks to share files, without any knowledge of how the networks operate or any special setup to get connected and start consuming and contributing to the shared content.

Since there is no central server or provider for peer-to-peer file sharing, there is no custodian of records to contact to obtain information. Any information that can be recovered from these applications must come from the computer that is using the peer-to-peer software.

Cellular phones began as radio telephones that could do no more than connect two phones over a short distance for the purpose of voice communications between two parties on the same radio network. Today, cellular phones are full-blown computers that can do everything a computer can do in a tiny package. Cell phones have become a gold mine of digital evidence. Whenever a cell phone is used to make a call, send an e-mail or text message, or used as a push-to-talk radio, a record is created by the cell phone company that can later be retrieved and used as evidence. The phones themselves record contact lists, call logs, pictures, video, e-mail, text messages, and in some cases, even GPS location information. Everything a cell phone does that uses the cellular network is recorded by the phone company. However, there are limits as to how long some of the data is stored by the phone company.

Digital cameras record not just pictures, but data about the pictures themselves. Inside the file created when the user snaps a picture, the camera records data such as the make and model of the camera, the date and time the picture was taken, the focal length and shutter stops. Depending on the model of the camera, there are many options for how the pictures are stored prior to being deleted or transferred to a computer or other storage device. Digital cameras can store their pictures on floppy disks, DVDs, CD-ROMs, and media cards.

SUMMARY

In this chapter we learned what digital evidence is, how it is created, some of the places it is stored, and the many ways that people are now connected electronically. We also learned about digital footprints and how they are created not only by you, but by others on your behalf. Digital evidence is everywhere, and knowing where it is and how to get access to it is half the battle.

Overview of Digital Forensics

INFORMATION IN THIS CHAPTER:

- Digital forensics
- A little computer history
- A brief history of computer forensics
- Computer forensics becomes digital forensics

INTRODUCTION

The widespread adoption of personal computers beginning in the early 1980s led to the need for computer forensics. Digital forensics began as computer forensics in the mid 1980s with the creation of the Federal Bureau of Investigation's Magnetic Media Program. In this chapter, we give a brief overview of the rise of the personal computer and the creation of computer forensics. We also look at how computer forensics became digital forensics and provide an introduction into what digital forensics is.

2.1 DIGITAL FORENSICS

Digital forensics is the application of forensic science to electronic evidence in a legal matter.

While there are many different subdisciplines and many types of devices, communication, and storage methods around today, the basic tenets of digital forensics apply to all of them.

These tenets encompass four areas:

- Acquisition
- Preservation
- Analysis
- Presentation

Each of these areas includes specific forensic processes and procedures.

2.1.1 Acquisition

Acquisition is the process of actually collecting electronic data. For example, seizing a computer at a crime scene or taking custody of a computer in a civil suit is part of the acquisition process. Making a forensic copy of a computer hard drive is also part of the acquisition process. In the digital forensics field, examiners refer to making these forensic copies of evidence as "acquiring" a hard drive rather than copying a hard drive. This is to avoid the confusion that could be caused by using the term "copy," since making a copy of something does not imply that the copy was made in a forensically sound manner.

Acquisition is the first step in the forensic process and is critical to ensure the integrity of the evidence. As acquisition is the first contact with the evidence, it is the point where evidence is most likely to be damaged or destroyed. Simply turning on a computer can lead to the modification of hundreds of evidentiary items including files, date and time stamps, introduction of new Internet history, and the destruction of files that could be recovered from areas of the hard drive that are in the area of unallocated space (see the section "Deleted File Recovery" in Chapter 29).

2.1.2 Preservation

As evidence is collected, it must be preserved in a state that is defendable in court. Preservation is the process of creating a chain of custody that begins prior to collection and ends when evidence is released to the owner or destroyed. Any break in the chain of custody can lead to questions about the validity of the evidence. Additionally, preservation includes keeping the evidence safe from intentional destruction by malicious persons or accidental modification by untrained personnel.

A chain of custody log best illustrates an example of preservation. Chain of custody logs should include every instance that a piece of evidence has been touched, including the initial collection of the device storing the evidence, the transport and storage of the evidence, and any time the evidence is checked out for handling by forensic examiners or other personnel. At no time should there be a break in this chain.

2.1.3 Analysis

Analysis is the process of locating and collecting evidentiary items from evidence that has been collected in a case. In a case involving spousal infidelity, the evidence that must be located can include e-mails and chat logs between the spouse and the paramour. In a fraud case, financial records would be the target of the analysis, as well as the possible deletion of records involving financial transactions. In a child pornography case, locating contraband pictures and movies would be the target of the examination. Each case is unique in this respect as the circumstances surrounding each case can vary widely, not only in the evidence being sought, but also in the approach used to perform the analysis. The analysis portion is also the area where the individual skills, tools used, and the training of the forensic examiner have the greatest impact on the outcome of the examination. For information on forensic tools used by examiners, see Chapter 5. Considering that electronic evidence appears in so many forms and comes from so many disparate locations and devices, the training and experience of the examiner begins to have an ever-greater impact on the success of the examination.

The analysis phase is also where the greatest disparity begins to become a factor between the skills and approach of a "computer expert" and those of a computer or digital forensics expert. While a computer expert may understand many aspects of computer usage and data, a properly trained forensic expert will be well versed in recovering data as well as in proper examination techniques.

Analysis of digital evidence is more than just determining whether something like a file or e-mail message exists on a hard drive. It also includes finding out how that file or e-mail message got on the hard drive, and if possible, who put the file or message on the hard drive.

2.1.4 Presentation

Presentation of the examiner's findings is the last step in the process of forensic analysis of electronic evidence. This includes not only the written findings or forensic report, but also the creation of affidavits, depositions of experts, and court testimony. There are no hard and fast rules or standards for reporting the results of an examination. Each agency or private entity may have its own particular guidelines for reporting. However, forensic examination reports should be written clearly, concisely, and accurately, explaining what was examined, the tools used for the examination, the processes used by the examiner, and the results of that examination. The report should also include the collection methods used, including specific steps taken to protect and preserve the original evidence and how the verification of the evidence was performed.

In general, a digital forensics report should include

- Background and experience of the examiner
- Tools used in the examination
- Methods used to verify the data
- Processes used to recover and extract the data
- Statement of what the examiner found
- Actual data recovered to support the statement of findings.

2.2 A LITTLE COMPUTER HISTORY

In the early days of personal computing, there were no networks accessible to the general public, and very limited storage options. The original personal computers to reach an audience outside of the pure hobbyist realm were the IBM Personal Computer, the Apple computer, the Commodore PET, and the Tandy TRS-80.

However, big businesses were still using mainframe computers and dumb terminals for their business applications such as word processing and financial tracking. This would soon change.

The IBM PC, introduced in 1981, would eventually become the de facto standard for all personal computers, resulting in the term "IBM compatible." With the introduction of Lotus 1-2-3, a financial spreadsheet program, IBM personal computers began to make inroads into the corporate computing world, driven by the desire of financial managers to have the ability to create electronic spreadsheets. Lotus 1-2-3 became the "super app" that drove sales of IBM personal computers and had a huge impact on the growth of the personal computer industry. As the demand for personal computers grew, companies like Compaq began to produce "IBM clones," making inroads into the market dominated by IBM. To combat this, IBM introduced Micro Channel Architecture (MCA) in an effort to force companies to purchase IBM parts in order to be compatible. However, the effort failed, and IBM soon returned to building personal computers using a common architecture based on industry standards.

Today, all computer hardware is based on well-known industry standards. The computing platform chosen by consumers today is driven more by aesthetics and specific software preferences than any proprietary hardware platform. However, the dominance of the Microsoft operating system on corporate desktops has resulted in the majority of businesses choosing Microsoft Windows for compatibility with the vast number of vertical market software applications built on the Microsoft Windows platform. Vertical market software is software created for a specific group of users, such as a loan management software application, a document management application, or an automotive shop management application.

Today these applications have been extended beyond the personal computer to portable devices. The popularity of smart phones and pad computers like the Apple iPad and Motorola Xoom has revolutionized the way people work with business documents and e-mail in what amounts to a handheld portable office.

2.3 A BRIEF HISTORY OF COMPUTER FORENSICS

In 1984, the FBI created the Magnetic Media Program, which initially only handled three cases in its first year. The Magnetic Media Program later became the FBI Computer Analysis and Response Team (CART) program. At the end of 2009, the FBI had fourteen Regional Computer Forensic Labs (RCFLs) in operation, with two more under construction.

In addition to the FBI CART program, there are other law enforcement programs in operation today that deal with computer forensics. One example is the Internet Crimes Against Children (ICAC) task force, which trains local and federal law enforcement agents to investigate Internet predators and perform computer forensics. Another is Operation Fairplay, a program that provides software and trains law enforcement agents to investigate peer-to-peer file sharing for child pornography cases.

In recent years, there has been an explosion of growth in computer forensics in the private sector as well. This is primarily driven by electronic discovery in civil suits and internal investigations into employee conduct, and the prevention of data loss by internal and external agents. In addition, companies must protect their customers' private data stored on their servers by maintaining constant vigilance against attacks both from within and outside the organization. A breach by hackers into a corporate network poses a great financial and reputation risk to any company that is a victim of such an attack. A case recently in the news was the attack on Sony's PlayStation Network and their other major gaming network maintained by Sony Online Entertainment. In this case, the private information of millions of subscribers to these game networks was stolen, putting this information at risk of being used for nefarious purposes by the hackers who breached these networks.

2.4 COMPUTER FORENSICS BECOMES DIGITAL FORENSICS

As technology has progressed, the field of computer forensics has been forced to expand to cover other types of electronic data, created by a myriad of devices.

Originally, computer forensics examiners only had to be concerned with what evidence might reside on a single computer or floppy disk. With the advent of networked personal computers, and especially with the connection of those networked computers to the outside world, and to each other over the Internet, the field of network forensics or incident response has grown to be the largest area of digital forensics. Network forensics is the process of figuring out how a network has been attacked, stopping the attack, and attempting to locate the attacker. The incident response team that performs the network forensics will examine routers, firewalls, server logs, and other data to attempt to remediate and prosecute network intrusions. Governments and corporations spend billions of dollars each year attempting to protect networks from outside intruders, and when that fails, remediating the damage done when someone breaches a network and causes damage or steals information. As more devices have come online, new areas of digital forensics have also come online, such as cell phone forensics. It is no longer possible to look at a piece of electronic evidence in isolation, where the assumption is that the sum total of the data resides in one place, on a single computer or floppy disk.

With the war on terror, there has been a tremendous increase in demand for trained computer forensics personnel in the military who are able to properly seize and analyze computer data in the field and in the lab.

The tremendous growth of the Internet has also increased the demand for trained network and computer forensics personnel to assist in responding to attacks on corporate and government networks, cyber-warfare, and cyber-defense activities.

SUMMARY

In this chapter, we learned a brief history of the personal computer, computer forensics, and the transformation of computer forensics into digital forensics. We also looked at what digital forensics is and introduced the four areas of digital forensics: acquisition, preservation, analysis, and reporting.

Digital Forensics: The Subdisciplines

INFORMATION IN THIS CHAPTER:

- The subdisciplines

INTRODUCTION

Originally the field of digital forensics only included computers, primarily personal computers. Over the last 20 years or so, as computers have become connected through small local networks and ultimately through the largest network of them all, the Internet, the term computer forensics has become too limited to encompass the entire field. Because of this, most examiners who practice more than just computer forensics have taken to calling their discipline digital forensics.

The field of digital forensics has expanded to include network forensics as well, and includes such areas of expertise as investigating network security breaches, hacking attempts, and data theft.

With the introduction of computer processing into other devices, such as global positioning system (GPS) units, automobiles, truck black boxes, cellular phones, answering machines, copy and fax machines, and so forth, the field has expanded to add additional subdisciplines.

Each of the subdisciplines can be part of a digital forensic examiner's expertise, but not all have to be. Some examiners choose to specialize in one area, such as computer forensics, without ever adding cellular phone forensics or GPS to their repertoire of skills.

3.1 THE SUBDISCIPLINES

This is not a comprehensive list of all the subdisciplines in the digital forensics field. To enumerate and explain them all would be a book in itself. However, the subdisciplines covered in this chapter are the ones you are most likely to hear about or encounter in the course of your legal practice or as part of your business if you're involved in a legal matter involving some type of digital evidence.

3.2 COMPUTER FORENSICS

Computer forensics is the oldest of the subdisciplines that make up digital forensics. In many cases, practitioners only focus on this one area. Computers are often the main source of digital evidence in a case, and with good reason. Computers can contain a massive amount of useful information in a case in and of themselves. They also can contain useful information about other devices like USB thumb drives, cell phones, digital cameras, and portable hard drives because almost all devices at one point or another circle back around to a computer. For instance, to create a backup of the information on your cell phone, it has to be connected to the computer. The same is true if you want to remove the pictures from a digital camera or USB thumb drive.

Computer forensics is primarily the examination of evidence found on a computer hard drive, such as user accounts, log files, time stamps, images, e-mails, and in some instances the examination of data on other hardware components within the computer, like the memory. The foundation of computer forensics is data recovery, and much of this subdiscipline revolves around that aspect.

3.2.1 Incident response

Some examiners consider incident response to be a subdiscipline of digital forensics, while others prefer to think of it as a field unto itself. There are many facets of incident response, and many books are dedicated to the field of network forensics or incident response, including network security, hacking and counter-hacking, intrusion detection, malware, and rootkits. That being said, the "incident" in incident response refers to a network security breach or attack. This attack can come from the efforts of a hacker, from a person within an organization, or from malicious code in the form of a worm, Trojan horse, or other malware. An incident response expert works to identify possible attacks against a network, determine whether the problem has spread and how to contain it, and then take measures to eliminate any malicious code. If necessary, steps will be taken to restore the data that has been compromised with clean backup files. Incident response experts also work to educate information technology (IT) personnel within an organization on how to protect their network with the appropriate security measures.

For a more complete treatment of incident response, we suggest visiting the SANS Institute website at www.sans.org where you can find numerous white papers and other information explaining incident response in detail. In our opinion, the SANS institute is the de facto standard in training and education for incident response professionals. Another excellent resource to learn more about incident response is the blog of Rob Lee, who is an industry leader in the area of incident response. You can find his blog at http://computer-forensics.sans.org. We also suggest the books by Harlan Carvey, a well-known practitioner in incident response. You can find Harlan's blog at http://windowsir.blogspot.com.

3.2.2 **Cell phone forensics**

Cell phone forensics includes the examination of cell phones, as well as the records created by cell phone service providers like cell phone billing information and call detail records (CDRs).

The examination of cell phones has become as common as the examination of computers due to their widespread use. This is easy to understand; just try to think of someone you know who does not own a cell phone. Cell phones contain a wealth of information, and examining them can recover data of evidentiary value. Some examples include the contacts on a phone, text messages, images, videos, audio recordings, and e-mail. Deleted information can be recovered on some cell phones as well. Due to the thousands of different models and makes of cell phones, in addition to the different types of cell phone networks and service providers, the ability to recover data from a cell phone is on a case-by-case basis. The general rule of thumb is that the more like a computer a cell phone is, a Blackberry or iPhone for instance, the greater the likelihood of being able to recover all of the data from it, especially deleted data.

While the number of digital forensic professionals who examine cell phones is increasing, the number of those who examine call detail records (CDRs) is growing at a much slower pace. Call detail records contain information about the numbers that were called from a particular phone, the duration of the call, the date and time of the calls, and the cell site information for cell phones. Cell site information can provide information as to the general location of a person and their movement based on their cell phone activity. However, using cell phone records to establish the whereabouts of a person by their cell phone activity is highly subject to the proper analysis of the cell site location information, the call detail records, and the correct historical analysis of the cell site data. Additionally, the United States has the emergency 911 location service, which is triggered whenever a person dials 911 on their cell phone. This type of geolocation of the person's cell phone can be very accurate and should not be confused with geolocation from cell site information. This is covered in detail in Chapter 37.

3.2.3 **GPS forensics**

A few years ago it was uncommon to see a car with a global positioning system (GPS) in it. As prices have dropped for GPS units, and the technology has gotten better, they have become much more common. Today, many vehicles have GPS tracking devices in them, such as rental cars, that the driver probably doesn't even know about. GPS forensics includes the examination of GPS units as well as GPS records. The examination of GPS units can yield information such as recently visited locations, favorite locations, and locations navigated to by address or street intersection. It is also possible to recover deleted information from many GPS units.

GPS records are also valuable as evidence, even if you cannot get the actual GPS unit. Records can be used to see the movement of a person or vehicle. By examining the data available in GPS units, it is possible to estimate how fast someone was driving, and if they made any stops and for how long.

If a person is suspected of a crime, GPS records can be helpful in determining if that person went to the location where the incident happened, whether they were ever near it in the vehicle, or if the timeframe even allows for the possibility of that person being a suspect. For instance, assume that a suspected person is accused of committing a murder at one location, and then dumping the body at another within a one-hour timeframe. If it takes an hour and a half to drive the distance from the scene of the incident to the location of the body, the plausibility of that argument based on GPS records takes a serious hit. However, it is also important to note that GPS units and GPS tracking are not perfect. There are situations where the recorded data can be highly suspect and have no correlation to the actual location of the GPS device. This can happen when a GPS unit's information is being collected by a third party and errors creep in due to data errors in the transmission of the GPS unit's locations, faulty GPS devices, and areas where the GPS unit may not have a clear view of the sky.

3.2.4 Media device forensics

Digital music players, digital audio recorders, personal data assistants, USB thumb drives, portable hard drives—these are media devices. The examination of media devices can provide useful data, including the files that exist on them and the recovery of deleted files from these devices. When they are plugged into a computer, these devices also leave information about themselves, such as the files that have been transferred to or from them and the time and date when these transfers took place.

There are many possibilities of finding data of evidentiary value on media devices. For instance, on a digital audio recorder, deleted audio recordings can be recovered. A music player, like an iPod, can be used like a portable hard drive to steal or hide data. Just because these devices might be designed with the intention to play music or keep up with your calendar, at their base level they are still storage devices, and most function exactly like a normal hard drive when connected to a computer.

3.2.5 Social media forensics

The past decade has seen an explosion of interest in the number and popularity of social media websites and programs. Programs like MySpace, Facebook, Twitter, and LinkedIn are commonly used social media outlets. It is common for people to have accounts with multiple social media outlets. For instance, someone might have a Facebook account to communicate with their friends and family, and a LinkedIn account to keep up with their business associates and other professionals. Social media has become the preferred method of communication for many, even surpassing e-mail in its popularity. This is especially true for the younger generations, who in many cases communicate solely via social media outlets.

Any type of communication inevitably leads to the possibility of evidence. The popularity of social media has brought about the need for social media forensics. This subdiscipline of digital forensics focuses on the ability to locate and examine social media communication on the Internet and as artifacts left on hard drives and cell phones. For instance, when a forensic examination is performed on a computer, social media programs could be installed, or data concerning websites like Facebook or MySpace could be found. This information could then be used to perform a social media investigation to find information about the online activity and communication of the person of interest.

3.2.6 Digital video and photo forensics

Digital video and photo forensics are grouped together for a reason. A photo is a still image, and a video is a sequence of still images. When you watch a video, it is a sequence of still images changing so fast that it appears as continuous movement. If you watch five minutes of television, you are actually watching thousands of still images changing so fast that the human eye cannot comprehend the individual slides. You can think of this like a cartoon flipbook. Each page has a particular drawing that is a still image. When you flip the pages quickly, however, the image appears to be in motion.

Digital video and photo forensics is the enhancement and analysis of these individual slides. The primary difference between video and photo forensics is that with a photo, you would enhance them one at a time, and with a video, you might enhance a thousand at a time. Stringent care must be taken in the enhancement and analysis of videos and photos. Either too much enhancement or the wrong kind of enhancement can damage the photo or video from an evidentiary perspective, because these processes can create anomalies or features within the photo or video that were not there originally.

3.2.7 Digital camera forensics

Digital cameras have all but replaced film cameras, with the exception of disposable cameras. A traditional film camera contains only the actual picture taken. A digital camera contains the pictures taken, and a great deal of information about the pictures themselves embedded as metadata. This metadata within a digital picture can include information of evidentiary value, like the model of camera used to take the picture, and the date and time the picture was taken.

It is possible to recover deleted pictures from a digital camera. Even if you do not have the camera itself, the pictures alone can be useful as evidence. If an examination is performed only on a computer, and pictures taken with a digital camera are found, the metadata within the pictures can be used to link them back to a specific camera.

3.2.8 Digital audio forensics

Digital audio forensics consists of the enhancement and analysis of audio recordings created with any type of digital recording device. Audio forensics can be used to verify the integrity of audio recordings, or to show that an audio recording has been tampered with. If a recording is of poor quality, it can also be used to enhance the audio track so that voices become more legible, or background noise that is of interest could be more easily heard.

It is also possible to perform voice pattern recognition with specialized forensic software. These software programs allow for the possible identification of voices with particular people within an audio recording. The software also has safeguards to reduce the possibility of a false positive. The other method of voice pattern recognition is the manual examination of a spectrograph. A spectrograph is a visual representation of auditory data. Just as sheet music is used to explain how a song should be performed using musical notes and how long the song should be, a spectrograph represents the different sound waves over time in frequency and intensity.

3.2.9 Multiplayer game forensics

The most popular form of games today is multiplayer games, especially Massively Multiplayer Online Role Playing Games (MMORPGs). There are tens of millions of people who play MMORPGs. These games typically consist of a person creating a character, with which they then explore an online world, level up, and join guilds and clans composed of other people who subscribe to the game. It is not uncommon for people to play online games for as much as 60 hours a week. We have seen instances where people have played a MMORPG for over 100 days in a single year. The 100 days is not the life of a character; it is in fact the actual amount of time a person is sitting in front of a computer, logged in to their character, and playing the game. The actual amount of time someone has spent playing one of these characters can be shown in the game itself by typing the */played* command into the game interface.

These games keep track of a lot of information about the people who play them. The programs store information about each session played and the length of that session, the in-game chat logs, and the characters associated with an account.

The records created by multiplayer games can be used to build timelines, establish alibis, and find in-game chatting of interest. Multiplayer online game evidence in covered in Chapter 41.

3.2.10 Game console forensics

Game consoles today, like an Xbox, Nintendo Wii, or Sony PlayStation, are all basically computers: they contain a hard drive just like a computer, and they operate using an operating system, just like a computer.

Since they are basically computers, they store information in a similar fashion. Many people use their gaming system to browse the Internet and watch movies, not just for playing games. This information is stored on the hard drive inside the gaming console. This means that information can be recovered, including deleted information from a gaming console.

To play games online using a console gaming system, a person must create an online account. With an Xbox, for instance, a person has to subscribe to Xbox Live. This creates information that can be used as evidence since that person now has an online identity, and parts of that information are saved on the gaming console.

A gaming console and a computer can be used in conjunction as evidence. With some games there is the option to have e-mails sent to you detailing your performance in a match. For instance, with the Madden football games, you can have an e-mail sent to you upon the completion of a game that details your performance. Information like this may seem insignificant, but it can be used to place the person at their gaming system at a particular date and time, and therefore establish an alibi.

SUMMARY

In this chapter we looked at a summary of the different subdisciplines in digital forensics, with a brief description of each. The purpose of this chapter was to look at a general overview of the different subdisciplines that make up the area of digital forensics and would most commonly be seen in legal matters involving electronic evidence.

The Foundations of Digital Forensics: Best Practices

INTRODUCTION

This chapter looks at who establishes best practices and what those best practices are. Specifically, this chapter provides a narrative of the processes for the collection and preservation of electronic evidence by forensic practitioners and first responders. This is not a step-by-step forensic collection manual, but an overview of the steps that should always be taken in the collection and preservation of electronic evidence, based on industry accepted best practices, when the evidence is being collected on scene or later on in the lab. It is important to know these best practices when assessing the validity and admissibility of evidence collected by anyone.

4.1 WHO ESTABLISHES BEST PRACTICES?

Guidelines published by the National Institute of Justice and the Association of Chiefs of Police set minimal standards for the collection and preservation of digital evidence. These guidelines are developed with the participation of law enforcement, government, academic, and industry practitioners. The best practices are then propagated to the industry through publications and digital forensic training programs. Certifications for persons in the field, such as the EnCase Certified Examiner (EnCE), the Computer Certified Examiner (CCE), the Access Certified Examiner (ACE), the Computer Forensics Certified Examiner (CFCE), and the GIAC Certified Forensic Analyst (GCFA), to name a few, reinforce these best practices by ensuring that the person being certified has a grasp of the proper procedures to correctly collect and preserve electronic evidence. These certification programs are covered in more detail in Chapter 9.

4.2 WHO SHOULD BE FOLLOWING BEST PRACTICES?

Anyone who proposes to work as a computer or digital forensics examiner should always follow the established best practices in the field. This is vitally important in a field where the results of the examiner's actions are to be used to provide evidentiary findings based on the collection, preservation, and analysis of evidence. Failing to follow accepted best practices leaves the work of the forensic examiner open to challenge and the possibility of the evidence collected being suppressed. The very least of the results of failing to adhere to accepted minimal best practices in the collection and preservation of evidence can be to cast doubt on the skills and qualifications of the examiner and the entirety of the examiner's work and potential testimony. It is also highly likely that an examiner will be questioned about these best practices when testifying in court.

4.3 SUMMARY OF BEST PRACTICES

Best practices apply to the collection and preservation of evidence. These are the two critical parts of ensuring that evidence will be accepted in a court of law as being authentic and an accurate representation of the original evidence. Modification of evidence, either intentionally or accidentally, can have a devastating effect on the entire case. Understanding best practices is critical for the legal professional so that attorneys and judges can properly assess the authenticity of the evidentiary findings. This is also critical for business and information technology professionals to understand that even if they are preserving evidence for the possibility of future litigation, these practices must be followed to protect the evidence.

If we look at preserving evidence as the overarching part of the collection and acquisition of digital evidence, we can see that the need to protect and preserve evidence begins *before* anything is collected, copied, or analyzed, and ends only at the final disposition of evidence. Whether that final disposition is to return the items collected to the owner, permanent seizure of the items by the government, or the destruction of that evidence via a destruction order, the preservation of the evidence must persist. In the digital forensic field, preservation is the overall protection of evidence, while acquisition is the actual act of making forensic copies of digital evidence either from hard drives, some other physical media, or live memory.

4.3.1 Volatile data and live forensics

Some evidence is only present while a computer or server is in operation and is lost if the computer is shut down. Evidence that is only present while the computer is running is called volatile evidence and must be collected using live forensic methods. This includes evidence that is in the system's RAM (Random Access Memory), such as a program that only is present in the computer's memory. These programs are considered TSRs or Terminate and Stay Resident programs. Many types of malware such as Trojan horse programs, viruses, and worms are designed to be only memory-resident programs, present in the computer's memory when it is operating, and they disappear when the computer is turned off, in many cases leaving no traces. There are also many types of other volatile evidence that are only available while the computer is running, including certain temporary files, log files, cached files, and passwords. RAM is cleared when the computer is turned off and any data that is present is lost. This can be a critical step if there is suspicion that any kind of data encryption is enabled that prevents the hard drive or portions of the hard drive from being viewed. In many cases the only way to recover the password needed to remove the encryption on a hard drive is to collect the "live memory" before the computer is turned off. Also, if the computer is running, the encrypted portion of the data storage would be accessible, but only until the computer is turned off, making it essential that the hard drive is copied while the computer is still turned on. There are tools available to make copies of RAM and hard drives on running computers and line-of-business servers that cannot be shut down, and still ensure that those copies are forensically sound.

4.3.2 **Preservation best practices**

As evidence is collected, it must be preserved in a state that is defendable in court. Preservation is the process of creating a chain of custody that begins prior to collection and ends when evidence is released to the owner or destroyed. Figure 4.1 shows the preservation process in graphical form.

Preservation steps include:

- **Identification:** Identifying the type and location of digital evidence can be a challenge. In order to prepare a subpoena or search warrant, it is critical to include any location and item in which digital evidence may reside in that particular case, including but not limited to computer hard drives, cell phones, digital cameras, GPS devices, and personal storage devices such as portable USB hard drives and even media players like iPods. This is the first step that precedes collections. It is not acceptable to simply collect everything once you get to a scene;

FIGURE 4.1

Preservation begins before data is collected and ends at final disposition

what you are going to collect must be previously identified in search warrant language and in civil subpoenas in order for the collection to be legal and allowable in a court of law. Collecting items not previously identified can cause that evidence to be suppressed in a legal action. Identification language must be specific and must have correct terminology; using language such as "CPU" instead of computer would mean that you can collect only the Central Processing Unit of a computer and not the computer itself. Collecting the CPU would be a waste of time since it does not contain any storage. Using language in which you specify collecting the "hard drive" would allow you to remove and collect the hard drive inside a computer, but not the computer itself. While the hard drive would contain evidence, you would not be able to verify the clock setting for the computer without access to the computer as a unit. This could lead to a challenge relating to the time stamps on files and activities on the computer hard drive since you would not have a method for verifying the time setting on the computer that created the time stamps. For more information, see Chapter 30.

- **Collection:** The collection step is critical since this is the first real contact with evidence. Not following proper collection procedures can lead to the destruction or modification of evidence, lost evidence, and subsequent challenges of the evidence collected. If someone attempts to collect a device and does not understand the proper methods to shut down the computer, operates the computer prior to shutdown, or shuts down a critical business server improperly, it can lead to data loss, civil liability for lost business, and the loss of critical evidence that could be collected prior to shutdown. Collection may include any or all of the following:

  - Photographing the evidence in place prior to collection or duplication.
  - Completing a complete inventory of each item including identifying information such as serial numbers, manufacturer, and descriptions.
  - Tagging each item for tracking and identification.
  - Securing each item to prevent inadvertent operation. This includes placing tamper-proof tape over power outlets, CD-ROM drives, USB ports, and floppy disk trays.
  - Bagging each item in a forensically sound manner, into a secure container that is sealed with tamper-proof tape to ensure that the evidence is not modified or damaged during transport.
  - Placing collected items in secure storage areas.
  - Proper check-in and check-out procedures with a maintained chain of custody for any access to or movement of the evidence.
  - Final disposition of the evidence, recorded in the chain of custody for any evidence that is released or destroyed.

4.3.3 Acquisition best practices

Acquisition is the part of the forensic process during which actual data is copied or duplicated. Following proper procedures is critical to ensure the integrity of evidence. The acquisition portion can be further broken down into two steps: duplication and verification.

- **Duplication:** This is one step that is easily performed incorrectly, especially if it is performed by someone who is not trained to properly duplicate electronic evidence. The only accepted method for duplicating electronic evidence requires that the original be protected from any possibility of alteration during the duplication process. This requires the use of accepted tools and techniques that allow the duplication of the evidence in a forensically sound manner. Using nonforensic methods will always lead to modification of the original evidence and/or incomplete copies of the original evidence that cannot be verified using forensic methods.
  - **Forensic method:** The proper forensic method for duplicating evidence from a computer hard drive or other media storage device requires the use of write-blocking of the original storage device. Write-blocking can be accomplished either by using a physical hardware device that is connected between the original (source) and the copy (target) hard drive (see Figure 4.2) or by using a special boot media that can start a computer in a forensically sound manner. The best option for making a forensic copy of a hard drive is to remove the hard drive from the computer, connect it to a physical write-blocker, and then use a forensic workstation and forensic software to make the copy. However, in some cases it is not practical to remove the hard drive. The computer may be of a type that makes the hard drive removal very difficult, such as some types of laptop. When this is the case, making a copy of the hard drive using a software write-blocking technique is the correct method. To use a software-based write-blocking method, the computer must be started up in a forensically sound manner. When a computer is first turned on, it goes through a set of steps, beginning with a Power On Self-Test (POST), followed by loading of the Basic Input

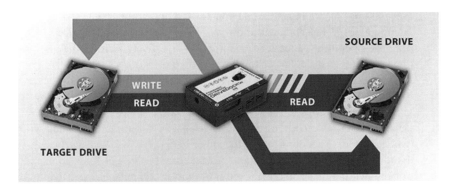

FIGURE 4.2

A physical write-blocker like the one shown here connected between the hard drives prevents any modification of the source hard drive

Output System (BIOS). The BIOS is software that is stored on the main board of the computer that tells the computer what types of hard drives are present; initializes the keyboard and other input and output ports, such as the USB ports; initializes the computer video card; and basically prepares the computer hardware to operate before it can load the operating system software. Settings in the BIOS tell the computer where to look for the operating system to start up, such as on a hard drive, from a floppy disk, a CD-ROM, or a USB device.

During normal operation, the computer will load the operating system installed on the hard drive, such as Microsoft Windows or the Mac OS. It is possible to prevent the computer from loading the operating system that is installed on the hard drive in favor of loading an operating system from a CD-ROM, floppy disk, or USB device.

When preparing to perform a forensic copy of a computer's hard drive(s), a forensic examiner would force the computer to load a special forensic operating system from a specially prepared boot media. This can be done by changing the settings in the computer BIOS to tell the computer to look for an operating system on a CD-ROM, a USB device, or a floppy disk. This can also be done by pressing a function key when the computer is first turned on to bypass the default setting in the BIOS for the startup location for the operating system. For instance, pressing F9 on many computers will bring up a menu where the examiner can choose which device to use to load the operating system. This can also be done on a Mac by pressing and holding the C key while powering on the computer.

This boot media can be a floppy disk, CD-ROM, or USB device that is specially prepared to load a forensically sound operating system. This is critical because when a computer starts up (boots) normally from the installed operating system, whether Windows or Mac OS or Linux, these operating systems automatically "mount" the hard drive(s) in read/write mode. This allows the user to read and write files, such as documents, to and from the hard drive.

Special boot media is media that contains an operating system that can start a computer up, but does not allow writing to the original hard drive. These forensic operating systems are modified to effectively turn off the ability of the computer to make any changes to the hard drive(s).

Once the computer is started up, either with a hardware write-blocker in place or by using a forensic operating system, the forensic examiner would make a forensic copy of the hard drive(s) installed in the computer.

Making a forensic copy of a hard drive means getting a "bitstream" copy, which is is an exact duplicate of the entire hard drive recording surface.

- **Nonforensic Method:** Personnel not trained in the proper forensic methods for duplicating electronic evidence may start a computer up and then make copies of the data on the hard drive. When a computer is started up in this manner, the operating system can write to the hard drive and change file dates, change log files, and other types of files, effectively modifying and destroying critical evidence. Figure 4.3 shows two hard drives connected

FIGURE 4.3

An unprotected hard drive will always be modified when a computer starts up

without any protection in place for the original evidence hard drive, putting the evidence at risk.

Nonforensic methods usually include just simply copying files from a hard drive to another storage device or using a backup program like Norton Ghost. While Norton Ghost has the ability to make a forensically complete (bitstream) copy, it is not generally accepted as forensically sound because Ghost copies are difficult to verify using hash values. (Hash values for verification are covered in detail in Chapter 26.) The reason for this is that Norton Ghost does not have a method for creating a hash value of the evidence being copied during the copy process. Additionally, a nonforensic copy of a hard drive will get only the data stored on the hard drive, such as documents, spreadsheets, and Internet history. A nonforensic copy will not get deleted files or areas of the hard drive where evidence can still reside that is not visible to the computer user.

- **Verification:** This is the final step in the forensic copy process. In order for evidence to be admissible, there must be a method to verify that the evidence presented is exactly the same as the original collected. Verification is accomplished by using a mathematical algorithm that calculates a number based on the contents of the evidence. Figure 4.4 illustrates the drive and file hashing process used to calculate the verification hash.

This is called creating a "hash value" and is performed by using either the Message Digest 5 (MD-5) algorithm or a Secure Hash Algorithm (SHA). The MD-5 is the most commonly used method for verification in computer forensics at this time. Forensic duplication tools automatically create a "verification" hash for the original and the copy during the duplication process. If these hash values do not match, there is an opening for a challenge to the authenticity of the evidence as compared to the original.

4.4 WHAT REALLY HAPPENS IN MANY CASES

The propagation of computers, cell phones, and other digital devices as potential evidence has far exceeded the resources of law enforcement to properly dissimilate

FIGURE 4.4

A hash value is calculated and stored for each data item copied and for the entire source hard drive

and train crime scene first responders in the proper best practices for handling this evidence on scene and in custody. In many cases, law enforcement personnel will modify evidence accidentally, simply because they do not have the training, or their department has not had the opportunity to establish procedures for handling digital evidence.

On the civil side, due to the lack of qualified examiners for hire, private attorneys are using computer support personnel rather than forensic examiners to collect and process evidence. This is especially true in small civil cases and domestic cases. Computer personnel are not trained in these best practices and are not following any type of methodology to protect and preserve the original evidence; not only is the training a prerequisite for following best practices, but the proper tools for the collection and preservation of the evidence are required as well. Lacking knowledge of best practices goes hand in hand with not having and applying proper tools for safe collection of evidence.

SUMMARY

In this chapter we covered who establishes best practices for the collection and preservation of evidence, by looking at some of the organizations who publish best practices and some of the certifications that include best practices in their programs. We also discussed what those best practices are, including the specific parts of the best practices for handling digital evidence. Finally, we looked at who should be following these best practices and why some examiners are not following them.

Overview of Digital Forensics Tools

5

INFORMATION IN THIS CHAPTER:

- What makes a tool forensically sound?
- Who performs tool testing?
- Computer forensics tools: An overview
- Classes of forensics tools
- Mobile device forensics tools

INTRODUCTION

Since this book is written for legal professionals, you may be asking yourself why this chapter was included. While all this talk about tools may seem unnecessary, our objective is to familiarize you with forensic tool validation and common forensics tools. In our experience, we faced numerous people claiming to be digital forensics experts who frankly didn't know which end was up when it comes to the proper tools in the digital forensics field. By having an idea of how the forensic tool validation process works, and common tools that are used, we hope to give you the information necessary to question examiners you might potentially hire, to see if they are qualified or not. If they do not possess any of these tools and cannot explain to you why a particular tool can stand up in court, chances are they will do you and your client more harm than good.

In the realm of digital forensics, a variety of tools are in use today. There are tools for acquiring digital evidence and tools for analyzing digital evidence. There are both hardware tools and software tools. There are tools commercially developed and available to anyone who can afford the price, open source tools available for free, and tools that are only available to law enforcement agencies. However, all of these tools, independent of their origination or who may use them, must meet minimum criteria to be considered forensically sound. These criteria are based on engineering and scientific principles that are translatable into the creation of both a testing and validation methodology.

5.1 WHAT MAKES A TOOL FORENSICALLY SOUND?

For any tool to be forensically sound, it must be definable, predictable, repeatable, and verifiable.

- **Definable:** One of the fundamental aspects of any forensic process is that the desired outcome and purpose must be definable. In other words, you must be able to state the problem, articulate the desired outcome, develop an algorithm to describe the process, and finally, have a measurement system to validate the process. As an example, for a forensic imaging tool, you would define it as:

  - **Problem:** There is a need to have a forensically sound tool to make identical copies of digital evidence.
  - **Desired outcome:** To create a process and method and ultimately a device or software application that can create a forensically identical copy of digital evidence in a verifiable and repeatable manner. (Note that this does not specify any criteria for performance related to speed of the copy process.)
  - **Algorithm:** An algorithm is a description of a process, broken down into logical steps. Algorithms are normally used in computer programming, but can be applied to any process that uses a yes/no type of logic. A decision tree can be regarded as a graphical presentation of an algorithm. In this case, we would first express the algorithm in pseudo-code. Pseudo-code is an informal description of an algorithm, basically a plain-language way to describe what the algorithm should do when it is actually written in real code. In this case, the pseudo-code for the forensic copy tool would look like this:

```
If system is on, write-blocking is enabled: (Protect the original
   from modification)
Okay to start copy process
While copy process is running
Check each block of data for errors
If no errors, accept and store
Calculate MD-5 hash value and store for that data block for
   verification purposes
Otherwise, reject data block, and re-copy
Re-copy previous data block
Re-check for errors
If still contains errors after this many tries, mark as bad blocks
Store bad block information
Proceed to next data block
Repeat until all data is copied and verified.
```

  The algorithm shown in pseudo-code is far from complete and is only shown as an example of how a high-level description of an algorithm for making a forensically sound copy would look.

- **Predictable:** Any function that the tool is going to perform must be predictable. If the tool cannot give predictable results, then it is not forensically sound, and all bets are off. Predictability in this case means that the tool will perform in a predictable manner across any usage of the tool for a specified function. In plain language, if the tool is supposed to find pictures of certain types, the prediction is that it will always find those types of pictures.

- **Repeatable:** The function must be repeatable within a tolerance of error. Let's take an example from the field of robotics: One of the defining characteristics in robotics is repeatability. If a robot arm is to move to a certain point, and then deposit a part in a certain location, can it repeat that exact movement hundreds of thousands of times within a defined tolerance of error? When you are looking at a forensic tool, can it repeat the function reliably, and what is the tolerance for error? Can it find 100 percent of the selected type of pictures 100 percent of the time or only 95 percent of the time? Is that 5 percent margin of error tolerable?

- **Verifiable:** One of the most important criteria for a tool in the arena of forensics is the ability to verify the results of the tool, not only within a particular testing environment, but also with other tools of the same type. For instance, if one examiner in a case is using EnCase forensic software and the other examiner is using Forensic Tool Kit forensic software, do they both produce the same result? If they do not, then the question must be raised: Is the difference a software error or an examiner error? This is not a matter of interpretation by the examiner, but a matter of exactness in a particular function of the tool. The idea is that no matter what forensic tool is being used by an examiner, the results of his or her examination must be verifiable by another examiner, independent of the tool being used as long as the tools are comparable in specification and function.

5.2 WHO PERFORMS TOOL TESTING?

The overall governing organization for the testing and validation of digital forensics tools in the United States is the Computer Forensics Tool Testing program (CFTT) at the National Institute of Standards and Technology (NIST). The CFTT develops testing methodology for specific tools. The following description of testing methodology is from the CFTT website:

> *The goal of the Computer Forensic Tool Testing (CFTT) project at the National Institute of Standards and Technology (NIST) is to establish a methodology for testing computer forensic software tools by development of general tool specifications, test procedures, test criteria, test sets, and test hardware. The results provide the information necessary for toolmakers to improve tools, for users to make informed choices about acquiring and using computer forensics tools, and for interested parties to understand the tools capabilities. A capability is required to ensure that forensic software tools consistently produce accurate and objective test results. Our approach for testing computer forensics tools is based on well-recognized international methodologies for conformance testing and quality testing.*[1]

5.3 COMPUTER FORENSICS TOOLS: AN OVERVIEW

Forensic software and hardware tools come in a variety of shapes and sizes, some designed to do everything in an examination and some designed to perform a specific function. In this section we will look at some of the better-known tools, without attempting to create a catalog of all tools. First we will look at forensic software tools and then forensic hardware tools. The tools are broken down into classes, and then by function.

5.4 CLASSES OF FORENSICS TOOLS

While there is no formal classification of forensic software tools, it is an easy task to put different forensics tools into general categories both by availability and by function:

- **Availability**
  - **Commercial.** Commercial software includes tools that are available to anyone who is willing to pay the purchase price. Prices for forensic software tools range from less than one hundred dollars for some single-purpose tools up to tens of thousands of dollars for enterprise level forensics and e-discovery tools.
  - **Open Source.** Open source tools are those that are developed under the Open Source Initiative[2] and are covered by one of the various licenses approved under that initiative. Open source tools are distributed free to anyone and are developed and supported by interested community members. The most well-known of these is the SleuthKit developed by Brian Carrier, author of "File System Forensic Analysis."[3]
- **Law Enforcement Only (LEO).** Some digital forensics tools are developed for use by law enforcement only. One such program is iLook. iLook is one of the more well-known law enforcement only forensics tools. It was developed by Elliot Spencer, and then maintained by the Internal Revenue Service Criminal Investigation Division (IRS-CI). In 2008, federal funding ended for the product, but Elliot Spencer's company Perlustro now sells a commercial version of the software.[4]
- **Function**
  - **Suites.** Forensic software suites are those programs designed to "do it all." The typical software suite operates as a single program to handle all aspects of a computer examination. All of the suites also include ancillary programs for the acquisition (forensic copying) of digital evidence in a forensically sound manner. These comprehensive forensic software suites are designed to handle acquisition of evidence, verification, analysis, and preservation all in one place. This enables the forensic examiner to perform all of the processes and functions needed for a complete forensic analysis from collection though reporting results for use in court testimony.

    Guidance Software (www.guidancesoftware.com) and Access Data Corporation (www.accessdata.com) have extensive documentation citing court cases that have involved EnCase and Forensic Tool Kit available on their websites.

- EnCase (Guidance Software Corporation)
- FTK Forensic Tool Kit (Access Data Corporation)
- iLook LEO and iLookPI (Perlustro Corporation)
- SMART (ASR Data, Data Acquisition and Analysis, LLC)
- P2 Commander (Paraben Corporation)
- X-Ways Forensics (X-Ways Software Technology AG)
- MacForensicsLab (MacForensicsLab, Inc.)
- BlackLight Mac Analysis (BlackBag Technologies)

- **Task-Specific or Single-Purpose.** Many software programs are available that perform a specialized task or function such as forensic triage, e-mail forensics, peer-to-peer forensics, chat program forensics, and Internet history forensics. This list includes software designed to handle specific tasks in the major evidence categories. Here we list some of the more well-known task-specific or single-purpose forensics tools.
  - **Forensic Triage Products.** Forensic triage is the process of conducting an examination of a computer to either eliminate it or include it for a full forensic analysis. Forensic triage is becoming more popular today as the number of cases involving computers continues to grow, swamping law enforcement agencies with computers waiting for a forensic examination. Forensic triage is seen as a way to reduce the backlog of computers that must be given a full forensic examination.
    - Drive Prophet (Guardian Digital Forensics)
    - Triage Examiner (ADF Solutions, Inc.)
  - **E-mail Only Products.** E-mail forensic software is used to recover and analyze stored e-mail in a variety of formats, including corrupted e-mail stores.
    - Email Examiner and Network Email Examiner (Paraben Corporation)
    - Email Detective (Hot Pepper Technology)
    - Mail Analyzer (Belkasoft)
  - **Chat Programs.** Chat program forensic software is designed to recover chat logs from chat services such as Yahoo Messenger, MSN, Trillian, Hello, Miranda, Skype, and others.
    - Forensic IM Analyzer (Belkasoft)
    - Chat Examiner (Paraben Corporation)
  - **Internet History**
    - NetAnalysis (Digital Detective)
    - Browser Analyzer (Belkasoft)
- **Acquisition (forensic software and hardware for making forensic copies of evidence)**
  - **Software for Acquisitions**
    - EnCase Forensic Software (Guidance Software Corporation)
    - Linen (Guidance Software Corporation)
    - FTK Imager (Access Data Corporation)
    - Forensic Replicator (Paraben Corporation)

- MacQuisition (BlackBag Technologies)
- Helix (e-fense)
- **Hardware for Acquisitions.** Forensic acquisition hardware comes in the form of write-blockers for protecting original evidence as well as in the form of forensic drive duplicators. There are far too many individual write-blocking products to list them by name. Below is a list of companies that produce and sell write-blocking and drive-duplication products.
  - Tableau
  - Logicube
  - Weibetech
  - Intelligent Computer Solutions
  - Voom Technologies

5.5 MOBILE DEVICE FORENSICS TOOLS

Mobile devices require their own set of unique tools to acquire and analyze the data contained on cell phones, personal data assistants, iPods, iPads and even GPS units. The following is a list of the major products available for mobile device forensics.

- Paraben Device Seizure (Paraben Corporation)
- Cellebrite (Cellebrite USA Corporation)
- Susteen SecureView (Susteen Inc.)
- CellDEK (Logicube)
- Mobilyze (BlackBag Technologies)
- BitPim (Open source free application)
- XRY (Micro Sysemation AB)
- Berla Corp GPS Forensic Software (Berla Corporation)

SUMMARY

In this chapter we looked at the criteria for a forensically sound tool, and the organizations that provide testing and validation for forensics tools. We looked at the various classes of forensics tools and discussed the types of forensic software and hardware tools currently in use today. We also included a list of all of the manufacturers of the tools covered in this chapter for further reading.

References

[1] National Institute of Science and Technology, Information Technology Library, *NIST Computer Forensics Tool Testing Program.* <http://www.cftt.nist.gov> (accessed 11.05.16).

[2] Open Source Initiative, *Mission*. <http://www.opensource.org/> (accessed 11.05.16).

[3] B. Carrier, The Sleuth Kit (TSK) & Autopsy: Open Source Digital Investigation Tools. <http://www.sleuthkit.org> (accessed 11.05.16).

[4] L.P. Perlustro, iLookPI powered by PSIClone <http://www.perlustro.com/solutions/ ilookpi-powered-by-psiclone> (accessed 11.05.16).

Digital Forensics at Work in the Legal System

6

INFORMATION IN THIS CHAPTER:

- Mitigation
- Pre-trial motions
- Trial preparation
- Example trial questions
- Trial phase

INTRODUCTION

Digital forensics evidence is used in many ways in legal matters not only as part of civil and criminal trials, but also during the pre-trial and post-trial phases. Sometimes a forensic examination can result in charges being dropped, sentences being reduced, and civil matters being settled, all without ever going to trial. The other side of the coin is that the result of a forensic examination may help a defendant to understand that going to court is too risky versus taking a plea bargain. As part of an informal poll of examiners, the number of cases where examiners actually testify is extremely low, less than 5 percent of the time according to an unscientific poll conducted by the authors. However, depending on the individual examiner and their area of expertise, this percentage can be significantly higher than the 5 percent.

On the other hand, digital forensics examiners can play a significant role at trial both in presenting evidence and in assisting attorneys preparing for the examination of opposing experts. In this chapter we will look at how some of these roles are played out through case examples.

6.1 MITIGATION

There are cases where an examiner's role is to perform examinations for mitigation purposes where the evidence could be used for pre-sentencing hearings. In the case study "Pre-Sentence Mitigation in an Internet Predator Case," the pre-sentencing computer forensic examination brought to light more than one mitigating factor in getting the sentence of a client who was more than 60 years old reduced from 25 years to 14 years.

6.1 PRE-SENTENCE MITIGATION IN AN INTERNET PREDATOR CASE

In one particular case, the client was charged in federal court with solicitation of a minor via the Internet. As part of the sentencing enhancement, the prosecution's computer forensics expert was claiming that the client had downloaded child pornography. He was not charged with the four images claimed as child pornography; they were being used only for sentence enhancement.

In addition, this client claimed that while he was chatting with people on the Internet, someone had offered to sell him an underage girl. In light of that claim, the judge had offered to reduce the client's sentence if the evidence of the chat could be produced.

A firm was brought in by the defense attorney to see if the claims being made by both sides could be verified. An examination of the computers proved that three of the four images were not child pornography. This also revealed that the one image that could be child pornography had been placed on his computer via the old Microsoft Messenger Service. The Microsoft Messenger Service was included in the Windows 98 operating system and ran on startup as a service, and was not controlled by the user of the computer. It was common to receive spam messages via this service, including files. The examination also showed that the images were placed on the computer four years previously and had never been opened.

On the claim by the client that he had been offered the sale of an underage girl, the examiner was able to locate and reconstruct his Yahoo chat logs from unallocated space on the computer hard drive. This allowed the examiner to present not only the chat text where the offer had been made, but the city and telephone number of the person who made the offer.

When this information was provided to law enforcement, the client received a sentence reduction of 11 years.

6.2 PRE-TRIAL MOTIONS

One of the ways that digital forensics experts assist attorneys is during the pre-trial phase. Experts can assist and testify in the support or opposition of motions to suppress evidence, motions to dismiss civil actions, and spoliation or discovery compliance motions. While this is for the attorney to decide, the examiner can certainly assist with the technical aspects and provide factual information in support of the motion. The examiner may also testify during the pre-trial motion hearings in support of the evidence at issue.

6.3 TRIAL PREPARATION

One major role of the expert during the pre-trial phase is to clearly answer any questions the attorney may have regarding the digital evidence in the case. Attorneys are smart people, but they are not typically experts in all forms of evidence. It is critical to make sure that the attorney understands the evidence being presented and has the proper technical foundation to proceed with the digital evidence portion of the case.

As part of trial preparation, the expert can also provide questions for the attorney to use in preparing for the examination of the opposing expert based on the opposing expert's report and the findings of the engaged expert. Of course, it is up to the attorney to decide which, if any, of the questions he or she wants to use, as he or she is the one who is deciding case strategy, not the expert.

One critical aspect of the expert's role in this phase is to provide the attorney with questions that will assist in bringing out the facts in a way that clarifies the issues at hand for the jury.

While this may seem obvious, providing questions without the expected and/ or correct answers would be like only giving someone half a hammer to drive a nail. The question set must be prepared so that the attorney will know in advance how the opposing expert may or should respond. It is part of an expert's role to anticipate the testimony of the opposing expert and prepare for rebuttal testimony.

However, no one is ever able to predict what may happen once testimony begins, so the ability to adjust is critical as examining an expert about digital evidence can take unexpected turns. The best situation is to have your expert at the table during direct and cross so he or she can listen to the testimony and provide new questions based on the expert's responses. Whether or not this will be possible depends on the case, the judge, and the jurisdiction. If the expert is not at the table, he or she can still take notes and be ready to pass them to the attorney at a convenient time.

6.4 EXAMPLE TRIAL QUESTIONS

These example question sets are designed to be part of trial preparation. Included here are two example question sets; one written for a civil hearing and one written for use at a criminal trial.

As these are from actual cases, they have been sanitized to remove any possible identifying information and the opposing expert is simply called Mr Examiner.

6.4.1 A civil case example

In this example the questions are for a civil case where the client has been accused of spoliation of evidence by using a file destruction program. This question set was used at a court hearing to question the plaintiff's expert on his examination of the defendant's computer. A preservation order had been issued previously in the case, and the discovery of the file destruction program was at issue in the production of discovery documents. The plaintiff's contention was that not all responsive discovery documents were produced and that the file destruction program was used as a method by the defendant to destroy evidence. The defendant's claim was that the file destruction program was used only to remove sensitive information in the normal course of business and had been removed from the computer immediately after the issue of the preservation order.

Q. Mr Examiner, you have in front of you a copy of your summary report dated March 27th, 2008. Is that correct?
A. Yes.
Q. Mr Examiner, is this the report you wrote regarding your investigation of the computer?
A. Yes it is.
Q. Mr Examiner, referring to your report, you state that this is the summary report of the procedures and findings of the computer investigation you did. Is that correct?
A. Yes it is.
Q. Mr Examiner, the word "summary" implies that there is a detailed report to support the summary. Did you do a detailed report?
A. No.

> **Q. If he answers No: So you did not write a detailed report of the steps taken during your investigation?**
> **A.** No.
> **Q. And you did not write a detailed report to support your summary report?**
> **A.** No.
> **Q. Mr Examiner, if you did not write a detailed report, how did you manage to write a summary report?**
> **A.** (No way to anticipate the answer.)

Q. Mr Examiner, in your summary report you state that on March 21st of 2008 that you; and I quote: "Received a computer laptop for investigation." Is that accurate according to the document you have in front of you?
A. Yes it is.
Q. Mr Examiner, can you describe for the court the methods you used to receive the laptop?
A. At this point he should be able to articulate his method for beginning the chain of custody. If he cannot, then question him about chain of custody specifically:
Q. Mr Examiner, are you familiar with the phrase, "chain of custody?"
A. Yes.
Q. Mr Examiner, can you describe for the court what chain of custody is?
A. (Correct Answer): Chain of custody is a process for ensuring that evidence is properly identified, collected, and protected from any changes from the first contact with the evidence and continuing through the end of litigation.
Q. Mr Examiner, referring to your summary, you state that at 11:13 AM you: "Removed hard drive from laptop and began imaging." Is that a correct reading of your summary?
A. Yes.
Q. And your summary then states: "Disk Imaging process began." Is that correct?
A. Yes.
Q. Mr Examiner, can you describe for the court the steps you took to protect the original hard drive from my client's computer prior to and during this disk imaging process?
A. He should describe here how he performed this in a forensically sound manner. If he is not specific about how he protected the hard drive, then ask him:
Q. Mr Examiner, did you use any special tools or equipment to protect the hard drive from any possible changes before and during the disk imaging process?
A. If Yes, have him describe them.
Q. Mr Examiner, can you describe for the court exactly how you went about protecting the evidence on the hard drive?
A. If No, attack his methods.
Q. Mr Examiner, are you telling this court that you did not take any precautions of any kind to protect the evidence provided to you by my client?
A. Yes.

Q. Mr Examiner, do you have any idea of how to conduct a forensically sound examination of a computer?
A. If Yes: Mr Examiner, if you know how to conduct a forensically sound examination of a computer, why didn't you?
A. If No, attack his expertise.
Q. Mr Examiner, you have presented yourself here today as an expert in computer forensics. But now you are telling this court that you really have no idea about computer forensics. Is that a correct assessment?
A. Yes.
Q. Mr Examiner, did you take any steps to validate the disk image you made from the hard drive?
A. He should say here that the tool he used created a verification hash value for the hard drive. If not, then ask about hash values.
　Q. Mr Examiner, are you familiar with the term hash value?
　A. Yes.
　Q. Mr Examiner, specifically in the realm of computer forensics, can you explain for the court what a hash value is?
　A. (Correct Answer): A hash value is a mathematical operation that computes a unique value for the contents of a hard drive or a file. This acts as a fingerprint so that the contents of the hard drive or file can later be validated as unchanged by recomputing the hash value against the original evidence. This is the only accepted method for verifying that evidence has not been changed in some way.
　Q. Mr Examiner, did the tools you used to create the image of the hard drive from my client's laptop computer compute this hash value?
　A. No, it did not.
Q. Mr Examiner in your report, you state that at 2:46 PM: "Started data recovery process on disk image." Is that correct?
A. Yes.
Q. Mr Examiner, what is data recovery?
A. (Correct Answer): Data recovery is the process of locating and rebuilding files that have been deleted on a computer hard drive.
Q. Mr Examiner, can you tell the court what software you used to perform this data recovery?
A. (Not in his report)
Q. Mr Examiner, have you received any training for this particular data recovery software?
A. (Not in his report or CV)
Q. Mr Examiner, can you explain for the court what happens when someone deletes a file on a computer?
A. (Correct Answer): When the user "deletes" the file, the operating system marks the file for deletion and puts it in the Recycle Bin. The operating system does not allow the space used by the deleted file to be used just in case the user changes their mind and wants to get the file back out of the Recycle Bin.
Q. What happens when the user empties the Recycle Bin on their computer?
A. (Correct Answer): Initially when a file is deleted it goes into the Recycle Bin. However, when the computer user empties the Recycle Bin, the operating system, in this case Windows, just stops keeping track of the file since the user has indicated that they no longer care about the file. The file itself is not actually deleted. Only the information about where the file is located is deleted. In effect, the operating system now "releases" the space used by the deleted file so that the operating system can use that space again for new files when the space is needed.
Q. Mr Examiner, is there a name for the space you are talking about when you refer to files that have been removed from the Recycle Bin?
A. (Correct Answer): Yes, this area is called "free space," or the correct term is "unallocated space."

Q. Mr Examiner, can you explain for the court how files are recovered by the software you used?
A. (Correct Answer): Data recovery software uses three methods for recovering files.

The first method is the equivalent of just looking in the Recycle Bin and restoring the file from there. This will result in the entire file being recovered.

The second method involves "reading" the file table that is maintained by Windows. This allows the recovery software to locate at least the first piece of a file. Then the recovery software follows a method called chaining, in which each piece of the file it finds contains information about the next piece of the file. This method may get some or all of the file.

The third method uses file signatures to recover files from unallocated space. This method will result in many files that cannot be opened.

Q. Mr Examiner, can you explain to the court what a file signature is and how it is used to recover a file from this unallocated space?
A. (Correct Answer): Nearly every kind of file has something called a header and sometimes a footer as well. A file header is in the first little bit of the file and describes what kind of file it is. The footer is at the end of the file itself and tells the software where the end of the file is.

For example, a Microsoft Word document has a specific header that tells the recovery software what kind of file it is. When the recovery software sees the header for a Microsoft Word document, it will then attempt to recover that document beginning at the point where it finds the header. However, this method only knows about the very first part of the file that contains the header information. From that point the software grabs everything until it either locates a footer for that file or finds a new header for a different file.

This method has to assume that all of the file pieces are next to each other on the hard drive. If all of the pieces of the file are together on the hard drive, the file can be recovered and can probably be opened. However, if all of the pieces are not together on the hard drive, the recovery software will still attempt to recover the file. This results in a lot of files that cannot be opened.

Q. Mr Examiner, did you at any time during your investigation operate or use my client's computer after you made the disk image? (This is a reference to the notes of the witness who observed the examination.)
A. Yes.

Q. Mr Examiner, are you aware that by doing so you altered and destroyed some of the original evidence?
A. He might say here that he asked the client for permission. If he does, then ask:

Q. Mr Examiner, is my client a computer forensic expert?
A. Not that I am aware of.

Q. Did you inform my client that by operating his computer you would be altering and destroying evidence contained on his hard drive?
A. No.

Q. Mr Examiner, in your summary you stated that on March 22, at 11:11 AM you identified that program "File Wiper" was used on the subject hard drive on January 27, 2008 at 3:03 PM. Is that an accurate reading?
A. Yes.

Q. Mr Examiner, are you certain about the date and time that you show in your report as being accurate?
A. Yes I am.

Q. Mr Examiner, can you tell the court what time zone you are referring to for the time to be 3:03 PM?
A. (Correct Answer): GMT.

Q. Mr Examiner, if the time you show in your report is GMT, what time would it be in the current time zone for my client's computer?
A. (Correct Answer): 11:03AM Eastern Daylight Time

Q. Mr Examiner, you stated that the program "File Wiper was used on the subject hard drive." Is that an accurate reading of your report?
A. Yes.

Q. Mr Examiner, how do you know that the program was used on the subject hard drive on that date and time?
A. Here he will probably say that was the last accessed time, which would indicate the last time the program was run.

Q. Mr Examiner, I don't see anything in your report that shows where that date and time came from. Is it in here and I just cannot see it?
A. This information is not in the report.

Q. Mr Examiner, is there some other report that contains this information? (If so, where is it?)
A. No.

Q. Mr Examiner, can you tell the court exactly where you obtained the date and time that you indicate is the last time the File Wiper program was run?
A. He should say that he got this from the thumbs.db file in the File Wiper folder.
If Yes then:

> **Q. Mr Examiner, is this thumbs.db file you are referring to part of the File Wiper program?**
> **A.** (Correct Answer): No it is not.

> **Q. Mr Examiner, can you explain for the court what a thumbs.db file is?**
> **A.** (Correct Answer): The thumbs.db file is a file that is automatically created by the Windows operating system that contains little pictures of the program's icons, documents, and so on.

> **Q. Mr Examiner, can you explain to the court how and when the dates and times get updated for a thumbs.db file?**
> **A.** (Correct Answer): The dates and times in a thumbs.db file are updated any time the files in the folder where the thumbs.db file is located are changed in some way.

> **Q. Mr Examiner, would deleting a file in that folder be a change to that file?**
> **A.** Yes.

> **Q. Mr Examiner, would the thumbs.db file be updated when the files in the folder are deleted?**
> **A.** (Correct Answer): Yes.

Q. Mr Examiner, can you explain for the court what the program "File Wiper" does?
A. (Correct Answer): It permanently destroys data on a computer hard drive.

Q. Mr Examiner, can you explain for the court how this program accomplishes the permanent destruction of data on a computer hard drive?
A. (Correct Answer): The software writes over the file with new data, usually in the form of ones or zeroes. Once data is overwritten in this manner, it cannot be recovered.

Q. Mr Examiner, on the second page of your report you have a paragraph title "Findings." Is that correct?
A. Yes.

Q. And in that paragraph you have two sentences. Is that correct?
A. Yes.

Q. In the first sentence you state and I quote, "File Wiper" is software that is designed to permanently destroy data from computers. Is that an accurate reading of your statement?
A. Yes.

Q. Mr Examiner, in the second line of the paragraph you have labeled as Findings in your report, you state, and I quote, "Because this software was being used on the hard drive, many of the files recovered were unreadable." Is that an accurate reading of your statement?
A. Yes.

Q. Mr Examiner, if as you indicate in your findings that File Wiper permanently destroys data, how it is possible that the files recovered were unreadable?

A. (Correct Answer): It is not possible.

Q. Mr Examiner, if as you state, the program that the File Wiper was run on January 27th of 2008, how is it possible that any files were recovered that existed prior to that date?

A. (Correct Answer): It is not possible.

Q. Mr Examiner, you are telling this court that this File Wiper program was run on a particular date and time. Is that correct?

A. Yes.

Q. Mr Examiner, is there any kind of evidence to back up your statement in your report?

A. Not directly.

Q. You mean not at all, don't you?

A. Yes.

Q. So you offer your opinion based on your report, but offer no evidence of any kind to support your statement?

A. Yes.

6.4.2 Criminal trial example

While criminal and civil matters share many characteristics and evidence types, evidence in many criminal cases depends heavily on timelines and user attribution, that is, who was at the computer when something happened, and who had access to the computer. When computer evidence is being relied on to show when someone performed a map search, ran an Internet search, downloaded a file, had an online chat and so forth, getting the time right is critical. Failing to perform basic examination steps like making sure the time is correct on a computer or other digital device can make a huge difference in the reliability of the timeline evidence.

The same is true when one side or the other is trying to prove that a particular person performed some action on a computer; knowing who had accounts and whether or not any or all of those accounts were secured by passwords can be used to show that only one person or any one of multiple people could have performed the map search, Internet chat, or other action.

Another issue that comes up in a lot of cases is whether or not the computer clock could have been changed to disguise when something occurred.

This set of questions was prepared for a death penalty trial. However, the case never went to trial and the defendant received 17 years as part of a plea bargain.

Q. Mr Examiner, can you tell us what physical evidence you received in order to conduct an examination of the computer evidence in this case?

A. I received three hard drives.

Q. When you say you received three hard drives, does that mean that you did not receive the actual computers?

A. Yes.

Q. Mr Examiner, did you ever have an occasion to examine the computers themselves?

A. No.

Q. So you conducted your entire examination on the hard drives and not the computers?

A. Yes.

Q. Mr Examiner, do you know who removed the hard drives from the computers?
A. No.
Q. Mr Examiner, do you know if the person who removed the hard drives from the computers examined the computers in any way?
A. No, I do not.
Q. Moving on to the analysis of the hard drives. When you examined the hard drives in this case, did you locate and examine the user accounts for each of the computers?
A. No. (See below.)

> **Q.** If Yes, then: Mr Examiner, you say that you did locate the user accounts on each of the computers?
> **A.** Yes.
> **Q.** Did you include this listing in any of your reports?
> **A.** No.

Q. Mr Examiner, in regard to user accounts on the hard drive evidence, did you check to see if any of the computers were password protected?
A. No. (See below.)
Q. Did you include this information in any of your reports?
A. No.
Q. Optional question: Mr Examiner, if a computer is password protected, but the password is known by several people, and those people are authorized to all use the same password, would this be the equivalent of no password protection for that group of people?
A. Yes.
Q. Optional question: Mr Examiner, if a computer has a blank password, in other words, you just press Enter to log on, would that be the same as no password?
A. Yes.
Q. Mr Examiner, I would like to go back for a moment to the physical evidence you examined in this case. You stated that you only received the hard drives, and not the computers. Is that correct?
A. Yes.
Q. Mr Examiner, would you consider examining the computer itself to determine such things as the current setting of the computer clock time to be a normal part of a forensic analysis?
A. Yes.
Q. In this case, Mr Examiner, are you aware of anyone examining the computers to determine the accuracy of the clocks on the computers?
A. No.
Q. Mr Examiner, in your experience, when you receive a complete computer as evidence, do you examine the computer to get the computer clock time?
A. Yes.
Q. Can you walk us through how that process should go?
A. (Correct Answer): First, you disconnect any hard drives in the computer to prevent them from accidentally being written to during this part of the examination. Then you start the computer up into BIOS. (This is the part of the computer that contains information about the computer itself, including the real-time clock information.) Then you record the time from the computer's real-time clock and check it against an external time source for accuracy.
Q. Mr Examiner, would you consider this to be an important step in a complete computer forensics examination?
A. Yes.
Q. Can you explain to the jury why this is an important part of a complete computer forensics examination?
A. (Correct Answer): It is important to know the time from the computer to make sure that when you review items on the computer hard drive, the time recorded for each of those items is accurate.

Q. And why is it important to know if the times that items are recorded are accurate?
A. (Correct Answer): If you are trying to say that someone did something on the computer on a certain date at a specific time, you must have this information. If the computer clock is wrong and you don't have a comparison to an external time source, you cannot say for certain when something happened.

Q. Would it be fair to say that you *don't know* if the clocks on the computers in this case are accurate?
A. Yes.

Q. Mr Examiner, I'd like to ask you about Item 17. This is the hard drive from a computer that was located at my client's business. Is that correct?
A. Yes.

Q. When you examined the hard drive for evidence, did you determine if more than one person used this computer on a regular basis?
A. No. (See below.)

> **Q. How did you determine that more than one person used this computer on a regular basis?**
> **A.** (Correct Answer): By examining the folders and e-mail accounts on the hard drive. Several folders had names such as .... Also, several e-mail accounts were present with different identities.

Q. Is it possible that more than one person used this computer on the same account?
A. Yes.

Q. Mr Examiner, in your report you stated that "the computer user logged in to Item 17 under my client's user account." Can you explain what that means exactly?
A. (Correct Answer): Someone logged in to the computer using the defendant's account rather than a user account of their own.

Q. Does that mean that the user was my client and could only have been my client?
A. No.

Q. So it could have been anyone with access to the computer?
A. Yes.

Q. You stated that someone logged in to the computer under my client's user account and visited the website www.mapquest.com on 12/4/06 from 11:23AM EST until 11:42AM EST. Is that an accurate account of what you stated in your report?
A. Yes.

Q. But you cannot say that the user logged in to the computer was in fact my client. Is that correct?
A. Yes, that is correct.

Q. As part of the statement I just read, you gave the exact date and times for the www.mapquest.com website. Now Mr Examiner, without knowing what the actual time was on the computer, can you say without a doubt that the times stated in your report are accurate?
A. No.

Q. So it could have been some other time than the time you stated in your report?
A. Yes.

Q. Mr Examiner, let's talk about Item 15. This is the hard drive from the laptop computer from my client's home. Is that correct?
A. Yes.

Q. Was the real-time clock information for this computer checked and recorded as part of the forensic analysis for the computer?
A. No.

Q. So you don't know if the computer clock was accurate on the computer taken from my client's home?
A. No, I do not.

Q. Is that because you only received the hard drive from the computer and not the whole computer?
A. Yes.

Q. And do you know if this computer was password protected?
A. No, I do not.
Q. Do you know if access to this computer was restricted in some other way? Locked in an office in his home, for instance?
A. No, it was not.
Q. Would be fair to say that someone other than my client could have used this computer?
A. (The correct answer could be "Yes," or "I don't know," or "It is possible.")
Q. But you cannot say if there was anything that would prevent someone other than my client from using this computer, correct?
A. Yes.
Q. In your report you stated that several Internet searches were made on this computer for keywords such as death, murder, and accidental deaths, as well as searches for videos and images based on the search term "death." Is that correct?
A. Yes.
Q. But you cannot say with certainty that my client was the person who made these searches, can you?
A. No.
Q. It could have been someone he allowed to use his computer. Is that correct?
A. Yes.
Q. The actual web pages returned by these searches were not recovered. Is that correct?
A. They were not.
Q. Did you attempt to find out what kind of results would have been returned by these searches?
A. No.
Q. So you don't know what the user saw once these search terms were entered into the computer. Is that correct?
A. Yes.
Q. Did you locate any web pages or other information from the computer hard drives related to committing a murder?
A. No.
Q. Did you locate any web pages or other information on the computers related to disposing of a body?
A. No.
Q. Item 16 is a hard drive from one of the computers at my client's place of business. Is that correct?
A. Yes.
Q. You stated in your report that a text fragment was recovered from that computer hard drive that contained references to "death, murder, and revenge through guns." Is that correct?
A. Yes.
Q. Mr Examiner, I have a printout of that text fragment here. Would you classify this as a document that has any meaning, or would you say it is just a bunch of words typed over and over?
A. Yes, it is words typed over and over.
Q. Would it be fair to say that someone reading this document would not receive any useful information about death, murder, and revenge through guns?
A. Yes.
Q. Mr Examiner, fax machines were also collected by police in this case. Were you or anyone at your agency ever asked to examine these fax machines?
A. No.

6.5 TRIAL PHASE

When a case does go to trial where digital evidence is to be presented by one or both sides through expert or fact witness testimony, the examiner can be of assistance in parsing the responses of the opposing expert during direct and cross examination.

SUMMARY

In this chapter we looked at the various ways that digital forensics experts participate in the legal system. We also looked at some case examples for mitigation and pre-sentencing. Finally, we looked at some question sets developed for real cases that demonstrated lines of questioning about digital evidence in a civil and a criminal case.

Experts

Why Do I Need an Expert?

7

INTRODUCTION

For convenience, digital forensics examiners will be referred to as experts throughout this book, even though the term "expert" is a legal term and is only valid in a court of law when someone passes the qualification tests of the court to be accepted as an expert.

As there are different subdisciplines in the area of digital forensics, there are different types of digital forensics experts. Some specialize in one area of technology, while others may have expertise in many areas including computers, cell phones, cell tower technology, video, and so forth. This chapter discusses why and when you should engage an expert in a matter involving digital evidence.

7.1 WHY HIRE A DIGITAL FORENSICS EXPERT?

While it seems that the answer here should be obvious, our experience over the years has shown us that many attorneys choose not to hire experts in cases involving digital evidence.

In some cases it is a matter of expense; in other words, why pay an expert's rates when you can have a computer specialist do the same thing much less expensively? This is most often seen in domestic cases where money is a serious issue or where the extent of what is being sought is pornography or Internet history and maybe some e-mails. Testimony is very rare in domestic cases as the evidence is primarily used to force one side to admit to an affair or to settle some dispute rather than go to court. If there is no need to be concerned about chain of custody, authenticating the evidence, or having to appear in court, then hiring a non-expert could save the clients some money if they can engage a computer technician to recover this information at a small percentage of the cost of a engaging a fully qualified expert.

The question is whether or not the higher rate you may need to pay to engage an expert will provide the appropriate value to you or your client. Value can be somewhat determined by the risks for the client in not engaging a qualified expert. In cases involving large amounts of money or criminal cases where the client's freedom is at stake, the cost of engaging an expert is very small in the grander scheme of things.

In a civil case where tens of thousands to millions of dollars are at stake, paying a digital forensics expert a few thousand dollars is a small part of the overall cost of litigation.

In criminal cases where your client is facing loss of freedom or even loss of life, the cost of engaging a digital forensics expert should not even be a consideration. One thing you can be certain of in criminal cases involving electronic evidence is that the prosecution will have a digital forensics expert on their side.

Proper collection and protection of digital evidence, efficient and accurate analysis of digital evidence, and the ability to properly interpret the results of examinations are all critical factors in knowing whether you need to hire an expert.

The proper interpretation of digital evidence is critical. There is a school of thought that digital evidence either is there or it isn't, and that is the sum total of an examination. Reducing the value of a digital forensics examination to this binary type of thinking is a mistake. Even with a single piece of digital evidence, there can be more than a single interpretation of that evidence. A good expert can use the entire body of digital evidence to come to a conclusion that takes into account the possible variables. There are many times when something can be proved conclusively concerning digital evidence, but just as frequently it often comes down to an expert opinion based on the interpretation of the evidence.

It is not uncommon to see experts make overstated claims concerning what digital evidence might mean in a case, or to simply interpret digital evidence incorrectly. It is even more common to see non-experts used in cases make interpretations that are flat out wrong, damage evidence in the process of their examination of the evidence, and fail to keep any kind of chain of evidence.

In cases that are complex and involve multiple computers, computer users, accusations, and complicated timelines, the use of an expert is even more critical. As more data is added to a case that must be analyzed and put into the overall context of the case, the ability to properly tie together seemingly disparate information and explain it in an understandable manner could be the difference in winning or losing.

Without a competent expert on your side, you are at the mercy of the conclusions drawn by the opposing side's expert. In situations like this, you need an expert to act as an equalizer; to determine whether or not the opposing expert has performed a sound forensic examination, to verify whether their claims concerning digital evidence in the case are accurate, and to combat those claims if necessary.

7.2 WHEN TO HIRE A DIGITAL FORENSICS EXPERT

When should you hire a digital forensics expert? The short answer is as soon as you determine that any type of electronic evidence will be part of your case.

Engaging a digital forensics expert early in your case will benefit you in many ways, especially if you have evidence that must be collected or a large volume of evidence that must be analyzed.

Performing tasks related to collecting and analyzing digital evidence takes a lot more time than you might think if you are not familiar with this type of evidence. The increasing size of hard drives makes them more time-consuming than ever to collect, process, and analyze. Hard drives are now being sold at your local electronics store that can contain three terabytes of data. That is roughly three thousand gigabytes or three million megabytes. Think of it as approximately 2.6 million floppy disks. That is a lot of data.

When you are presented with a case where original evidence must be collected, getting access to and subsequently getting a forensic copy of the evidence is a time-sensitive operation to make sure that evidence that may be critical to your case is not destroyed. Allowing an electronic device such as a computer, cell phone, global positioning unit, or one of the many other types of device that can contain evidence to continue to be operated raises the probability that evidence will be lost during the normal processes of the device. Many devices including computers and cell phones perform automatic updates to the operating system software that can modify the contents of the storage in the device, affect the way the device functions, and also modify the revision number of the software. Delays in completing forensic collections also increase the risk of evidence being intentionally destroyed or destroyed in the normal course of business where a company's data retention policy may include periodic disk-cleaning operations or purging of e-mail stores.

In cases where the other side has already collected and possibly analyzed electronic data, you will need time for your expert to perform his analysis. There are an alarming number of cases where the attorney has waited until the eleventh hour to contact an examiner to perform a collection or to do an analysis. A couple of cases in point: An attorney contacted a firm on a Friday afternoon. He and his client were scheduled to be in court on Monday morning where the client must either take a plea bargain or go to trial. In another case, an attorney brought in a global positioning unit to be forensically collected on a Wednesday and the attorney needed to have an expert report completed that following Monday. The collection wasn't possible because the unit's batteries were dead and the attorney did not have the power cable for the unit. Even with ordering a replacement cable overnight, the deadline was missed, caused by the delay in collecting the evidence.

In cases involving deleted items that are the basis for a spoliation claim, understanding how data is deleted and recovered, and what system artifacts are created that can be used to figure out how, when, and who deleted the data is a complex process involving computer time stamps, analysis of system artifacts like thumbnail caches, and examination of the raw data on the hard drive of a computer. These types of analysis require not only a skilled examiner, but the proper forensic tools to locate and examine these specific types of evidence.

Failing to make a decision to hire an expert early in the litigation process can lead to incomplete analysis, increased costs, and in some cases, failure to comply with court orders that may lead to sanctions or inadmissibility of evidence critical to your case.

SUMMARY

This chapter examined the need to hire an expert and when to do so. The need to hire an expert is dependent on several factors including the presence of digital evidence, the cost factor, the type of case, and the need to get a proper examination and interpretation of the evidence. Hiring an expert early in the litigation process can help to ensure that evidence is not lost and that your expert has sufficient time to perform a thorough and complete analysis and can help to prevent incurring extra costs.

The Difference between Computer Experts and Digital Forensics Experts

INFORMATION IN THIS CHAPTER:

- The computer expert
- The digital forensics expert
- A side-by-side comparison
- Investigation of digital evidence

INTRODUCTION

Digital forensics is a specialized area that encompasses technical, legal, and investigative knowledge. The area of computer expertise is a specialized area that encompasses technical knowledge about the planning, deployment, support, diagnosis, and repair of computers.

While the technical knowledge required to perform the two different types of work does overlap in a very limited way, the technical knowledge specific to digital forensics is focused on working within the legal system, where computer expertise is not.

8.1 THE COMPUTER EXPERT

The field of computer technology is very broad and can include computer hardware, software, networking, and security. Depending on the individual person's background and training, they may be a hobbyist who "tinkers" with computers or a highly specialized information technology support professional who designs and implements large-scale storage solutions, provides network security solutions, designs and writes software, and anything in between.

There are literally hundreds of thousands of technicians out there who fit somewhere in the range between tinkerer and specialized support professional. However, bear in mind that a software expert most likely will not have any knowledge of computer hardware.

The term "software expert" refers to persons who perform functions ranging from a QuickBooks consultant who sets up and configures that financial information for a small business to a person who actually creates software applications from scratch for end users. A person who is a software expert in this sense will probably not be someone who can set up and configure a server in a network.

This has become more prevalent as the number of specialized applications and systems has increased. In a large organization you are likely to find specialists on staff who are dedicated to handling a small set of the overall infrastructure. For instance, in a large IT (information technology) department, you may have persons dedicated to supporting, maintaining, and upgrading only e-mail servers or backup servers, or maintaining the database servers. There may be another person dedicated solely to network security who maintains firewalls and remote access to the network, and who monitors the network for intrusions and malware such as viruses and Trojan horses.

Software developers are more focused on designing applications for use by end users or for middleware. Website developers are focused on the mechanics of web applications and work hand in hand with designers who determine how the website will look and feel to a visitor.

Of course there are always exceptions, and some people have the ability to become a generalist and even develop a high level of expertise in several areas.

Computer hardware maintenance has become simpler over the years at the desktop level, but more complicated at the enterprise level. In the 1990s, building a computer from component parts was complicated. In those days one had to purchase a computer mainboard, a compatible processor, and compatible memory. That part has not changed at all. However, in the mid- to late 1990s, having integrated components such as the video card, network adapter, modem, and sound card was a rarity. Today, it is the norm for a computer mainboard to have all of the components built in at the factory so all you have to do to build a computer from scratch today is purchase the mainboard, processor (CPU), the memory (RAM), a hard drive, a DVD drive, and a computer case. Assembling a computer like this takes just a few minutes from unpacking the components to first startup.

Gone are the days when the technician had to manually set jumper switches on the mainboard for the processor speed and then install a bunch of add-in cards for the video, audio, networking, and modem and hope they would all actually work.

The same goes for a networking engineer. Someone who works on personal computers may have good knowledge of the operating system software and installing applications, and knowledge about the hardware of the computer; their expertise is in making a computer work, and fixing it when it does not.

It is very easy to make the mistake of thinking that someone who provides computer support services can also provide forensic analysis services. The mindset of a computer support person is to approach a computer as to what's wrong, versus approaching a computer as to what is of evidentiary value.

As shown in Fig. 8.1, a computer expert's focus and knowledge base is directed toward installing, maintaining, and repairing computer systems. While a computer support person may have the skills to recover a client's lost data, that is only one small area of computer forensics. Data recovery software is available off the shelf at most major computer stores. However, for that ability to cross over into the realm

FIGURE 8.1

Knowledge areas of computer support personnel

of computer forensics, the person handling the data recovery must understand and be able to explain exactly what the recovery tool is doing and how it does it.

8.2 THE DIGITAL FORENSICS EXPERT

Digital forensics examiners may or may not come from a background of working with computers. Many law enforcement examiners start out as police officers who do not have computer backgrounds, but who are selected for various reasons and then attend training for computer forensics. Others begin life as computer support people and subsequently get training in forensics.

Having in-depth knowledge of computers and software in general is not a prerequisite for a digital or computer forensics examiner. It can certainly be a plus, but it is not a requirement. A computer forensics examiner is trained to work with specialized tools to perform recovery of data and to analyze that data in a forensic manner. What that means is that a computer forensics examiner is focused on the examination of recovered data from an evidentiary standpoint. What does the evidence mean in light of the case at hand? The computer forensics examiner must be able to determine facts about the data, not just recover the data.

What matters in the training and development of a computer forensics expert is the focus on the handling of evidence, the investigation of the alleged acts, working within the law, and the ability to present findings in a legal matter.

To give an example, suppose that your client is accused of deleting data from a hard drive after a preservation hold has been put in place. Furthermore, add in the fact that when the computer is examined, a file-wiping software program is discovered to have been on the computer.

Examiner 1, who is a computer support person with no forensics training, examines the hard drive, runs a file recovery software application against the hard drive, and recovers hundreds of deleted files. Then in his report, he states that because the computer had file-wiping software installed on the computer, he was not able to open all of the recovered files. During his examination, he also operates the client's computer.

In his report Examiner 1 states the opinion that the computer owner had last run the file-wiping software two days after the court hearing. He also states that the file-wiping software permanently deletes files. Lastly, he states that because the file-wiping software was run two days after the court hearing, he could not open some of the files he recovered.

Examiner 2, who is a trained forensics examiner, also examines the hard drive from the client's computer. However, Examiner 2 first removes the hard drive and makes a forensic copy without ever turning the computer on. He then examines the hard drive forensic copy and also recovers hundreds of deleted files. He notes that the only evidence of a file-wiping program is the empty directory where the file-wiping software was installed. Inside that folder, he notes that the only file remaining is a system file with a date that is two days after the court hearing on the preservation order.

Next he locates and downloads a copy of the same version of the file-wiping program onto a clean test computer and then runs the software and subsequently uninstalls the software to determine how it works and what it does when it is uninstalled. He also determines that while the computer was in the custody of Examiner 1, over ten thousand files were accessed on the client's computer.

Examiner 2 determines that the file-wiping software is designed to permanently delete files by overwriting them with zeroes. By examining the raw data on the hard drive forensic copy, he notes that sets of zeroes are not found on the hard drive—that would be evidence of overwritten files.

Examiner 2 concludes that the file-wiping program was removed from the computer two days after the court hearing. He also concludes that the file-wiping software, while present, did not prevent the recovery of thousands of files, indicating that the software was never run against the client's drive to remove files of interest. He also concludes that if the file-wiping program were run against the drive, the evidence of such would be the presence of a known overwrite character repeated in sections in the raw data on the hard drive, and this was not present.

Examiner 2 notes that the conclusions of Examiner 1 are directly contradictory to one another.

Figure 8.2 illustrates the focus of digital forensics experts on the areas of technical knowledge, investigative techniques, and the legal system.

FIGURE 8.2

Knowledge areas of digital forensics

8.3 A SIDE-BY-SIDE COMPARISON

While both the computer expert and the forensics expert will both need technical knowledge, they differ markedly in the type and scope of the technical expertise needed to perform their functions.

Table 8.1 is a very small sampling of the technical differences between computer expertise and digital forensics expertise. The take-away from this is that while both disciplines have a technical foundation, they are not the same. Computer expertise begins with establishing a technical foundation of knowledge needed to provide and maintain computer infrastructure for computer users and does not have a requirement for the needed technical expertise specific for forensic handling and analysis of digital evidence. Computer forensics expertise requires technical

Table 8.1 Technical Expertise Comparisons

Computer Expert	Forensics Expert
• Installation and setup of computers, software, and networking	• Forensically sound acquisition of digital evidence
• Disaster recovery of failed systems from backups	• Forensic data recovery from multiple media types, including backups
• Troubleshooting and repairing computer problems	• Forensic data analysis
• Removal of virus, malware, and Trojan horse software from infected computers, not the evidentiary effect of such programs	• Determination of the effect of virus, malware, and Trojan horse software on digital evidence, not for the purpose of removing such programs
• Installation and maintenance of software applications for the end user	• Examination of artifacts left behind by software applications for the purpose of determining the effect on evidence
• Installation and setup of networking and Internet access for the purpose of allowing the end user to access the Internet or work network	• Examination of Internet artifacts in investigations for the purpose of determining their evidentiary value
• Formatting and using various file systems for the purpose of installing operating systems such as Windows, Mac OS, or Linux	• In-depth knowledge of how file systems work at the lowest level for the purpose of locating and examining artifacts recorded by the operating and file systems
• Works with common file formats such as DOS, Windows, Linux, Mac for the purpose of installing software, finding files, and making backups	• Understands and can use forensic file formats such as Expert Witness, DD Images, Access Data Images, and Smart Images for the purpose of chain of custody, authentication, and verification of evidence
• Can make backups of hard drives, files and directories; does not include deleted data, for the purpose of recovery of lost documents for business continuation	• Can make forensic copies of entire physical media including all deleted data for the purpose of forensic analysis

Table 8.2 Legal Expertise Comparisons

Forensics Expert	Computer Expert
• Chain of custody	• Unlikely
• Search warrant affidavits	• None
• Discovery motions and subpoenas	• None
• Assist with trial preparation	• Unlikely
• Can qualify as a computer forensics expert in court	• May qualify as a computer expert in court
• Adheres to ethics guidelines for forensics examiners	• Not applicable

training in forensic analysis techniques to examine file data, file system metadata, operating system artifacts, and discrete file evidence.

Table 8.2 begins to show the gap between the expertise of a computer expert and a digital forensics expert. This is a critical distinction when dealing with digital evidence in legal matters where your case may hinge on adhering to proper chain of custody, evidence handling, and whether or not evidence was obtained within the scope of a warrant or court order. The reason this is so important is that during the voir dire process of qualifying someone as a computer forensics expert, these areas will be addressed by the court through examination of the expert's work history, specific forensics training, specific forensic certifications, prior testimony, and prior publications.

8.4 INVESTIGATION OF DIGITAL EVIDENCE

Computer experts do not have a need to understand examination of digital evidence. No computer training course deals with this type of knowledge, nor should it.

If you attend computer training courses, you will find that the focus is on a specific topic such as using Windows, or writing applications, installing server software, or implementing network security. Whether the course is covering software development or installation and maintenance of a server, the ultimate goal is always to provide a service to end users.

Once a person begins to attend courses related to obtaining electronic evidence and subsequently examining that evidence, they are now crossing over into the forensics side. For example, taking courses in network security normally progresses from simply setting up perimeter devices such as firewalls, to analyzing the logs of the firewalls and intrusion detection systems, as well as server logs, to determine attack vectors, culpability, and remediation of a breach. This is network forensics.

8.4.1 What does it mean to "investigate"?

To the layman, investigating a computer might include determining what someone has been doing on the Internet; for example, has my employee been surfing porn on the Internet during working hours? Or perhaps, one might want to know if their spouse has been communicating with a paramour via e-mail. Are my kids going places they shouldn't go on the Internet when they are using the home computer?

While these are investigations that digital forensics experts perform on a regular basis, the difference is how thorough an investigation do you need and what is the expected next step?

If you are just trying to make sure your kids are safe on the Internet, a cursory review of the Internet browsing history will probably be sufficient to either confirm or assuage your fears. However, if the examination of the Internet activity on a computer is going to lead to potential legal proceedings, whether you are terminating an employee for violating your computer usage policy or planning to use evidence of an affair in a divorce proceeding, then having the ability to verify the information recovered can be critical in determining the admissibility of the evidence. Simply poking around in a computer to find this information without taking steps to protect the authenticity could result in losing your case.

In complex cases involving civil litigation where documents or e-mails are going to be a factor in determining the outcome of the case, the correct analysis could mean the difference between winning and losing. What this means is that beyond the recovery of a piece of evidence, the next step is to properly frame that evidence through correct interpretation. In other words, you can rarely look at a piece of electronic evidence in isolation. Suppose that you have a client accused of stealing corporate data. You hire someone to examine the computer to determine if the accusations have any merit. The questions that must be answered in such a case are as follows:

1. Was the data ever present in the first place in an area that the user had access?
2. If it was, what is the evidence that the user took a copy of the data?
3. Does evidence of the data being located on an external hard drive prove that the user "copied" the data for a nefarious reason?
4. If you find evidence that an external hard drive such as a USB stick was inserted into the computer, does that alone prove anything?

One of the most important factors in any investigation into digital evidence is user attribution. In other words, can you prove that the person accused is the person who was actually at the keyboard? In forensic examinations of digital evidence, the need to not only find a piece of evidence, but also determine who created that piece of evidence involves delving into the what, when, how, and who of the evidence.

If something was deleted, can you find it? Can you determine when it was actually deleted? Can you determine who deleted it? Is it possible to prove ownership of the deletion itself? Very few systems have any type of specific logging turned on that will record who modifies a file. In the case of a personal computer where the user does not have a password protecting their individual account, then attributing the deletion to that person just became extremely difficult.

These are all basic questions that must be answered, if they can be answered, in any digital forensics investigation. To simply say, "I found this on Sally's computer" is not enough to ensure that your evidence will be allowed, or that you can show that Sally actually is the one who put that e-mail or document or picture on the computer.

When one gets into the actual investigation and examination of computer or other digital evidence, the complexity increases by orders of magnitude when an examiner must not only locate the evidence, but find all the facts surrounding that piece of evidence. Who was logged on to the computer at the time the evidence was created? Was the account password protected? Is the date accurate? Is it relevant? Was the original evidence protected when this item was located to ensure that the evidence wasn't modified or planted? Did the person who examined the computer have a legal right to do so?

Dealing with these types of questions is the area where the differences between a computer expert and a digital forensics expert begin to really assert themselves. Does the person you are considering using to perform a computer forensics examination have the background and training to ensure that the results will be legally obtained, properly protected, completely analyzed, and ultimately allowed in court?

SUMMARY

This chapter examined the differences between computer experts and digital forensics experts, delving into the technical, legal, and investigative aspects of their training and experience. Information in this chapter also touched on the basics of the examination of digital evidence.

Selecting a Digital Forensics Expert

INFORMATION IN THIS CHAPTER:

- What is an expert?
- Locating and selecting an expert
- Certifications
- Training, education, and experience
- The right forensic tools

INTRODUCTION

In the field of digital forensics, there is no governing body at the national or state level that accredits examiners as being competent in their field. The industry does not have a bar exam or other accreditation system to ensure that experts have even the minimum qualifications necessary to practice in this field. This means that anyone can call themselves a digital forensics examiner regardless of their capabilities, experience, or competence. This is why the selection process of a digital forensics expert is so critical. It also gets more complicated; an examiner may be an expert in computer forensics, but not in cell phone forensics, cell tower technology, or GPS forensics, for example. If your case contains a particular type of digital evidence, it is important to hire an expert who has particular experience and credentials in that specific type of evidence, be it computer forensics, cell phone forensics, GPS forensics, or cell tower technology. A computer forensics expert isn't going to do you much good in a case involving cell tower evidence, and in all likelihood will not be able to qualify as an expert witness in court in the area of cell tower evidence analysis. This chapter will cover what you need to look for in an examiner regarding their credentials, experience, and competencies as it comes to the different subdisciplines of digital forensics and the evidence associated with them.

9.1 WHAT IS AN EXPERT?

Depending on your state or jurisdiction, the test used to determine whether or not expert testimony will be allowed by the court may be the Frye test (*Frye v. United States*, 293 F. 1013 (D.C. Cir. 1923))[1], Daubert test (*Daubert v. Merrell Dow*

Pharmaceuticals, 509 U.S. 579 (1993))[2], Porter test (*State v. Porter*, 241 Conn. 57, 698 A.2d 739 (1997))[3], cert. denied, 523 U.S. 1058, 118 S. Ct. 1384, 140 L. Ed. 2d 645 (1998) (Sec. 7-2 Connecticut Code of Evidence)[4] or other test outlined in that state's code. Many states have practice manuals and a set of specific statutes that govern experts and expert testimony. Contacting your state bar association is an excellent way to locate this type of information.

The federal system uses Section 700 of the Federal Rules of Evidence, and specifically Rule 702 to define expert witness testimony.

> *Federal Rules of Evidence: Rule 702. Testimony by Experts:*[5]
>
> *If scientific, technical, or other specialized knowledge will assist the trier of fact to understand the evidence or to determine a fact in issue, a witness qualified as an expert by knowledge, skill, experience, training, or education, may testify thereto in the form of an opinion or otherwise, if (1) the testimony is based upon sufficient facts or data, (2) the testimony is the product of reliable principles and methods, and (3) the witness has applied the principles and methods reliably to the facts of the case.*[6]

No matter which rule governs your particular case, all experts must first qualify as an expert in any case in the United States where they will be asked to provide expert testimony. However, depending on the court and the judge, this qualification process can be all over the board. Some judges are willing to qualify anyone as a computer forensics expert if they have any computer background at all, since many judges lack the basic understanding of what a computer forensics expert does and what should be a minimum floor for qualification as an expert.

Using experts in court is a battle not only of expertise, but of perception. Experts who look good on paper may not be the best choice if they have limited public speaking experience, do not present themselves professionally, or have trouble explaining complex technical concepts in a simple, easy-to-understand way, which can be a problem when taking the expert to court.

While prior court testimony experience is a big plus, lack of testimony experience is certainly not a reason not to hire an expert.

While the legal definition of an expert is outlined very specifically, the practical side of determining whether someone is an expert in a particular field is equally if not more important than making sure that the expert you engage can qualify in court. Also, it is important to make sure that the expert is the right one for you and your case.

An important step in your initial hiring process is to interview the expert, preferably face to face. In any event, you will want to judge the demeanor of your expert early on, just as a precaution. While an expert might have a great resume, if he is abrasive or condescending or unable to communicate in a nontechnical way, he could become a problem in front of a jury.

Having said that, it is still important that your examiner be able to qualify as an expert in the event that you need the expert to testify in a court of law, bearing in mind that even if she is not required to testify in the initial matter, she may need to testify in the event of an appeal or may have to go through the deposition process.

From a practical standpoint, an expert is someone who not only has technical training and experience in the area that you wish to engage their services, but they should also have references to back up that expertise.

The same holds true for certifications in the field of forensics. Forensic certifications are expensive to pursue and difficult to obtain, and while they add confidence to the credentials of the examiner, they are not required for an examiner to qualify in court or to be engaged to provide expert services.

However, beware of the expert who does not have at least a minimum of experience or training specifically in the area of expertise that you need. The reason for this is that the expert must have specific knowledge of forensic methods and processes. The danger for the unaware is that you can hire someone who has expertise in computers, for instance, but does not have specific training or expertise in dealing with computer or cell phone data as evidence. This lack of expertise in the forensic aspects of technology can become a real problem if your case involves an opposing expert who does have that expertise and can show where your expert has failed to properly protect evidence or even destroyed evidence.

The second part of prequalifying an expert as a practical matter is to understand that having experience and or training in forensic investigations is of particular importance where the case involves complex civil or criminal litigation. These cases go beyond simple data recovery and production and can involve multiple persons, specific types of data such as financial records, proprietary software formats, complex relationships between user accounts, data-hiding techniques, and correlation to external devices.

For example, a marital infidelity examination normally involves locating e-mails, Internet history, chat logs, and perhaps pictures, and may not go beyond simply producing this information to show a connection to a paramour.

A criminal case, on the other hand, will always have an expert on the side of the government who has already performed a forensic investigation into the digital evidence. In these cases, if the defense employs an expert, and they certainly should, the expert must not only be able to duplicate and verify the prosecution examiner's work, but they must also be able to properly perform their own examination to ensure that the claims being made by the prosecution are in fact valid and have been properly interpreted.

9.2 LOCATING AND SELECTING AN EXPERT

The best method for locating an expert is through referrals from others who have used experts in the area of expertise that you need. Use of your local state's list serve is an excellent way to locate experts as well as national list serves such as the National Association of Criminal Defense Lawyers.

Failing that option, locating an expert using the Internet search engines like Google, Bing, and Yahoo is an option. While you may get a lot of results or "hits" when you perform the search, sifting through the experts is particularly important when you begin the prequalification process prior to engaging an expert. Remember that the web is used for marketing and can contain a significant amount of hyperbole in the stated expertise of experts.

There are expert witness locator services; some are services where the expert pays a fee to be listed and others are services that qualify experts and the client pays a fee to the locator service when hiring them. One such service that stands out is the Round Table Group (www.roundtablegroup.com). When the expert is paying the freight to be listed on an expert witness list or website, it is just another marketing tool. In any event, you will still need to go through your own prequalification process.

9.2.1 Establishing your selection criteria

The first step in locating and selecting an expert is figuring out what criteria you want to use to filter down the type of expert you need.

9.2.2 What evidence is part of your case?

If your case includes multiple types of evidence such as computers, cell phones, cell phone records, and so on, finding a firm that can handle all of those types of evidence can be a plus. This leads us to the first criterion: What types of evidence do you need to deal with and what kind of expert do you need?

Computer evidence is still the most common type of evidence out there. However, that is quickly being matched by portable devices such as cell phones and pad computers like the Apple iPad. Other common types of evidence are video and audio. Less common evidence includes global positioning units (GPS) evidence, cell phone records, wiretaps, and pen trap evidence.

If you are looking for an expert in computer forensics, then that is going to be the broadest category of experts in the field as that was the beginning of the digital evidence discipline. Experts who can interpret and testify about cell phone call detail records are much less common. If you are dealing with pen traps or wiretap evidence, then an expert in that specific area is a must due to the legal and technical and evidentiary complexities of those types of cases.

9.2.3 What type of case do you have?

The second criterion is a little more difficult to work with because every forensic examiner will handle some type of case, but not all will take every type of case. The broadest divide is in criminal and civil cases. You can expect that nearly every examiner will be willing to take a civil case, with the exception that some may not take domestic cases. Examiners who will take criminal defense cases are in the minority. To further break that down, examiners who will take criminal defense cases involving child pornography or other sex crimes is an even smaller minority.

Some ways to determine if the examiner will take a criminal case is to look at their professional affiliations. Most examiners who have websites will list these professional memberships. Anyone who is a member of the High Technology Crimes Investigation Association (HTCIA) is barred by the association's bylaws from working for the defense in a criminal matter. Many HTCIA members perform criminal work for local, state, and government agencies on the prosecution side. On the other hand, if the expert is an associate or full member of the National Association of Criminal Defense Lawyers, you can be certain that he will take some type of criminal case for the defense.

Also, many private forensic examiners are prior law enforcement personnel and still maintain a relationship with various law enforcement agencies. These examiners rarely take a criminal case for the defense.

9.2.4 The prequalification process

Once you have a list of potential experts, the next step is to go through a prequalification process. This involves reviewing their resumes or curriculum vitae as well as checking their references.

9.2.4.1 Prequalification questions

- Does the examiner have forensic training and experience?
  - While an expert's resume may be impressive with a listing of certifications and experience, unless those certifications and experience are specific to forensics, you are not getting the right kind of expert. Certifications are detailed later in this chapter.
- Does the examiner have experience in the type of case I have?
  - When hiring an examiner, it is helpful if they have prior experience in the specific type of case. In most cases, this is not much of a barrier unless the case involves some area that is specialized, such as child pornography cases, complex financial cases, or intellectual property.
- What are the fees charged by the examiner? Are they reasonable?
  - Having read about some cases that are real horror stories regarding fees, it is important to have some idea of what a reasonable fee estimate should be. If the examiner you are considering hiring is talking in the tens of thousands of dollars for a case, there should be a very good basis for those fees. The simplest way to check the reasonableness of the proposed fee engagement is to get quotes from more than one examiner. While this seems elementary, it is not often done when hiring experts. Watch for experts who claim that they will need to bring a truckload of equipment to do an examination of a couple of computers for some exorbitant amount of money.

9.2.5 What is a reasonable fee?

Fees for cases can vary significantly from one examiner to the next. While a low hourly fee does not guarantee a less skilled examiner, be aware that the low fee may be a red flag in other ways. It may indicate lack of experience, a part-time examiner who works somewhere else full-time, lack of proper insurance, or lack of commercial forensic tools. Getting work done cheaply may end up costing you and your client far more in the end. The difference in fees between an examiner who is ultimately not skilled enough to handle your case and one that is more expensive but better suited to your case needs can be significant.

A reasonable fee in one case may seem completely unreasonable in another. Some of the factors that will impact the fees for a particular case are:

- **The amount of evidence to be examined.** Looking at a single small hard drive is far different from examining multiple large hard drives.
- **The complexity of the case.** Complex cases where many different types of evidence have to be analyzed also impact the costs of doing a case. Recovering data that is hidden or located in the unallocated space on the hard drive is more expensive than simple recovery and analysis. If the case involves a combination of complex file recovery, e-mail, Internet history, visual image analysis, keyword searches, user account analysis, timeline analysis, and other functions, the case will take a lot more time and hence be more expensive.
- **If the case involves child pornography images**, the examiner must travel to and perform all of the work at a law enforcement agency. This will add to the expense as the examiner must charge for all the time spent at the agency, including computer processing time that might not be charged for if the case were analyzed in the examiner's lab.
- **Court preparation and testimony**. As cases increase in complexity, court preparation time increases as well.

9.2.6 How can you tell what is a reasonable fee quote?

The more experience an examiner has with a type of case, the more accurately she can quote you an estimate of what your case will require. However, the caveat here is that every case has its surprises, and the quote may change once the examiner actually starts work. Table 9.1 gives some general estimates for different types of cases. These estimates are exclusive of court testimony. The most accurate way to quote a case is for the portion of the examination through report writing, but exclusive of court testimony.

Most cases tend toward the minimums in the table. Some of the variables that can make case estimates balloon are hard drive size, number of drives to analyze, and other analysis tasks such as keyword searches and searches in unallocated space, and if the case is in a language foreign to the examiner. A good example of an extreme would be a case where there were over one hundred e-mail accounts and over one million e-mails on a single computer being used by a single user that had to be

Table 9.1 General Time Estimates by Case Type

Case Type	General Estimate of Hours Required
Simple domestic case: Forensic copying of original evidence in the lab, recovery of Internet history, e-mail, chat logs, pictures.	10 to 20 hours
Forensic software-based single cell phone examination	4+ hours
Manual examination of a single cell phone	4 to 8 hours
Civil case	10 to 50+ hours depending on complexity
Criminal case	15 to 50+ hours depending on complexity
Child pornography case	20 to 60+ hours depending on complexity and location. Cost is higher due to Adam Walsh Act requirement that has the examiner onsite during the entire process. Additionally, travel cost to and from the location is required if it is not local to the examiner.
Simple hard drive imaging: A single hard drive in a computer that is easy to access.	2 hours if done in lab (many examiners charge a flat fee for making forensic images of hard drives). 3 to 12 hours if onsite (depends on size of drive).
Complex hard drive imaging: Complex RAID setups, odd formatting, extremely large size (multiple terabytes).	2 to 25 hours depending on size, hardware type, operating system, and formatting.

recovered and analyzed. There is no way to anticipate when a case that appears to be a simple e-mail recovery might turn into a massive amount of e-mails like this case.

The more complete information you have about the type of equipment to be examined and what you will need from the case, the more accurate the estimate will generally be. If you do not have specific information about the number of computers to be copied and/or examined or the type of computers, then the examiner can attempt to provide an estimate on a per-machine, per–hard drive, or per-device basis, with the dollar amount being calculated after an inventory of the items to be examined is completed.

9.3 CERTIFICATIONS

There are not that many computer and other forensic certifications that apply to this field. However, there are dozens of certifications in the computer field. Rather than trying to list every possible computer certification here, only the prominent computer forensic certifications are listed. The list is not exhaustive and lists only the most prominent certifications. If the certification your potential expert has is not on this list, then it is in your best interest to look it up to make sure it is a forensic certification. Having a certification is not the sole deciding factor in hiring an expert. There are a lot more uncertified examiners out there than certified ones, and lacking a certification does not mean that an examiner will not be able to perform proper work or that they will not be able to qualify as a forensics expert in court.

- **EnCase Certified Examiner (EnCE)**
  - This is probably the most widely known and recognized certification. This is a vendor-specific certification that is provided through Guidance Software, the publishers of the EnCase Forensic Software. EnCase is widely used in law enforcement and in the private sector. (www.encase.com)
- **Access Certified Examiner (ACE)**
  - This is the vendor-specific certification for the Forensic Tool Kit (FTK) software by Access Data Corporation. FTK is widely used in law enforcement and in the private sector. (www.accessdata.com)
- **Certified Computer Examiner (CCE)**
  - This is a vendor-neutral certification administered by The International Society of Forensic Computer Examiners. The CCE is one of the oldest certification programs. (www.isfce.com)
- **GIAC Certified Forensic Examiner (GCFE) and GIAC Certified Forensic Analyst (GCFA)**
  - These are vendor-neutral certifications administered by SANS Institute and are supported by extensive training programs. (www.giac.org)
- **Certified Forensic Computer Examiner (CFCE)**
  - These certifications are offered by the International Association of Computer Investigative Specialists (IACIS). Until recently the certification has been open only to active or retired law enforcement officers. As of July 2011, the certification is open to the general public. (www.iacis.com)

9.4 TRAINING, EDUCATION, AND EXPERIENCE

Until a few years ago, degree programs in computer forensics or digital forensics were nonexistent. These days there are numerous universities offering programs in digital forensics.

Traditionally, computer forensics examiners and digital forensics examiners have received training from vendors, from other experts, and from their own in-house training programs. Law enforcement examiners typically receive training through law enforcement–sponsored training programs as well as from vendors of forensic software tools.

The more training the examiner has, the greater the confidence you can have in hiring her to perform forensic services.

The greatest practical value of all is real case experience. This means that the expert has been in the trenches performing the work and can be vetted through references from clients.

Ultimately, the ideal expert is going to have a combination of certifications, experience, and education specific to the field and specific to the type of evidence in your case.

Once you have narrowed down your selection to the top one or two, always take a minute to run a Google search on the expert. You just want to be sure that some derogatory information isn't going to show up about your expert that might have an impact on her ability to testify in court. See if she has a Facebook or MySpace page that is publicly accessible and if she does, make sure you review it. Another good resource to check on the expert is LinkedIn (www.linkedin.com).

9.5 THE RIGHT FORENSIC TOOLS

One thing you want to make sure of when you are selecting an expert is whether or not the expert has the appropriate forensic tools. It may seem silly to think that anyone would put themselves into the market without owning some type of forensic tool, but it happens more often than you might think. The reason for this is that commercial forensic tools are expensive. If the expert you are going to hire is going to use free, open source tools, then you should consider asking them if the tool they are going to use has been used in court and what the results were if the tool was challenged. If they cannot answer that question, they are probably not the right expert for you.

As to what are the "right" tools, the debate could go on about open source tools versus commercial tools; however, the fact is that the vast majority of law enforcement agencies and forensic consulting companies use commercial tools. They are well supported, have been tested in court many times, and are, for the most part, more efficient than open source tools.

Owning and using commercial tools is evidence of a significant monetary investment by the examiner in his or her business and craft. Not only do many commercial tools have a high purchase price, but they also have an annual maintenance fee that must be paid to keep the tool up to date.

Some open source tools are well accepted by the forensic community, such as the Linux DD copy method. It is forensically sound and verifiable. Another open source tool used by many in the forensic community is a cell phone tool called BitPim (www.bitpim.org).

When it comes to computer forensic tools, commercial tools like EnCase and FTK (Forensic Tool Kit) dominate the marketplace worldwide and one or the other, or both, are used by nearly every law enforcement agency in the world. Other commercial tools that are out there that are used by consultants and agencies are Paraben's P2 Commander, X Ways Forensics, and Smart for Linux by ASR Data.

Even if the expert is not using one of the flagship commercial packages like EnCase or FTK, he should at least know about them and be able to deal with the forensic file formats these software packages create. If you are thinking about hiring an expert and he does not know these tools, that should be a major red flag.

Other types of digital forensics require specialized tools specifically designed to deal with a particular type of hardware such as cell phones or GPS units.

It is in your best interest to check out whatever tools the expert says he owns and knows how to use. Every commercial tool is easily located via a Google search.

SUMMARY

In this chapter we looked at aspects of locating and selecting a digital forensics expert, including education, training, and certifications. We also examined a method for prequalifying an expert and how to check up on an expert to make sure you are not unpleasantly surprised by his online background. We also took a look at some ways to determine whether the quoted fees for your case are reasonable. We also discussed the types of tools an expert should have and know how to use.

References

[1] *Frye v. United States*, 293 F. 1013 (D.C. Cir. 1923), *available at* <http://scholar.google.com/scholar_case?q=FRYE+v.UNITED+STATES.+293+F.+1013+%28+D.C..+Cir+1923&hl=en&as_sdt=2,34&case=827109112258472814>.

[2] *Daubert v. Merrell Dow Pharmaceuticals*, 509 U.S. 579 (1993), *available at* <http://scholar.google.com/scholar_case?case=827109112258472814&q=Daubert+v.+Merrell+Dow+Pharmaceuticals,+509+U.S.+579+%281993%29+%29&hl=en&as_sdt=2,34>

[3] *State v. Porter*, 241 Conn. 57, 698 A.2d 739 (1997), *available at* <http://scholar.google.com/scholar_case?case=4686561469800639820&q=State+v.+Porter,+241+Conn.+57,+698+A.2d+739+%281997+%29&hl=en&as_sdt=2,34>

[4] *Official 2000 Connecticut Code of Evidence*, Connecticut Judicial Branch. <http://www.jud.ct.gov/Publications/code2000.pdf>, 2009 (accessed 11.05.19).

[5] Legal Information Institute at Cornell Law School. *Federal Rules of Evidence (LII 2010 ed.)*. <http://www.law.cornell.edu/rules/fre/rules.htm> (accessed 11.05.19).

[6] Legal Information Institute at Cornell Law School, *Federal Rules of Evidence (LII 2010 ed.)*. <http://www.law.cornell.edu/rules/fre/rules.htm> (accessed 11.05.19).

What to Expect from an Expert

10

INFORMATION IN THIS CHAPTER:

- General expectations
- Where to begin?
- The examination
- Court preparation
- Expert advice

INTRODUCTION

Depending on the type of service you need in a particular case, an expert should be expected to assist you with all of the steps regarding digital evidence. Many attorneys and commercial clients are dealing with digital evidence for the very first time, and there is a significant knowledge gap as to the handling of cases involving digital evidence. It is the expert's role to bridge this gap by assisting the attorney in identifying and obtaining evidence through discovery, reviewing expert reports and providing an assessment of the case, making sure that any evidence is properly collected and handled in a forensically sound manner, educating the attorney about the specific evidence in the case, and assisting the attorney with trial preparation.

10.1 GENERAL EXPECTATIONS

When you contact a forensic expert, you may have no idea of what you need to do to deal with this type of evidence. And depending on the type of case, the steps that must be taken can vary considerably.

The most basic considerations are obtaining the evidence via motions or orders to access the evidence, what type of evidence to ask for it if is not already clearly spelled out, and a review of the opposing expert's work if one is involved in the case.

If you are the plaintiff in a case, it will fall on you to obtain all the evidence you will need to litigate the case. Unless you are already well versed in the many types and forms of evidence and evidence storage, you may be at a loss as to what to ask for and where to get it. An expert can assist you through the process of identifying potential evidence, creating motion language to obtain the evidence, and finally, analyzing the evidence.

If you are representing a client in a criminal case, you will be dealing with search warrants and affidavits that are technical in nature, especially in cases involving Internet stings and file-sharing programs. An expert can and should assist the attorney in reviewing warrant affidavits, assessing the forensics performed by law enforcement experts, and in answering questions for your client about the digital forensics aspect of their case. In many cases, a digital forensics expert can assist you and your client with assessing the merits of a case where digital evidence is the primary evidence in the case.

Engaging a properly experienced expert can also be critical in assisting you with your pre-trial motions by providing assistance with understanding the way evidence was gathered and preserved, analyzing the probable cause in search warrant affidavits, and assisting in the assessment of cost burdens for processing various types of evidence in civil cases.

10.2 WHERE TO BEGIN?

The question of where to begin comes up in every case. And the answer many times is dependent on the need in the particular case.

If the case is a civil case, the process of identifying and then getting and collecting evidence is the first step. The expert should be able to assist with motion language to make sure that the evidence is made available and also be able to outline, if needed, the processes and procedures that will be used to collect the evidence in a forensically sound manner.

For example, the expert can provide a protocol or set of requirements that can be included in production motions to ensure that the evidence is properly collected. This is particularly important when you are using third parties to collect and copy digital evidence, or if the other side is producing the evidence using their own experts or personnel.

10.2.1 Sample protocol for evidence collection by a third or opposing party

The following protocol shall govern the collection, copying, and preservation of evidence to be produced by the plaintiff:

1. All media shall be copied in a forensically sound manner in compliance with accepted best practices for the handling, copying, verification, and preservation of digital evidence.
   a. No computer or other device shall be operated, previewed, copied, or otherwise "powered on" without proper write-blocking hardware or software in place to protect the original evidence.

  b. All collection, handling, and copying of digital evidence shall be performed by a properly trained forensics examiner with specific experience and training for the type of device that is to be copied; computers and computer storage media shall be handled and copied by trained computer forensics examiners; cell phones and mobile devices shall be handled and copied by trained cell phone forensics examiners.

  c. Any type of digital evidence that requires that a representative of plaintiff or defendant, or a third party, assist in the collection and copying of said evidence, such as NetApp shares and snapshots, server file shares, mail stores, backup volumes, and so forth, shall be performed under the supervision of a trained digital forensics examiner.

  d. All forensic copies shall be made using a standard forensic collection tool, which may include but is not limited to FTK Imager, EnCase, Helix, Forensic Talon, or Tableau. Any such tool used must have the capability of generating a verification hash for the evidence copied.

  e. All forensic copies shall be delivered in a standard encapsulated format such as the Expert Witness (E01) Format, EnCase Logical Format (L01), Access Data's Logical Format (AD1), or the Linux DD format.

  f. Mobile devices such as cell phones and GPS units shall be copied using forensic tools designed for the specific purpose of analyzing such devices in a forensically sound manner. Forensic tools for this can include but are not limited to Paraben's Device Seizure, Susteen's SecureView, XRY, Cellebrite, CellDek, or Blackthorn. Any tool to be used for the forensic copying of mobile devices shall be disclosed and approved by the supervising digital forensics examiner prior to collection of any mobile device data.

  g. In the event those copies cannot be made in the following formats due to technical issues, the supervising digital forensics examiner shall be notified as to the reason and propose an alternative collection method to be employed.

2. Documentation Requirements

  a. A complete chain of custody shall be created and maintained for all evidence collected.

  b. An acquisition report shall be created for all evidence collected, by item, and shall include at a minimum the following information:

    i. The name and contact information of the person who performed the collection and copying of the evidence.

    ii. The qualifications of the person who performed the collection and copying of the evidence.

    iii. The acquisition hash values in MD5 and/or SHA1 format for each item of evidence collected.

    iv. The specific process used for the collection and copying of each item of evidence, including the manufacturer, name, and version of the tool used for both hardware and software tools.

    v. The method used to protect the evidence, including the make and manufacturer of the write-blocking method employed.

   vi. The origination of the evidence item including the originating location (server, computer, cell phone), device name and serial or asset tag number, file path(s), manufacturer, make and model of the device, and the corresponding custodian name or owner of the data.

  vii. The name and contact information of any person who assisted in the collection or copying of the device.

The reason such a protocol is critical is that many times, especially in small civil cases, one side may decide to use a non-expert to perform collections. In many cases, the person handling the collection and examination of evidence had no training or experience in forensics, did not use any forensic tools for protecting the evidence or making forensic copies, and modified the evidence during the collection and examination process. Rarely does this come to light until you get to court and the person's qualifications are revealed to be that they "helped out neighbors and friends with recovering their lost family pictures, removing viruses, and generally fixing their computers."

When you get contaminated evidence in a case like this, it becomes a much larger job for your expert to sort out what has been done, and verification of the evidence and facts may become impossible.

Once the evidence is collected, the expert may be required to write an affidavit outlining the processes and procedures used and documenting the chain of custody. Alternatively, your expert may be required to prepare an affidavit challenging the methods used and the chain of custody for evidence collected and produced by the opposing side.

In a criminal case, the expert should be able to discuss the case with you and assist with motions and subpoenas for getting either a copy of the evidence, or in the case of an Adam Walsh Act contraband case, motions to get access to a copy of the evidence for analysis.

For example, in a criminal case where there is a serious risk of contamination, to the point where the issue will be brought up at trial as part of your defense argument, then an expert can assist you in assessing the risk of tampering and also to prepare a motion that will allow your expert to make a new forensic copy of the evidence in question for comparison to the forensic evidence provided by law enforcement. However, this will add significant expense to the case due to the additional work that must be performed to make new forensic copies and compare them to the copies made by law enforcement. Not only would you need to justify the additional expense to whoever is paying for the expert's services, but you will probably meet stiff resistance from the prosecution in getting such a motion approved by a judge.

At this point, you may need an affidavit from your expert to support the motion and/or testimony at a pre-trial hearing by your expert to explain why it is necessary to recopy what the prosecution has already provided.

Different types of evidence will require different language specific to obtaining that evidence. For instance, the subpoena language to get the proper records from a cell phone provider is very different from the language needed to get forensic copies of computers and cell phones in the hands of law enforcement.

For example, to obtain call detail records from a cellular carrier, you will need to specify exactly what you want to get in the subpoena response. In a case involving cell tower locations for a cellular phone, just getting the call detail records is not enough to properly perform an analysis. You will also need to have language in your subpoena to obtain engineering and maintenance information about the cell towers of interest. Motion language for call detail records and cell tower information is covered in Chapter 24.

In the case of cell phones, there are still many police departments and law enforcement agencies that do not have the resources to examine cell phones. If this is true in your case, it is doubly important to get any cell phones properly collected and examined by your expert before they are damaged in some way or returned to the owner.

In any of the cases, the expert should already have or be able to write the technical language needed to obtain evidence and assist you with this process.

10.3 THE EXAMINATION

Once the evidence has been gathered, the expert will perform an examination or analysis of the evidence. Based on information provided by you as the attorney and your client, and the expert's review of an opposing expert's forensic report, the expert is expected to perform the following steps:

1. Verify the work of an opposing expert.
2. Perform an independent analysis of the evidence to ensure that all of the facts are accurate and also that the evidence has been completely analyzed if an opposing expert is involved in the case.
3. Once the analysis has been completed, the expert should be able to advise you on the findings and in some cases, the merits of the digital evidence in the case.
4. Assist you with trial preparation based on the analysis of the digital evidence.

10.4 COURT PREPARATION

Part of the process is assisting the attorney with court preparation. This involves anticipating what the opposing expert may testify about based on their forensic reports. As part of the process, a series of questions should be developed by the expert to assist the attorney with cross-examination of the opposing expert.

Some examples of such questions include:

1. During your examination of the computer in question, did you check and verify the accuracy of the date and time of the computer's built-in clock?
2. Is there a possibility that the computer clock was set to an earlier time to cover up the fact that the witness could have planted this evidence on the computer?

3. Did you take any steps to verify that the computer clock was not manipulated in some way by setting to an earlier time and then setting it back to the current time?
4. Can you tell the court whether or not my client had his own personal login for the computer?
5. Can you tell the court if my client's login was password protected?
6. Can you explain the steps you took to protect the evidence on the hard drive when you made your copy?

The expert may also be required to testify and should be able to provide testimony as to the ownership of the computer, ownership of various files, the handling and collection of the evidence, specifics relating to the software installed on the computer, and dates and times of computer activities.

10.5 EXPERT ADVICE

Before a case goes to court, the expert may be asked to advise the attorney as to the merits of the case in regard to the digital evidence located or presented. This is mostly true in criminal cases where the expert has had an opportunity to review the digital evidence and form an opinion of the strength of the evidence if presented at trial.

10.1 MERITS OF THE CASE

Larry had a case where an attorney contacted him late on a Friday afternoon. His client was charged with possession of child pornography, and he was scheduled to attend court the following Monday to either accept a plea bargain or enter a not-guilty plea and to go to trial. The attorney and the client met with Larry that evening and Larry reviewed the discovery in the case, including the computer forensic report compiled by the law enforcement agency.

After reviewing the discovery and asking the client some pointed questions with his attorney present, Larry advised the client that going to court would be a high risk compared to the plea offer he had on the table. While the client maintained that he did not know about the presence of the child pornography located on his computer and external hard drive, he could offer no explanation for how it got there. He said that he did not know of anyone else using his computer and that he was the only one who had ever used his external hard drive, which was stored in his bedroom closet. He could think of no witnesses to anyone seeing someone using his computer. It boiled down to his only being able to state that he didn't do it, but there was no evidence or witness he could name to contradict the forensic report provided by law enforcement. Other elements of the case added to the problem as he was also charged with secret peeping for installing a hidden camera in his bathroom for him and his girlfriend to record their sexual encounters. He had a plea offer on the table to only serve probation and register as a sex offender for five years. The client decided to take the offered plea. When he attended court the following Monday, the judge told him after he accepted the plea bargain that if he had not done so and lost at trial, the judge would have put him in prison until he was an old man. The client was in his early twenties and based on the sentencing guidelines, if he had lost at trial he could have been sentenced to prison for over 25 years.

SUMMARY

In this chapter we discussed what you as an attorney or client should expect from a digital forensics expert. We looked at motions and discovery and some of the ways an expert can assist in getting discovery in the correct manner. We also looked at what to expect in a computer forensics report and included a sample of the minimum information you should expect to be provided in computer or other digital forensic reports. This chapter also covered trial preparation, some sample questions for court testimony, and how an expert can assist in assessing the merits of a case based on the forensic evidence.

Approaches by Different Types of Examiners

11

INFORMATION IN THIS CHAPTER:

- Standards
- Training and experience
- Impact on examinations
- Ethics
- The approach to an examination

INTRODUCTION

Digital forensics examiners come from many different backgrounds: law enforcement, private sector computer and software professionals, military, academia, and the private investigator community. Some examiners are primarily self-taught, while others have extensive training through government or private entities or are recent college graduates of one of the digital forensics programs at various universities.

Examiners can be full-time, where digital forensics is their primary function, while others are part-timers, only doing digital forensics as a small part of their primary job, or doing it as a second vocation. Some examiners handle dozens of cases each year, while others may only handle one or two cases in a year. All of these variables result in examiners taking different approaches to cases.

11.1 STANDARDS

The digital forensics field has no overall governing body that establishes standards for examiners. While the National Institute of Justice (NIJ) in the United States (http://nij.gov/nij/topics/forensics/evidence/digital/welcome.htm) and the Association of Chief Police Officers (ACPO) in the United Kingdom (www.acpo. police.uk/) have published several guides for law enforcement personnel, these are not widely known. This puts the field into a variable situation where digital forensics examiners are out there following their own rules, no rules, or have adopted the standards of the NIJ, ACPO, or one of the member organizations available, such as the High Technology Crime Investigators Association (HTCIA) (http://www.htcia.org), International Associations of Criminal Investigative Specialists (IASCIS) (http://www.iacis.com/), the American Society of Digital Forensics and E-Discovery (http://www.asdfed.com/), or the Digital Forensics Certification Board (http://www.dfcb.org), to name a few.

Not only are standards not widely followed, but internal procedures vary considerably between agencies, firms, and individual examiners. The result is that the quality and thoroughness of examiners can vary based on the individual who is performing the examination. Key questions that should always be asked of an examiner are whether they are aware of the standards organizations and publications, and if they follow any of them. Memberships in these types of organizations are no guarantee that the examiner is following best practices but do indicate that the examiner is aware of them. At the very least, the examiner should be aware of best practices in the field and where those best-practice standards come from. If they do not have that minimal knowledge, they could be a major liability for you and your client if you engage them to provide digital forensics services.

11.2 TRAINING AND EXPERIENCE

As we discussed in Chapter 10, training and education for digital forensics examiners also varies, with no particular training program being seen as a "standard." Add to this that some examiners are out there practicing with no training at all, and you add to the variability of the examinations. Bear in mind that training programs are primarily focused on teaching technique rather than standards.

A major factor in the approach taken by an examiner is going to be their amount of practical experience in the conduction of digital forensics examinations. No matter where the examiner works, be it as an independent consultant or for a major firm or large law enforcement agency, the number of cases she actually works will have a major impact on her examination. Even examiners who have had extensive training may have little practical experience in conducting examinations. As examiners perform more examinations, they learn from practical experience far more than any training program can ever offer. The reason for this is that training programs prepare the examiners to practice by providing them with the knowledge they need to begin to practice. Experience is the only teacher that can further an examiner's practical knowledge, making her more efficient and better prepared to handle the variances in the types and complexity of cases and the enormous variety of software programs that create evidence.

Inquiring into the experience and training of the examiner you propose to use in a case is one of the most important things you can do. But you must be specific in your questions about the training and experience actually being in digital forensics and not just some general area of computer expertise. The key term when dealing with computer and mobile device forensics will always be "forensics" unless you are looking for a particular type of expert, such as someone with extensive software development background for an intellectual property case or someone with training in cellular technology for a cell-tower-tracking case.

11.3 **IMPACT ON EXAMINATIONS**

The combination of variations in training, standards organizations, and internal policies and procedures leads to the reality that if you are working with an expert in the private sector, your results will vary depending on whom you hire or if you are in a corporate environment, who is managing your forensic program. This also holds true for law enforcement agencies, especially very small agencies where the examiner is doing very few cases a year and has limited access to training.

Probably the worst-case scenario is someone who has decided that computer forensics is an "easy money" field and has purchased a forensic software tool and started practicing without investing the time or money to make sure that they have at least a minimal understanding of the standard areas of digital forensics: collection, preservation, analysis, and reporting.

The results of examinations differ as widely as the diversity of examiners from a wide variety of backgrounds. The worst ones are the computer support guy who is hired by an attorney to "take a look" at a computer and pull out some evidence. They approach the case based on their knowledge of computers and file recovery. They fail to protect the evidence, do not maintain a chain of custody, perform their work directly on the subject computer rather than a forensic copy, and have no idea of the legal ramifications of what they are doing. Do they even have the legal right to do what they are doing? These types of amateur computer sleuths can seriously jeopardize a case through lack of knowledge and expose you and your client to potential lawsuits and sanctions.

On the other hand, professionally trained and experienced examiners tend to be efficient, taking less time to perform complex examinations; they prepare thorough and complete reports and have the tools and expertise to find that elusive piece of evidence that can make or break a case. Their approach will be methodical, follow logical steps, and be properly documented, and they will be able to articulate their findings in court.

11.4 **ETHICS**

Every examiner should subscribe to a code of ethics. A couple of examples are the code of ethics from two prominent organizations, the High Technology Crime Investigators Association (http://www.htcia.org/htcia_code.shtml)[1] and the American College of Forensic Examiners Institute (http://www.acfei.com/about_acfei/principles/).[2]

While ascribing to a code of ethics is not going to make a difference in the technical aspects of an examination, at a minimum it sets a standard for how examiners should conduct themselves in the course of handling examinations.

Probably the most important ethical factor for digital forensics experts is that they must never have a stake in the outcome of a case, whether that stake is financial or due to the examiner having some kind of connection to the person or a conflict of interest in the case.

Secondly, the digital forensics examiner or expert is not an advocate. While he may not be neutral, he must remain independent. A law enforcement examiner is not a neutral examiner because he works for the prosecution. The same is true for an examiner working for the plaintiff or defense. However, no matter which side the examiner is working for, he must keep an unbiased stance that allows him to stick to the facts in a case and report those facts independently of the desires or goals of the advocates in the case. A digital forensics examiner is ethically bound to report the truth, even when that truth does not match the claims of the parties. It is the advocate's responsibility to deal with the facts of the examination and decide how to proceed in a case.

11.5 THE APPROACH TO AN EXAMINATION

How a digital forensics expert approaches an examination is going to be dependent on several factors; experience with that particular type of case, experience with the tools she is using, her training and background, and restrictions placed on the examination by a court order or search warrant.

In order to conduct a completely thorough examination, the examiner should have access to multiple forensic tools. For example, the examiner may use Forensic Tool Kit (FTK) as her primary examination tool; digging into the details of an examination could require the use of a specialized tool that extracts Internet history in detail, or a tool that is designed to read a particular file type such as a chat program archive.

When someone purchases a forensic software tool and does not take the time to study how to use that tool or what steps to take with the tool, the chances are greater that they will either miss potential evidence or get bogged down in looking at evidence that would not be relevant to the case. It is just as important for an examiner to know not only how to look for a piece of evidence, but what evidence to look for. Some of what the examiner will be looking for is determined by the type of case.

For instance, in a case involving Internet chats, the examiner would focus on locating and extracting evidence for the many types of chat programs someone can use on the Internet. These would include not only dedicated chat programs like AOL Instant Messenger or Yahoo! Chat, but chats embedded in web pages that may have originated on a MySpace or Facebook page.

In a civil case involving a sexual harassment claim where one party claims he or she was sent harassing e-mails, the examination would focus on recovering and documenting these e-mails. Knowing where to look for e-mail and how to recover and document it would be a critical part of this type of examination. The other part of this type of examination would be authenticating the e-mails to provide evidence as to whether or not the alleged offender actually sent them in contrast to their being faked in some manner by the accuser.

Law enforcement examiners will normally be at least partially restricted by the terms in the search warrant. For instance, if they have a warrant to search for contraband images, they would normally focus on recovering and examining images and movies and the source of those images or movies. If the warrant is for a financial fraud case, the focus would be on recovering evidence of financial transactions and documents such as spreadsheets, e-mails, banking, credit cards, and so forth. They would not normally be looking at pictures or movies as these would not be included in the scope of the warrant. However, if during the examination they locate contraband images, these can become the basis for a search warrant for going back to look specifically for illegal materials.

However, in many cases, the search warrant language for computers has become so broad that the warrants allow searching for just about anything.

In a civil case, the digital forensics examiner might be looking for keywords in e-mails or documents. There would be no reason for the digital forensics examiner to waste time looking at pictures or movies unless the case specifically involves such potential evidence.

The number one factor in how a digital forensics examiner approaches a case is going to be the examiner's level of experience. As digital forensics examiners gain experience, they tend to become more efficient in performing examinations by learning what to focus on and most importantly, when to stop an examination. Cases where no evidence is found can be frustrating and time-consuming, especially if the client is convinced that evidence exists in spite of the findings of the examination.

SUMMARY

In this chapter we discussed the factors that affect the approaches taken by different types of examiners. We looked at some of the standard-setting organizations and how the examiner must know and follow these standards or guidelines. We also looked at the impact of the training and experience of an examiner on his or her approach to a digital forensics examination. We also looked at ethics and provided information on some organizations that have published ethical statements for their members.

References

[1] High Technology Crime Investigation Association, *HTCIA Code of Ethics and Code of Values*. <http://www.htcia.org/htcia_code.shtml> (accessed 11.05.20).
[2] American College of Forensics International, *Forensics Principles of Professional Practice*. <http://www.acfei.com/about_acfei/principles/> (accessed 11.05.20).

Spotting a Problem Expert

12

INFORMATION IN THIS CHAPTER:

- Beyond the window dressings

INTRODUCTION

Unless you are already familiar with the digital forensics expert you wish to hire, chances are you are buying a pig in a poke. You really don't know much about the digital forensics expert unless you have the benefit of having had that digital forensics expert referred to you by a colleague or someone you trust. Or you may have had some type of direct contact with the expert at a conference or training event. In this chapter we will discuss some of the warning signs of a problem expert and how to spot them.

12.1 BEYOND THE WINDOW DRESSINGS

In Chapter 9 we discussed how to go about selecting an expert. However, there is only so much you can do in the prequalification process to be certain that the expert you are engaging is the right expert for you. Many times, you won't know what you really have until the engagement begins. That is when you get to peek behind the window dressing of the fancy website and see the real person you are working with. While the expert may seem really knowledgeable and impressive based on the information he put on his website, how do you really know?

12.1.1 Verifiable experience and criminal records

As discussed in Chapter 9, having a certification is an optional part of an expert's qualifications. However, a digital forensics certification can give you some assurance about the examiner. The reason is that most certifications require that the examiner have some amount of verifiable experience prior to allowing her to take the examination.

At the time of this writing, information for some certifications that require the candidate to pass a criminal background check are: the Certified Computer Examiner (CCE) (http://www.isfce.com), the Digital Forensics Certified Practitioner (DFCP) (www.dfcb.org), and the Certified Forensic Computer Examiner (CFCE) (http://www.iacis.com). As you can imagine, it would be very embarrassing to put an expert on the stand only to find out that he or she has a criminal record. There is no reason not to ask the examiner if he or she has passed a criminal background check as part of your selection process.

While having a certification is a plus, it is certainly not enough to overcome the deficiencies of an expert who may have other issues that can negatively impact your case.

12.1.2 Attitude

How does the expert interact with you and your team? Does she seem arrogant or superior? Does she take the time to properly explain technical concepts in easy-to-understand language?

An expert who comes across as arrogant or impatient with nontechnical people will probably not present very well on the witness stand, especially if his attitude is, "I'm the expert, take my word for it." Experts who have a tendency to talk down to laypersons will continue that behavior in court at the risk of alienating the jury or coming across as less than completely honest.

12.1.3 The bull factor

When the expert is asked a question for which he does not have the answer, does he try to convince you that he does anyway? This is a great risk if the expert must testify. When asked a question about the forensics in a case, the expert must be able to stick to the facts and offer only opinions that are fact based and relevant. If the expert starts trying to confound you with his vast knowledge rather than simply saying, "I don't know the answer to that question," you may be in trouble. This can be a sign that he is using jargon to overcome a real lack of in-depth expertise in the subject matter. Chances are that you will be looking for an expert who knows a great deal more than you. The problem is when someone does know more about a subject than you do, how can you judge how much they really know compared to another subject matter expert? Being able to clearly answer technical questions in a manner that is understandable to a layperson is one of the most important skills of an expert. If you are getting the impression that the expert will fall back on jargon rather than clear explanations, you are detecting one of the trouble signs that could become a real problem as the case develops and potentially goes to court, where the expert will need to be able to explain complex technical issues to people who may not use a computer at all.

12.1.4 Appearance matters

Does the expert have a professional appearance? While our society has a tolerance for many different styles, when dealing with subject matter experts, that tolerance diminishes rapidly. The expert you engage should present herself in a manner that is acceptable in your local culture and that will convey an image of professionalism and competence. The old saying, "Never judge a book by its cover" does not apply. Everyone has an initial reaction to the appearance of an expert, and that reaction can color their impression of that expert's testimony. If the impression is negative, that expert will have to overcome the initial reaction caused by her appearance and demeanor.

12.1.5 **The big problems**

Does the expert have the time to handle your case properly? If you are having trouble getting the expert to actually examine the evidence in a timely fashion to comply with your court schedule, you will be left with the problem of not having been able to properly prepare for trial or to advise your client as to the forensic evidence in his or her case.

In a federal case in the Midwest, the defense expert was put on the stand even though he had never reviewed the evidence in the case. In the trial transcripts of his testimony, his excuse was that he didn't have time to review the evidence due to his schedule. This was in spite of the fact that he had been retained for several months prior to trial and the evidence was available for examination at his convenience. This particular expert made grand claims on his website about how he is the best expert available. His trial testimony was arrogant, combative, and he made all kinds of statements that had no factual basis. Needless to say, he didn't help the case, yet he still got paid a lot of money for his "expert" services.

12.1.6 **Aversion**

Some experts will take cases that they really shouldn't take if they cannot handle the content of the evidence. This is especially true for experts who will take a case involving child pornography, yet they cannot view the images due to a personal aversion to the evidence. (One of the roles of a defense expert in these cases is to verify that the images charged are in fact child pornography as described by law enforcement. It is critically important that the examiner you hire to handle one of these cases have experience.) The only way to do that is to view the images. This is of real importance in cases where the prosecution is not required to provide a list of the specific images being charged. In this instance, the only recourse for the defense expert is to review all of the images and attempt to ascertain what images the prosecution might be using to bring the charges against the defendant. Being unwilling to review the actual contraband images in a case should be a reason for the expert to withdraw from the case or refuse to take the case at all.

SUMMARY

In this chapter we looked at various signs of problems that can arise with digital forensics experts and how to detect them. We dealt specifically with the issues of experience, criminal history, appearance, and demeanor, as well as aversion to dealing with select types of evidence on the part of the expert. We also discussed the problem with experts who are not responsive, who do not actually review evidence, and who try to "bull" their way through testimony or questioning.

Qualifying an Expert in Court

13

INFORMATION IN THIS CHAPTER:

- Qualifying an expert
- Qualifying experts in court

INTRODUCTION

Before attempting to qualify an expert in court, it is important to determine whether he or she has the necessary qualifications in the first place. This may seem obvious, but if we look at it a little more closely, it makes sense. Before hiring an expert, it is important to determine if he has the qualifications necessary to be an expert witness when it comes to the evidence in your case. For example, just because an examiner may be an expert in computer forensics, this does not mean he is an expert in cell phones. Likewise, an examiner may be proficient in cell phone forensics, but this has little to no bearing on being an expert in cell tower technology forensics. While expertise in computer forensics can lend credibility to the examiner's knowledge of other areas, this expertise is no substitute for actual experience and training in a specific subdiscipline of digital forensics. Work with your expert to make sure he has the needed qualifications in the specific area of forensics you will be qualifying him in, and work with him to prepare the qualification questions to be used in court.

One way to compare the difference is to look at the difference between a medical pathologist and a medical forensic pathologist. They are both medical doctors and both have training in pathology. The study of pathology is the training needed to determine the cause of a disease or ailment. Forensic pathology includes specific training to determine cause of death. Only one of these two areas requires specific forensic training.

13.1 QUALIFYING AN EXPERT

To qualify an expert in court, she must meet the standards set forth by the local jurisdiction for expert testimony. The issue with qualifying experts in the various areas of digital forensics is that the field is not very well known and assumptions are made about what a digital forensics expert is. This becomes more complex as you attempt to qualify an expert in a specific area such as cell phone forensics.

13.1.1 **Federal Rules of Evidence: Rule 702 Expert Witnesses**

Rule 702 of the FRE[1] states

If scientific, technical, or other specialized knowledge will assist the trier of fact to understand the evidence or to determine a fact in issue, a witness qualified as an expert by knowledge, skill, experience, training, or education, may testify thereto in the form of an opinion or otherwise, if

(1)   *the testimony is based upon sufficient facts or data,*

(2)   *the testimony is the product of reliable principles and methods, and*

(3)   *the witness has applied the principles and methods reliably to the facts of the case.*

The key points in this rule are that an expert witness may be qualified by knowledge, skill, experience, training, or education.

Where this gets sticky is when the judge making the qualification decision has no expertise or knowledge in the area of qualification. This can easily lead to completely unqualified individuals being allowed to offer expert testimony and opinions in a case where they do not have the proper training or experience. As you prepare for the qualification process, pay special attention to the expert's resume or curriculum vitae for strengths and weaknesses. Your expert should be able to assist you with examining the opposing expert's qualifications prior to trial.

You will want to focus on your expert's strengths during qualification. During cross-examination of the opposing expert, you would want to do the opposite and press any weakness in his qualifications.

13.1.2 **The resume or curriculum vitae**

The expert's resume or curriculum vitae will include information on their education, training, and experience that provide a foundation for their claim of knowledge or skill in a particular area. The problem is that some experts will overstate their qualifications to the point of perjury. This can be especially problematic when an expert claims a degree she does not have, as has happened in some cases. That is one reason to make sure that the expert has actual verifiable experience, knowledge, education, and skills.

You can verify these areas by having the expert, at a minimum, supply along with her resume or CV, copies of training certificates, copies of certifications, and copies of college degrees or diplomas. If you have any doubts, check up on the area you are concerned about by contacting the college or university that issued the degree or the organization that issued any certifications and checking to make sure the expert earned them and that they are still valid. Many certifications expire if the expert does not pay the renewal fee and/or fails to meet the continuing education requirement to retain the certification.

13.1.3 **Certifications**

One aspect of certifications that can be very positive is that many, but not all, certifications in the forensics field require a minimum amount of verified training and work experience before the examiner can take the examination. When an expert presents certifications as part of his qualifications, it is important to ask upon cross-examination whether any training or experience was required in order to obtain the certification.

For any certification presented as part of an expert's qualifications, she should be asked to explain the type of certification and how it applies to the specific area of forensics in which she will be expected to testify. There are dozens of computer and software certifications that have no bearing on forensic analysis of digital or electronic evidence.

If in doubt, ask the expert to explain the qualifications required to obtain the certificate and who the certifying body is that issued the certificate.

13.1.4 Training

If an examiner claims hours of training specific to digital forensics, copies of the training certificates should be included for inspection by both sides as a form of verification. Watch closely for training specific to the area of forensics involved in your case, as the expert's training may indicate expertise in some area of computing, but it is not an indication of forensic training.

13.1.5 Experience

When an expert presents work experience, it is important to ask upon cross-examination if his job includes specific forensic duties. One way to attack this section is if the expert's place of employment is known prior to the hearing, you look up the company website or any other information that may help you to determine if the company that employs the expert even offers any forensic services. If he is working as a paid consultant on a case and relying on expertise gained in his employment, digging into his specific job function and tasks can assist in either supporting or weakening his qualifications.

13.1.6 Education

If your expert has a degree related to the field that you want to qualify them in, this is another area that can be used to assist in getting the expert qualified. There are degrees that can be earned specifically in digital forensics or computer forensics. However, other degrees in the computer science and information security fields cross over and can be used as a foundation for qualifying the expert witness as well. On the other hand, if your expert does not have a degree in a digital forensics area or in a computer science field, or does not have a degree at all, it may be better to not ask about education but concentrate more on experience and training. Many people in the computer or digital forensics fields do not have degrees, and the lack of a degree, if the expert is strong in other areas, should not be a barrier to getting them qualified.

13.2 QUALIFYING EXPERTS IN COURT

What you will want to accomplish through questioning of the expert witness is whether or not she has enough of any of the above to qualify her as an expert in the area in which she will be testifying. The ongoing challenge with experts is that lawyers and judges do not know enough about this particular field to adequately make a determination in many cases of whether an expert is actually qualified or not.

There are a couple of ways to attack this particular issue:

1. Cross-examination specific to the area of expertise compared to the expert's resume or curriculum vitae
2. Cross-examination on the underlying principles and practices that form the basis of the area of expertise

13.2.1 Sample qualification questions

These sample questions will use computer forensics as the focus; however, you should substitute the specific area of forensics when applicable (GPS, cell phone, cellular technology or cell tower technology, audio, video, and so on).

1. Please state your full name.
2. What is your business address?
3. Where are you employed?
4. What is your position there?
5. How long have you been employed at this company?
6. What is your job function at this company?
7. Where were you employed prior to your current job?
8. What was your position there?
9. How long were you employed there?
10. What was your job function at that company?
11. How long have you been doing computer forensics?
12. Have you ever been hired as a computer forensics expert in the past?
13. Approximately how many times have you been hired as a computer forensics expert?
14. Have you ever testified in the area of forensics?
15. How many times?
16. Have you received any training specific to computer forensics?
17. Do you hold any certifications specific to computer forensics?
18. Are those certifications current?
19. Do you have a degree or certificate in computer forensics?
20. Can you briefly explain what computer forensics is?
21. Can you briefly explain chain of custody?
22. Have you published any articles or books in the area of computer forensics?
23. Have you ever been invited to speak at any conferences related to computer forensics?

24. Are you a member of any professional organizations specifically in the field of forensics?

SUMMARY

In this chapter we looked at Federal Rules of Evidence Rule 702 regarding the qualification of expert witnesses. We also covered the types and nature of qualifying documents and statements of expert witnesses in digital forensics. Lastly, we looked at questions for the purpose of voir dire regarding the qualifications of expert witnesses.

Reference

[1] Legal Information Institute at Cornell Law School, *Federal Rules of Evidence (LII 2010 ed.)*. <http://www.law.cornell.edu/rules/fre/rules.htm#Rule702> (accessed 11.05.20).

Motions and Discovery

Overview of Digital Evidence Discovery

14

INFORMATION IN THIS CHAPTER:

- Discovery motions in civil and criminal cases

INTRODUCTION

Creating effective discovery motions for digital evidence is not a cookie-cutter process. In order to get the information your expert will need to perform a comprehensive examination, the discovery motion will need to be tailored to the type of digital evidence that is of interest in the case. For example, a discovery motion created for data on a computer will not work for all computers; what if that computer is a live production server at a corporate facility that absolutely cannot be taken offline without completely crippling a company? A situation such as this will require forensic processes that are of a higher degree of complexity when capturing that data. Yes, the data can be collected, but a discovery motion designed for a generic computer is not going to provide information that could end up being critical to a case when it comes time to actually examine the data collected from a live production server.

The following chapters in this section will guide you through our process of creating discovery motions for types of digital evidence. The expert you hire should be able to assist you in creating your discovery motions. Your expert should be the one who knows all the intricacies regarding a type of digital evidence, and should also know all the peripheral information related to that evidence needed to examine it properly. If the expert you have hired cannot do this, his competence must immediately come into question. This is not asking a digital forensics expert to be proficient in lawyering; it is asking an expert to bring his expertise to bear by assisting you in creating the discovery motion so that he can perform his job correctly.

14.1 DISCOVERY MOTIONS IN CIVIL AND CRIMINAL CASES

When you are creating discovery motions for criminal defense cases, the evidence in question is usually in a postmortem state, meaning that it is not in use, it is offline, and it is probably in the custody of law enforcement. Forensic images have probably been made of much of the evidence, and if not, access can be gained to these items so that your expert can do so. Also, the evidence usually has decent chain of custody documentation. With civil cases, it is common for the evidence items to still be in use and online. Sometimes the digital evidence devices cannot be taken offline or powered off for full forensic acquisitions. This is especially true in e-discovery cases. Even when the devices can be taken offline and fully acquired, the window of time to do so can be as limited as overnight or a few hours. Since these items are often still in use, deliberate planning and scheduling must be done in order to forensically collect the evidence of interest. It is also common to see a lack of chain of custody documentation, if any exists at all, in civil cases. Getting your expert access to the evidence is always a critical component when creating discovery motions. Due to the differences between civil and criminal cases, the discovery motions have to be crafted differently to contend with the unique challenges that civil and criminal cases have, especially when it comes to getting access to the evidence.

14.1.1 Common challenges in criminal and civil cases

The following is the 30,000-foot view of the common challenges in civil and criminal cases that need to be addressed when creating discovery motions. The subsequent chapters will cover these challenges in greater detail, but for the moment it will suffice to bring them to your attention.

14.1.1.1 Common challenges in criminal cases

1. The evidence in the case contains contraband images, preventing you from getting a copy of the evidence and requiring that all forensic examination by the defense expert be performed on location at the law enforcement facility and under the supervision of a law enforcement officer.
2. Evidence items, such as cell phones, were returned to their owners by law enforcement before an opposing expert could examine them. It is also common for this to be done without law enforcement creating any kind of copy, forensic or otherwise, of the evidence.
3. All elements of the documentation created by the law enforcement examiner, such as reports and bench notes, are not requested in the discovery motion.
4. Evidence is not turned over because the law enforcement agency did not have the tools to make a copy of the evidence.
5. The evidence is in a form that is difficult to capture, such as a global positioning system (GPS) device.

14.1.1.2 Common challenges in civil cases

1. The chain of custody for an item of digital evidence is poorly documented or unknown. It is important for your expert to know, if possible, of everyone who has handled this digital evidence, and whether they did so in a way that forensically preserves the evidence.

2. Access to the evidence is limited. These limitations could be because the item cannot be taken offline, such as a live production server, or if the device can only be offline or out of the possession of the custodian for a short period of time, like a CEO's laptop.

3. All of the documentation created by the opposing expert, or about the opposing expert, has not been requested in the discovery motion. This is critical in civil cases, as we have encountered many people claiming to be forensics experts who have no forensic training, experience, or tools. In these situations, there is a high probability that the opposing expert has altered the evidence in some way or even destroyed evidence.

4. There is a tendency in many civil cases to perform self-collection where the producing party collects the evidence using their computer support persons, or the custodians themselves copy documents and such to an external hard drive. This poses many problems, including the alteration of metadata, lack of authentication, and the inability to reproduce the evidence in its original unaltered form for inspection by a third party at a later date.

5. The evidence is in a format that the receiving party cannot use such as backup tape, a forensic image format, or a database, or it is in a proprietary file structure.

6. The evidence may be in the control of a third party such as a cell phone service provider, an Internet service provider, or a third-party data backup or storage provider.

SUMMARY

In this chapter we learned about some of the common challenges to getting evidence in criminal and civil cases. Such challenges include incomplete discovery motions, self-collection, inaccessible formats, and items lost due to returns to the owners without an examination being performed.

Discovery of Digital Evidence in Criminal Cases

INFORMATION IN THIS CHAPTER:

- Sources of digital evidence
- Building the motion

INTRODUCTION

Criminal cases can involve many types of digital evidence. The key is to make sure that you are getting all of the evidence you need to defend your client effectively. To do this, you must first go through the initial discovery provided in the case and then determine what digital evidence might be available, either directly from the law enforcement agency or via subpoenas of third parties. If you can get a qualified expert involved early in the case, they can assist you with determining what digital evidence may be available and of interest in the case and how to ask for it in discovery motions.

The information in this chapter can apply to any criminal case; however, specific attention must be paid to cases involving contraband. For example, federal child pornography contraband cases are governed by the Adam Walsh Child Protection and Safety Act of 2006. Discovery in cases involving contraband is covered in Chapter 21.

15.1 SOURCES OF DIGITAL EVIDENCE

Every criminal case is unique; however, the method for determining what evidence to look for via discovery can be well defined. During the initial fact-finding process of reading initial discovery provided by the prosecution, pay particular attention to items collected as well as clues to items that may be available from third parties:

- **Search Warrant Returns**
  - Search warrant returns provide a listing of all evidence collected by law enforcement when they execute the warrants. It is important to pay special

attention to the items in the inventory to see if they might yield digital evidence. While it may appear obvious that you want to ensure that you get computers and cell phones, other devices, such as cameras, GPS units, and storage devices, can also contain critical evidence.

- **Paper Discovery**
  - It can be easy to miss potential digital evidence when working through paper discovery if you are not aware of some of the evidence that can be gathered based on clues provided by witness statements, investigative reports, and documents gathered from third parties.
  - Evidence in the paper discovery can include cell phone call records, GPS records from third-party monitoring services, web pages from social media sites, printouts of e-mails and file listings, and specific computer screenshots.

15.2 BUILDING THE MOTION

When you build your motion for discovery in these cases, it is important to make sure you include items in the motion that may not seem obvious. For instance, many law enforcement agencies collect items that may contain digital evidence, yet they may never examine those items. In many cases, the warrant is written in such a way as to allow the wholesale collection of anything and everything in the realm of electronics, including items like facsimile machines, cameras, video tapes, CD-ROMs, movie cameras, music players, and game consoles.

During the process of discovery review, your expert should also be able to assist you in identifying evidence that was collected improperly from third parties and evidence that was not requested from third parties. Call detail records are collected in many cases today, and in many circumstances they are not requested properly. Discovery of call detail records is covered in detail in Chapter 24.

15.2.1 Discovery motion specifics

- **The Inventory.** Defense requests a complete inventory of all items taken that may contain any type of digital data, whether or not such items were examined or copied by prosecution's experts.
- **Items the Defense Will Supply to Assist in Getting the Discovery.** Defense will provide sanitized hard drives for the forensic copies if requested by the law enforcement agency.
- **Specifying the Forensic Copy Format.** The preferred format for forensic images is EnCase (E01) Expert Witness Format. However, any forensically sound format is acceptable. (Expert Witness Format is a widely used format that can be opened by the majority of forensic tools available. It is also easily converted into other formats. Finally, it is a self-contained set of files that are not subject to contamination.)

- **Specifying Other Formats.** Defense requests that any items provided to the prosecution in electronic format including but not limited to call detail records, audio or video recordings, and GPS logs, be provided in the same format to the defense.
- **Requesting Supplemental Documents.** Defense requests a complete copy of all forensics reports, chain of custody records, and lab notes generated by the prosecution's experts pertaining to the acquisition, preservation, analysis, and/or reporting by said experts in the course of this investigation.

  Defense also requests a copy of the resume or curriculum vitae of any prosecution expert involved in the collection, handling, imaging, or examination of any electronic evidence and or items collected.
- **Computers and Related Items.** Defense requests a duplicate of any forensic copies made by the prosecution's experts of any computer hard drive, digital storage media, including but not limited to CD-ROMs, USB flash drives, floppy disks, memory cards, digital camera storage, smart cards, and portable hard drives.
- **Cell Phones, GPS Devices, and Other Portable Devices.** Defense requests duplicates of any forensic copies made by the prosecution's experts of any cell phone and/or SIM cards, media cards, GPS devices, media players, game consoles, video recording devices, audio recording devices, or any other electronic devices collected in this case.
- **Items Collected and Not Forensically Imaged.** In the event the prosecution's experts did not make a forensic copy of any original media, defense requests that forensically sound copies be made and furnished to the defense for examination by the defense expert.

  In the event the prosecution's experts are unable to make forensic copies of any evidence, the defense requests access to said evidence in order to make forensic copies for examination.

NOTE

Why They Don't Examine What They Collect and Why You Should

Many police departments and state law enforcement agencies are lacking in trained personnel and forensic equipment. For this reason, many of the items collected in search warrants are never examined, or in the case of cell phones, are examined informally without using proper forensic tools and procedures. That is why it can be important to make sure that your expert has the training and tools to collect and examine digital evidence from disparate devices. In some cases, this may require that you employ multiple experts depending on the evidence collected by law enforcement. In other cases, one firm may be able to provide experts in all areas of your case.

You can never tell when some odd device may contain evidence critical to your case. Something as innocent sounding as a PlayStation Portable, Xbox, or iPod can contain evidence you may be able to use in litigating your case.

15.1 EXAMPLE LANGUAGE FOR A CONSENT ORDER FOR DIGITAL EVIDENCE

(This is an example of a consent order from the State of North Carolina.)

 UPON MOTION OF THE DEFENDANT, by and through his counsel, _____, and it appearing to the Court:

1. That Defendant has been indicted for the offenses of _____;
2. That based upon discovery received to date by the Defendant, **(list items here if known)** were seized and removed from the alleged crime scene by law enforcement and are presently in the custody of the _____;
3. That counsel for Defendant has a reasonable belief that there exists information contained within the data files in the aforementioned computers that is necessary to ensure Defendant receives a fair trial and effective assistance of counsel and to adequately prepare a defense in this matter;
4. That the Defendant is entitled under the discovery statutes of Article 48 of the North Carolina General Statutes, as well as _Brady v. Maryland_, 373 U.S. 83, 83 S. Ct. 1194 10 L. Ed. 2d 215 (1963), and its progeny, to these requested items;
5. That the Assistant District Attorney, counsel for Defendant consent to the entry of this Order as indicated by the signature of each below.

IT IS THEREFORE ORDERED that:

1. The law enforcement agency or agencies provide to the Assistant District Attorney the following:
   a. A duplicate of any forensic copies made by the law enforcement personnel or by the prosecution's experts of any computer hard drive, digital storage media including but not limited to CD-ROMs, USB flash drives, floppy disks, memory cards, digital camera storage, smart cards, and portable hard drives, GPS units, or other devices capable of storing electronic data;
   b. Duplicates of any forensic copies made by state law enforcement personnel or by the prosecution's experts of any cell phone and/or SIM cards, media cards, or other storage used in conjunction with telephony;
   c. In the event law enforcement personnel or the prosecution's experts did not make a forensic copy of any original media, defense requests that forensically sound copies be made and furnished to the defense for examination by the defense expert;
   d. In the event that said law enforcement agencies are unable to provide copies of evidence from any of the devices seized, a defense expert shall be given the appropriate opportunity to make forensic copies of any such devices or storage media.
   e. A complete inventory of all items taken that may contain any type of digital data, whether or not such items were examined or copies made by law enforcement personnel or the prosecution's experts, and;
   f. A complete copy of all forensics reports, chain of custody records, and lab notes generated by law enforcement personnel or the prosecution's experts pertaining to the acquisition, preservation, analysis, and or reporting by said personnel or experts in the course of this investigation.
   g. A copy of the resume or curriculum vitae of any prosecution expert involved in the seizure, handling, copying, or examination of the items listed in this order.
2. That, upon receipt from the law enforcement agency, the Assistant District Attorney provide to counsel for Defendant copies of the aforementioned items.

SUMMARY

In this chapter we looked at the general language you can use to build discovery motions in the majority of criminal cases. If you follow these guidelines, you should be able to get what you need in the hands of law enforcement. Specific types of motions and subpoenas will be discussed in later chapters that deal with specific evidence types such as cell tower records and video and audio evidence.

Discovery of Digital Evidence in Civil Cases

INFORMATION IN THIS CHAPTER:

- Rules governing civil discovery
- Electronic discovery in particular
- Time is of the essence
- Getting to the particulars
- Getting the electronic evidence

INTRODUCTION

Discovery in civil cases can be challenging for many reasons: If you are the plaintiff, you will be faced with trying to figure out what evidence might exist in your case, where it might reside, and who has control of it.

The chance of evidence being lost or destroyed in a civil case is actually much higher than in a criminal case. The reason is that the person or persons involved may know well in advance that you will be seeking electronic evidence and may take steps to dispose of anything incriminating, whereas in a criminal case, evidence is typically seized with no forewarning of the persons in possession of the evidence.

Litigation holds, spoliation, cost shifting, undue burden, and sanctions against parties for failing to abide by discovery orders can occur in a criminal proceeding, but they are more commonly addressed in civil actions.

16.1 THE CASE OF THE NEW COMPUTER

A civil case required that a personal computer be produced and then forensically imaged (copied) for preservation and later forensic examination. At the beginning of the collection process, when completing the chain of custody form, it was noticed that the computer appeared to be new. When the manufacture date on the back of the computer was checked, it was determined that the computer had a build date of only two weeks prior to the computer being made available for copying. The defendant in the case claimed that the computer was not working properly and had returned the computer to the manufacturer for repair, and the manufacturer had simply replaced the unit with a new computer. Whatever evidence had been on the computer was now lost.

16.1 RULES GOVERNING CIVIL DISCOVERY

The general rules governing civil discovery in federal cases are provided in the Federal Rules of Civil Procedure (FRCP). Each state will also have its own rules for civil practice that set out rules for civil discovery.

The Federal Rules of Civil Procedure that govern civil discovery are Rules 26, 29, 34, and 45.

- **Rule 26** sets out the duty to disclose, required disclosures, disclosure of expert witnesses, discovery timing, and prediscovery conferences. Rule 26 is very important to understand as it defines the rules for required disclosure prior to any discovery requests being made by either party.[1]
- **Rule 29** defines the stipulations about the discovery procedures, including depositions and that other procedures governing or omitting discovery may be modified.[2]
- **Rule 34** specifically addresses electronic evidence, its form, and production.

  You must also bear in mind that other rules govern certain entities such as an Internet service provider that can limit or prevent you from obtaining evidence in a civil proceeding, most notably the Stored Communications Act (SCA), which is part of the Electronic Communications Privacy Act (ECPA). It is codified as 18 United States Code, Subsections 2701 to 2712. The SCA addresses voluntary and compelled disclosure of stored wire and communications and transactional records held by third parties, specifically dealing with Internet service providers and other online services.

  In denying subpoenas in civil cases, Facebook has routinely cited the SCA as its reason for failing to provide requested information, specifically any messages or wall posts in a user's account. The problem is that 18 U.S.C. § 2703(a) speaks of release of stored electronic communications to "a governmental entity" and doesn't mention private parties in civil cases.

  An excellent resource for understanding the Stored Communications Act is Orin S. Kerr's article, "A User's Guide to the Stored Communications Act, and a Legislator's Guide to Amending It", published in the *George Washington Law Review*, 2004.[3]
- **Rule 45** covers subpoena requirements.[4]

16.2 ELECTRONIC DISCOVERY IN PARTICULAR

Rule 34(a) of the Federal Rules of Civil Procedure states

A party may serve on any other party a request within the scope of Rule 26(b):

(1) *to produce and permit the requesting party or its representative to inspect, copy, test, or sample the following items in the responding party's possession, custody, or control:*

(A) *any designated documents or electronically stored information—including writings, drawings, graphs, charts, photographs, sound recordings,* *images, and other data or data compilations—stored in any medium from which information can be obtained either directly or, if necessary, after translation by the responding party into a reasonably usable form; or*

(B) *any designated tangible things; or*

(2) *to permit entry onto designated land or other property possessed or controlled by the responding party, so that the requesting party may inspect, measure, survey, photograph, test, or sample the property or any designated object or operation on it.*[5]

While the rule implies that you can go after pretty much anything in electronic form, defining what that "anything" is, is an important step, primarily because the FRCP also states in Rule 34(b) under contents of the request that you "(A) must describe with reasonable particularity each item or category of items to be inspected."

In other words, the bucket approach isn't allowed. You must describe in your discovery motion such items as computer hard drives, cell phones, e-mail, documents, pictures, diagrams, databases, drawings, and so forth specifically enough to satisfy the judge that you are being reasonable in your request and not opening yourself to a claim of undue burden being placed on the producing party.

16.3 TIME IS OF THE ESSENCE

It cannot be stressed strongly enough that the potential loss of electronically stored evidence is extremely high as time between the creation of the evidence and the time the evidence is collected increases. Computer hard drives crash, companies routinely delete data as part of their normal course of business, video surveillance systems overwrite their data storage on a short schedule, people buy new cell phones and discard the old ones. Technology changes and companies retire older systems for newer ones and may not preserve the data from the old system. Electronic data is volatile, and massive amounts of evidence can be destroyed at the click of a button.

16.4 GETTING TO THE PARTICULARS

One method for figuring out what you want to collect in a civil case is to take the What, Who, How, Where, and Who approach. This is an investigative process from the standpoint that you must take many of the same steps that would be used in a criminal investigation. In this instance, the purpose of the "investigation" is to locate and collect electronic evidence.

To expand the thought: What happened? Who was involved? How would electronic evidence be involved? Where might that electronic evidence be? And who controls the electronic evidence? We will work through this process from the standpoint of locating and eventually collecting the electronic evidence.

16.4.1 What happened?

All litigation requires a "what happened?" that is the cause for litigation in the first place. Someone or something did or did not do something that has resulted in injury or harm to another party, whether that result is physical or financial harm. Was it a person or persons involved or was it an inanimate object? Ultimately, everything is the responsibility of a person, and getting to the people involved is paramount to locating electronic data.

16.4.2 Who was involved?

Since litigation always has some intent to establish liability or culpability, figuring out who did something is the first step. In other words, who are the parties that had some interaction with or instrumentality concerning the alleged subject of the litigation? Once these parties are identified, either by name or by area of responsibility, the discovery order or conference can be used to determine who to collect data from. While the other side in a civil matter may be required to disclose the identities of persons who may be in possession of electronic evidence, don't be surprised if they fail to do so completely. This does not necessarily occur because of intent, while that may be a factor, but because they simply did not consider all of the possibilities.

16.4.3 How would electronic evidence be involved?

The multitude of ways in which an electronic record can be created should always be considered in reviewing any type of case. Everything from phones to automated parking systems can create an electronic record. Thinking about methods of doing things today as well as the physical surroundings and potential third-party connections to a case will lead to finding out how records were created that can be collected and analyzed. Are there records out there that were created directly by a person involved or by an automated process that was present in the physical space where the incident occurred? Consider all the electronic devices that can be present in a retail store at any moment in time: employee and customer cell phones, surveillance systems, alarm systems, computers, credit card processing machines, ATM machines with cameras, facsimile machines—all of these devices are capable of creating and preserving electronic data, even the DVD vending machine that customers use to rent movies and games requires the use of a credit or debit card.

16.4.4 Where might electronic evidence be stored?

Electronic evidence can be stored in so many places these days that it can be mindboggling once you start to ponder how an electronic record might be created and subsequently stored in even seemingly mundane circumstances.

If you are dealing with a business, you can expect that the business will be using computers, perhaps a network and the Internet. This means that electronic evidence can be stored on the individual computers; network servers; remote office locations; on computers used by teleworkers; company and personal cell phones; on backup tapes, USB drives, portable hard drives, off-site mail servers, public mail servers, off-site backup services; in remote storage such as Google, Microsoft SkyDrive, DropBox, Carbonite remote backup; and other places as well. Do they have an internal or external voicemail system where messages might be stored?

16.4.5 Who has control of the electronic evidence you need to collect?

Lastly, once you have identified who was involved, how records might be created, and where those records might be stored, your next task is determining who has control of the electronic evidence. Chances are that it will be a combination of persons directly involved as well as third parties such as cell phone companies, Internet service providers, transcription services, and even cloud-based data backup companies.

16.2 A SEXUAL HARASSMENT CASE SCENARIO

In a sexual harassment case, it is often a matter of "he said, she said." Getting verifiable evidence can be the deciding factor in supporting the claims of one side or the other by providing a record of what really happened. By walking through the process outlined in this chapter, you can see how the process would work in this type of case.

What happened?

An employee claims that her boss has been sexually harassing her on the job and even at home via her personal e-mail. She claims he has left her sexually explicit voice mails and even sent her sexual pictures via his cell phone to her cell phone in text messages.

Who is involved?

Directly involved are the employee making the claim and the employee being accused. However, who else might be indirectly involved that may have evidence in the matter?

The coworkers and possibly friends and family members of the accuser to whom she may have sent copies of the harassing e-mails, text messages, and pictures. Also indirectly involved may be the system administrator of the company network, who can locate e-mails in the company e-mail system, and third parties such as cell phone companies.

How would electronic evidence be involved?

The basis for evidence in the claim is e-mail, text messages, pictures, and voice mails. So you know you need to gather e-mail evidence, text messages, and voice mail recordings.

You would also want to remember that many smart phones are backed up to computers and can contain information that may no longer be present on the phones themselves. And since this case involves company computers and e-mail, there may be evidence still present on the company's backup system even if the e-mails were deleted or destroyed on the personal computers.

Where might electronic evidence be stored?

At this point, questioning the parties about what devices they use for electronic communication can lead to discovery of where this evidence may reside.

At this point you want to begin to create an inventory of devices and locations where the evidence may reside. This can be done through interviews with the parties.

What you will want to find out and catalog for discovery purposes are all of the devices used by the parties for communication:

- Computers (both home and company): Laptops, desktops, pad computers or tablets (like an Apple iPad)
- Cell phones (both company and personal)

Then you will want to attempt to identify other sources of electronic evidence storage:

- Voice mail recordings (on cell phones and the company voice mail system)
- E-mail accounts and storage (on the computers, cell phones, and any free e-mail accounts through third parties like Hotmail, Yahoo!, etc.)
- Cell phone records and internal company phone records

Who has control of the electronic evidence you need to collect?

The last part will be determining who has possession and control of the evidence items you need for the case and their names and contact information.

- The parties in the case for any devices they personally own or have permission to use at the company along with any online e-mail accounts they use that may be involved in the communication trail.
- System administrators for the company's computers, network, mail servers, e-mail backups, and telephone networks.
- Any phone company or cellular carrier that may be able to provide phone logs, call records, or stored communications.
- Any friends, coworkers, or family members who may be in possession of copied e-mails, text messages, or voice mails.

Once you have collected all of the information by following the steps in the case scenario, you should be in a good position to start crafting your discovery motions to get as much evidence as possible in support of your party's claims.

16.5 GETTING THE ELECTRONIC EVIDENCE

Depending on the size of the business or number of people (custodians) you need to collect evidence from, your approach will vary.

In a small action involving a few computers or custodians, the Civil Order Example shown in Fig. 16.1 can be specific enough to suit your needs; however, this order assumes that you will have the forensic personnel to go into the business and collect the information and does not make an allowance for production by the other side in the litigation.

The order example in Fig. 16.1 specifies what is to be collected, who is going to do the collection, as well as where and when the collection will take place.

In a larger collection scenario or in one where the opposing party will be producing the electronic evidence using their own forensic personnel, a motion would be used that contains the following information:

- What is to be collected
  - E-mail, user files, copies of computer hard drives or other storage media including any USB drives, backup tapes, CD- or DVD-ROM disks, network shares

Civil Order Example

Order for Expedited Discovery

THIS CAUSE came on to be heard before the undersigned Superior Court Judge Presiding over the Civil Session of_____Superior Court, on___, on Plaintiff's Motion for Expedited Discovery.

The Court, having reviewed the pleadings of record, finds that he Plaintiff has shown that reasonable grounds exist to believe the following:
1. This is an action by Plaintiff seeking damages relating to Defendant_____
_____at the Business Location.

BASED UPON THE FOREGOING FINDINGS OF FACT, THE COURT FURTHER CONCLUDES AS A MATTER OF LAW that an order should be entered granting expedited discovery to permit Plaintiff's inspecting and copying all of the computers; hard drives, disks, CDs, DVDs, memory sticks, thumb drives, or any other medium upon which information is stored electronically, which are at the Business Location.

NOW, THEREFORE, IT IS HEREBY ORDERED, ADJUDGED AND DECREED AS FOLLOWS:

IT IS FURTHER ORDERED, ADJUDGED AND DECREED as follows:

1. Defendants shall allow representatives of Plaintiff to enter the Business Location (_____) and conduct an examination of any of the computers; hard drives, disks, CDs, DVDs, memory sticks, thumb drives, or any other medium upon which information is stored electronically, which are at the Business Location. Such examination may include copying of all hard drives, disks, CDs, DVDs, memory sticks, thumb drives, or any other medium upon which information is stored electronically. Defendants may permit Plaintiff's representatives to remove such items to expedite copying process, or may permit the inspection and copying to be performed at the Business Location, as Defendants may elect.
2. Defendants shall permit the entry and copying described above beginning at_____on the _____day of_____and continuing until finished.
3. The _____Sheriff shall serve this Order for Expedited Discovery upon Defendants as immediately as possible.
4. The information discovered in response to the inspection and copying permitted herein shall be used by Plaintiff solely for the prosecution of its claims, and for no other purpose whatsoever, unless and until the Court orders otherwise.

_____
Superior Court Judge

DATE AND TIME ENTERED:_____

FIGURE 16.1

Example of a civil order for expedited discovery

- For the following persons named herein or
  - Provide the list of custodians you want to collect from.
- That contain any information, records, or correspondence related to the specific matter described herein
  - This relates to the specific case or complaint.
- When it will be collected
  - Specify a date and time for the collections to occur. Make sure to allow yourself and the other side time to comply; however, keep in mind that time is of the essence to avoid loss of evidence by user deletions, company retention policies, and the normal operations of computers and cell phones that can destroy evidence.
- That said collection will be completed by MONTH, DAY, YEAR
  - Specify an end date for the collection to be completed.
- How it will be collected
  - Whether or not the evidence is to be collected by a forensic examiner.
  - That proper forensic procedures will be followed in the collection of the electronic evidence.
  - In the event that the party cannot perform the collection in a timely and forensically sound manner, petitioner shall be allowed to perform such collections or a neutral party shall be selected to perform the collections.
- Conditions of the collection
  - That a chain of custody will be maintained and provided with the electronic evidence
  - That all electronic evidence shall be delivered in its native form or in forensic images of the electronic evidence, the format to be agreed upon by both parties in advance.

In most cases, failing to get evidence is a result of taking too long to perform these steps to get to the actual collection or simple missing items that could have been collected if they were identified early in the process. Not getting a preservation order in place in a timely manner can be the difference between getting evidence and getting nothing of value because electronic evidence is in a constant state of being modified and perhaps even destroyed during the normal operation of electronic devices.

SUMMARY

In this chapter we looked briefly at the rules governing civil discovery and how they can impact the discovery process. We also looked at a process that can be used to determine what to collect, from whom, and where. An example was provided to show how the process would work in a case scenario. Lastly, we covered a simple discovery order for electronic evidence and the additional steps for a large or more complex discovery scenario.

References

[1] Legal Information Institute at Cornell Law School, *Federal Rules of Civil Procedure: Rule 26.* <http://www.law.cornell.edu/rules/frcp/Rule26.htm> (accessed 11.05.21).

[2] Legal Information Institute at Cornell Law School, *Federal Rules of Civil Procedure: Rule 29.* <http://www.law.cornell.edu/rules/frcp/Rule29.htm> (accessed 11.05.21).

[3] Legal Information Institute at Cornell Law School, *Federal Rules of Civil Procedure: Rule 34.* <http://www.law.cornell.edu/rules/frcp/Rule34.htm> (accessed 11.05.21).

[4] Legal Information Institute at Cornell Law School. *Federal Rules of Civil Procedure: Rule 45.* <http://www.law.cornell.edu/rules/frcp/Rule45.htm> (accessed 11.05.21).

[5] Legal Information Institute at Cornell Law School. *Federal Rules of Civil Procedure: Rule 34.* <http://www.law.cornell.edu/rules/frcp/Rule34.htm> (accessed 11.05.21).

Discovery of Computers and Storage Media

INFORMATION IN THIS CHAPTER:

- An example of a simple consent to search agreement
- Example of a simple order for expedited discovery
- Example of an order for expedited discovery and temporary restraining order

INTRODUCTION

In this chapter we cover the language needed to get discovery of computer and storage media. We include here examples of language you can use for simple discovery orders, restraining orders, and a consent to search form. These are only examples and should be modified to suit your individual case. For language examples for criminal cases, see Chapter 15.

17.1 AN EXAMPLE OF A SIMPLE CONSENT TO SEARCH AGREEMENT

A consent to search agreement is used by law enforcement agencies to get permission to search electronic storage devices without having to apply for and receive a search warrant. These agreements are also used by private firms when needed to show that a person has provided his or her consent to search in lieu of having to obtain a court order to compel compliance. These types of forms are used when the person giving consent has agreed to voluntarily cooperate in a search in a criminal or civil case. In either case, it requires that the person signing the agreement have the legal right to give consent to search the particular item and also be legally capable of giving consent.

These types of consent forms are not usually notarized, but can be if that is desired for some reason to provide additional authentication of the document.

17.1 CONSENT TO SEARCH

DATE:_____

TIME:_____

I, _____, hereby authorize
_____to:

a. Conduct a search of my computer hard drives, floppy disks, CDs, cell phones, media
players and other data storage devices, identified as _____
_____
_____
_____
_____;

b. Said search may include any or all data contained on the referenced Hard Disk Drive
or other storage media, whether in files, tables, other data structures, or unallocated
space;

c. Said search may include removal of the computer and/or other data storage devices from
their present location at _____
_____, incidental production
and examination of a duplicate Hard Disk Drive or analysis files which contain all the
data on the referenced Hard Disk Drive, said duplicates, files, and data becoming the
sole property of _____.

This written permission is being given by me to the above named _____
_____ voluntarily and without threats or promises of any kind, and is given with my
full and free consent.

_____   _____

Signature of Person Giving Consent   Witness

_____   _____

Printed Name   Witness

_____Address

_____

Phone Number

17.2 EXAMPLE OF A SIMPLE ORDER FOR EXPEDITED DISCOVERY

This is an order used to compel discovery in a simple case where a motion has
been filed to allow collection of evidence from the opposing party. This is only an
example and should be appropriately modified by an attorney for use in a particular case.

17.2 _____

THIS CAUSE came on to be heard before the undersigned Superior Court Judge Presiding over the Civil Session of _____ (Superior, District, Other) Court, on _____, on Plaintiff's Motion for Expedited Discovery.

The Court, having reviewed the pleadings of record, finds that the Plaintiff has shown that reasonable grounds exist to believe the following:

1. This is an action by Plaintiff seeking damages relating to Defendant _____ _____ at _____ hereinafter known as "ADDRESS".

BASED UPON THE FOREGOING FINDINGS OF FACT, THE COURT FURTHER CONCLUDES AS A MATTER OF LAW that an order should be entered granting expedited discovery to permit Plaintiff's inspecting and copying all of the computers; hard drives, disks, CDs, DVDs, memory sticks, thumb drives, or any other medium upon which information is stored electronically, which are at the Business Location.

NOW, THEREFORE, IT IS HEREBY ORDERED, ADJUDGED, AND DECREED AS FOLLOWS:

IT IS FURTHER ORDERED, ADJUDGED, AND DECREED as follows:

1. Defendants shall allow representatives of Plaintiff to enter the ADDRESS (_____) and conduct an examination of any of the computers; hard drives, disks, CDs, DVDs, memory sticks, thumb drives, or any other medium upon which information is stored electronically, which are at the ADDRESS. Such examination may include copying of all computer hard drives, disks, CDs, DVDs, memory sticks, thumb drives, or any other medium upon which information is stored electronically. Defendants may permit Plaintiff's representatives to remove such items to expedite copying process, or may permit the inspection and copying to be performed at the ADDRESS, as Defendants may elect.
2. Defendants shall permit the entry and copying described above beginning at____ on the ___day of _____, 20XX and continuing until finished.
3. The _____Sheriff shall serve this Order for Expedited Discovery upon Defendants as immediately as possible.
4. The information discovered in response to the inspection and copying permitted herein shall be used by Plaintiff solely for the prosecution of its claims, and for no other purpose whatsoever, unless and until the Court orders otherwise.

17.3 EXAMPLE OF AN ORDER FOR EXPEDITED DISCOVERY AND TEMPORARY RESTRAINING ORDER

This is an order used to compel discovery in a simple case where a motion has been filed to restrain the party from destroying evidence and to allow collection of evidence from the opposing party.

This is only an example and should be appropriately modified by an attorney for use in a particular case.

17.3

THIS CAUSE came on to be heard before the undersigned Superior Court Judge Presiding over the Civil Session of _____ County Superior Court, on _____, on Plaintiff's Motion for Temporary Restraining Order and for Expedited Discovery.

The Court, having reviewed the pleadings of record, finds that the Plaintiff has shown that reasonable grounds exist to believe the following:

1. This is an action by Plaintiff seeking damages and injunctive relief relating to Defendants_____ and _____ breach of a contract containing a covenant not to compete: and relating to all Defendants' misappropriation and use of Confidential Information and trade secrets of Plaintiff.
2. Defendants do business in competition with Plaintiff, and using Confidential Information and trade secrets of Plaintiff, _____, from a location whose address is _____ ("The Business Location").
3. Defendants have misappropriated and used Confidential Information and trade secrets of Plaintiff: the Confidential Information and trade secrets are stored on computers owned or operated by Defendants which are at the Business Location (and which may be at other locations): and Defendants may secrete or destroy evidence of their use of the same irreparably and immediately injuring the Plaintiff if they are not enjoined from doing so.

BASED UPON THE FOREGOING FINDING OF FACT, THE COURT CONCLUDES AS A MATTER OF LAW that a temporary restraining order should be entered, preventing Defendants from removing, destroying, or tampering with any of the computers; hard drives, disks, CDs, DVDs, memory sticks, thumb drives, or any other medium upon which information is stored electronically, that they may have at any location.

BASED UPON THE FOREGOING FINDINGS OF FACT, THE COURT FURTHER CONCLUDES AS A MATTER OF LAW that an order should be entered granting expedited discovery by permitting Plaintiff's inspection and copying of all of the computers; hard drives, disks, CDs, DVDs, memory sticks, thumb drives, magnetic tapes, or any other medium upon which information is stored electronically, which are at the Business Location.

NOW, THEREFORE, IT IS HEREBY ORDERED, ADJUDGED, AND DECREED AS FOLLOWS:

1. Defendants are temporarily restrained and enjoined from removing, destroying, or tampering with any of the computers, hard drives, disks, CDs, DVDs, memory sticks, thumb drives, magnetic tapes, or any other medium upon which information is stored electronically, that they may have under their possession, custody, or control, at any location.
2. Hearing on Plaintiff's motion for preliminary injunction, extending the restraints set forth herein, shall be held in the _____, _____ of _____at_____ on the _____day of___, 20XX, or as soon thereafter as may be reached.
3. Plaintiff shall post as a bond, with respect to entry of the restraints set forth, the principal amount of $_____.

   IT IS FURTHER ORDERED, ADJUDGED, AND DECREED as follows:

4. Defendants shall allow representatives of Plaintiff to enter the Business Location (_____) and conduct an examination of any of the computers, hard

drives, disks, CDs, DVDs, memory sticks, thumb drives, or any other medium upon which information is stored electronically, which are at the Business Location. Such examination may include copying of all hard drives, disks, CDs, DVDs, memory sticks, thumb drives, or any other medium upon which information is stored electronically. Defendants may permit Plaintiff's representatives to remove such items to expedite the copying process, or may permit the inspection and copying to be performed at the Business Location, as Defendants may elect.

5. Defendants shall permit the entry and copying described above beginning at____ on the ___day of _____, 20XX and continuing until finished.

6. The _____Sheriff shall serve this Temporary Restraining Order and Order for Expedited Discovery upon Defendants as immediately as possible.

7. The information discovered in response to the inspection and copying permitted herein shall be used by Plaintiff solely for the prosecution of its claims, and for no other purpose whatsoever, unless and until the Court orders otherwise.

SUMMARY

In this chapter we looked at example language for various methods of discovery for computers and storage media. Included in this chapter was information covering a consent to search form, a simple order for discovery, and an order that includes language to protect the evidence prior to discovery by restraining the receiver of the order from destroying evidence.

Discovery of Video Evidence

INFORMATION IN THIS CHAPTER:

- Common issues with video evidence
- Collecting video evidence
- Example discovery language for video evidence

INTRODUCTION

Video evidence is one of the more difficult types of evidence to deal with in cases. It is hard to collect, and in many cases is improperly collected and mishandled. Video sources vary widely in their recording quality, and in many cases the cameras used to record video are poorly focused, have lights shining directly into the camera, or are at an improper angle to record properly.

Whenever you must deal with video evidence, in any format, you will want to attempt to have the evidence properly preserved by specifying early on that the evidence is not to be viewed on the original media. Taking immediate steps to issue a preservation order for the evidence and specifying that the evidence is to be properly handled, preserved, and copied are critical elements in having evidence that can be used in litigation.

The greatest issue dealing with video evidence is not actually getting the evidence itself, but the manner in which it is obtained. It is often the case that by the time an attorney receives video evidence, video recording has been damaged in some way through mishandling or repeated viewing of the original media.

18.1 COMMON ISSUES WITH VIDEO EVIDENCE

Many issues involving the collection and preservation of video evidence can have a major impact on the quality of the collected evidence, the ability to authenticate the evidence, and whether the video can be enhanced for use in a case. Depending on the type of recording media, recording device, and the settings for the recording device, the quality of a video recording can vary widely. In addition, collecting and preserving video evidence incorrectly can reduce its value a great deal.

18.1.1 Collecting and preserving tape media

With a VHS videotape, every time the video is viewed, the quality of that tape deteriorates. Unlike a digital video recording, a VHS tape is mechanical, with the tape running over spools, and the tape degrades as it plays, rewinds, fast forwards, and pauses. Usually with video evidence, only a small portion of the entire video is of interest. Let's say, for example, that there is a one-hour VHS video tape that contains the footage of a supposed wrongful death incident, and the incident lasts only a matter of seconds. If someone reviews that footage of interest numerous times by watching it, rewinding the tape, and pausing throughout, that section of the VHS tape that is of interest can be degraded significantly or destroyed completely. If no effort to preserve the original was made, by working from duplicates or making a digital copy for instance, then by the time your video forensics expert gets his hands on the VHS tape for examination, it could be beyond help because the time-frame of interest in the footage has been degraded to the point that no enhancement can be performed.

18.1.2 Video recording devices

Video recording devices come in many shapes and sizes from systems that still use analog VHS tapes to systems that are fully digital and record directly to a hard drive in the Digital Video Recorder (DVR) unit. The type of recording device will determine what kind of video recording is being performed and how that video must be collected.

18.1.2.1 Collecting video from multiplex systems

Multiplexing involves using one screen to display the video recording from multiple cameras at once, with one camera having a large view, while the other cameras in the system are shown in smaller "thumbnail" views on the display. These systems can be set to automatically cycle through each of the camera inputs, or the operator can switch between these camera views manually. Figure 18.1 shows a multiplex system with all of the cameras on the display in a "thumbnail" view.

Multiplexed recording systems bring their own host of collection challenges. The most common mistake is using the main screen only when video evidence is collected. This main screen shows the video recordings from multiple cameras on it, meaning that you have multiple small, usually low resolution depictions of video as shown in Fig. 18.1. However, most multiplexed video recording devices allow you to make each one of the camera video feeds fill the whole screen before exporting that video, shown in Fig. 18.2. The correct way to collect multiplexed video is to get the video feed from each camera, not just the main screen that shows all of them.

18.1.2.2 File formats and video programs

When you are developing discovery for digital video recordings, it is important to specify how you want the video produced, especially as it relates to the file format

FIGURE 18.1

Multiplexed device with all cameras shown in "thumbnail" views

FIGURE 18.2

Multiplexed device, showing recording from entire screen versus individual cameras

the video will be in. If at all possible, you want the video file in its original condition, meaning that it has not been converted from one file type to another. When a video file is converted from one file format to another, it is possible for the quality of the video to degrade. Whenever possible, you want to make sure that the video is exported from the recording device using a file format that allows for lossless compression. This makes for larger files, but it helps to ensure that no quality is lost in the digital video, as compression can cause the overall quality to deteriorate.

If the video has been converted, you also want to make sure that the converted video will be viewable using common video software programs, such as Windows Media Player or Apple QuickTime. This helps to negate a common scenario, where a video file is produced that can only be played by a specific piece of software. This is an issue because that piece of software may allow you to view the video, but will not allow you to rewind, fast-forward, or pause. This type of situation typically occurs when the video is delivered by a law enforcement agency in encrypted form or as the direct output from some digital video recording systems. This scenario can make reviewing video evidence an overly time-consuming process. If you have a video that is an hour long, but only ten seconds is of interest, having to view the entire hour of video footage just to see that ten seconds every time is extremely inefficient.

18.2 COLLECTING VIDEO EVIDENCE

Depending on the recording device, the methods used to collect the video from the device can vary greatly. For instance, with many surveillance systems, the only way to get the video from the device is to export it using the controls on the device itself. Sometimes quality and file format options are available when exporting the video when it is collected. When it comes time to enhance or analyze the video evidence, how the video was exported is critical. The higher the quality of the exported video evidence, the more likely it is that a video expert can successfully enhance the video or analyze it. The video evidence should always be exported at the highest possible resolution in a format that loses the least amount of quality through compression.

In other situations, the video recording system may not have any method for exporting video, and the only way to get the evidence is to record the screen using an external video camera.

- **Time Verification**

    Even if the video collected from a recording device is preserved correctly, it is usually the case that insufficient information concerning the recording device itself is documented. Many recording devices, such as surveillance systems and hand-held video cameras, require that the user input a time and date manually. If the time and date are wrong on the recording device by even 15 minutes, an entire timeline of events can be thrown off, or a legitimate alibi could be erroneously deemed false. To determine the correct time, check and record the time on the recording device at the time of the collection, and then compare to an external time source like a cell phone and record the difference or offset. Despite how easy this is, more often than not, this vital step in the evidence collection process is skipped.

18.3 EXAMPLE DISCOVERY LANGUAGE FOR VIDEO EVIDENCE

Included here is language for the technical items that should be requested when creating a discovery order for video evidence to make sure you get everything you can and in the proper format.

18.1 DISCOVERY LANGUAGE FOR VIDEO EVIDENCE

1. Any and all standard operating procedures (SOP) used by (Agency or Expert) regarding video evidence, to include but not limited to, standard operating procedures for the acquisition of video evidence, the preservation of video evidence, the storage of video evidence, the analysis and processing of video evidence, and the production of video evidence.
2. A resume or curriculum vitae containing the qualifications and experience of any persons involved in the acquisition, preservation, storage, analysis, processing, or production of video evidence.

3. A listing of all the tools used in the acquisition, preservation, analysis, and processing of video evidence, to include both hardware and software tools. With software tools, the version of the software should be included. The tools should be listed as used in the examination of video evidence in sequential order.
4. Any and all chain of custody records regarding the video evidence.
5. Any and all reports and documentation concerning the methods used to preserve the video evidence, to include but not limited to, reports and documentation pertaining to hardware or software forensic write-blocking, and reports or documentation pertaining to the hardware or software tools used to create any duplicates of the original evidence and the method of storage for the original video evidence.
6. Any and all information, documentation, or reports concerning the viewing of the video evidence from the original media should also be included.
7. A copy of any forensic reports that detail the work process used by the forensic examiner in the course of his or her examination for the video evidence in this case, including any logs created by the analysis software used to examine the evidence.

SUMMARY

In this chapter we looked at issues regarding the discovery of video evidence. We covered specific issues that arise when VHS video tape is not properly handled and preserved, the impact of different file formats and conversion on video evidence, and the problems that arise from improper collections of video evidence including failing to collect date and time information. Sample language was also included for use in discovery motions for video evidence.

Discovery of Audio Evidence

19

INFORMATION IN THIS CHAPTER:

- Common issues with audio evidence
- Example discovery language for audio evidence

INTRODUCTION

In order to have the best results possible in any enhancement or forensics work performed against an audio recording, it needs to be treated with care during the processes of collection, preservation, and copying. Also, simply getting a copy of the recording without specifying the output format and copy process may not be the best option, as there are numerous factors with audio recordings that can cause deterioration in the audio quality.

While the forensic processes performed to analyze video and audio evidence may be significantly different, the actual evidence types themselves are similar when it comes to preservation. They both are subject to distortion and data loss if the copying method is not carefully considered in light of reducing the amount of actual data loss that can occur during the copy process.

19.1 COMMON ISSUES WITH AUDIO EVIDENCE

A sound is a vibration at a set frequency. For instance, a dog whistle is a sound that vibrates at such a high frequency that only animals can hear it. A subwoofer is a bass speaker that actually can produce sounds that the human ear cannot hear, but the human body can "feel" the vibrations in the air. Depending on the recording device, the ability to record and play back sound at these extreme frequencies varies depending on the type of recording media.

Audio recording occurs in two formats, analog and digital. While music purists may maintain that analog recordings have the most natural sound, digital recordings support a wider range of frequencies during the recording and playback process. This means that a digital recording can record more sound in the form of overall frequency range. A sound that is not recordable in analog format due to a very high or very low frequency could appear in a digital format.

19.1.1 **Audio recording devices**

Audio recording devices range from tape-based recorders such as micro, mini, and standard audio cassettes and reel-to-reel tape recorders, to digital audio recorders that record on compact discs, hard drives, and media cards.

For this reason, if the original is in a digital format, any copies need to be made in a comparable digital format that uses lossless compression. Preferably, the recording method used to duplicate the original would have no compression at all.

On many digital audio recorders, deleted files can be recovered because the media is treated like a computer hard drive, as long as the files have not been over-written. Your expert will need physical access to the device in order to recover any deleted audio data, if it still exists. Overwritten analog audio tapes cannot be recovered.

It is becoming increasingly popular to recover deleted audio recording from smart phones. If you are able to get access to the physical storage on the phone, such as a media storage card, then recovery of audio files is very possible.

19.1.2 **Tape media**

If the audio evidence is on an audio tape, such as a cassette tape, any playback of the audio recording will cause the tape to deteriorate. You can think of a cassette tape as a miniature VHS tape. They both deteriorate whenever they are played, rewound, fast-forwarded, or paused. The original audio tape should never be worked from, just as the original hard drive in a computer forensics case should never be used for analysis. A duplicate recording should be made on another cassette tape, or in the best circumstance, a digital copy should be created.

Another issue with magnetic tape is that the tape itself is made from plastic coated with a metal oxide and the plastic does stretch a tiny amount each time the tape is played. This stretching that occurs as a result of repeated playing of a cassette or other audio tape will result in distortion of the recording over time and can cause the pitch of the audio to change.

19.1.3 **Audio metadata**

If only the audio recording itself is received in discovery, critical information can be missed that might reside on the audio recording device itself, such as the time and date the device was set to when the recording was made.

If the audio is being collected from a smart phone, the date and time information may be available as part of the file system metadata on the phone. This is also true of most digital devices that have a time stamp feature, including digital answering machines, and digital pocket recorders.

The Apple iPhone stores voice mails on the phone and the voice mails can be obtained, including the time stamps, by performing a backup of the phone and then analyzing the backup data itself.

19.1.4 **File formats and audio programs**

If possible, you want the audio recordings produced in discovery exactly as they were originally collected. Just as with digital video recordings, digital audio recordings can lose quality through file conversions. If this is not an option, you want the audio recordings in a format that is easily accessible using normal audio playback software programs, such as Windows Media Player or iTunes. You do not want the audio recordings to be dependent upon a single piece of audio playback software. A common scenario is that the audio is produced, but is dependent upon a single software program to be played at all, and sometimes these software programs will not allow for rewind, fast-forward, and pause functions. This occurs when a law enforcement agency produces the audio in an encrypted format that cannot be converted into a standard format and must be played using the supplied player only. This forces you to listen to the entire audio recording even when only a small section may be of interest.

19.2 **EXAMPLE DISCOVERY LANGUAGE FOR AUDIO EVIDENCE**

The following list includes the technical items you want to include in a discovery motion for audio evidence.

1. A copy of any audio evidence already collected or acquired from any device.
2. Access to any device currently in custody for the purpose of making a forensic copy of the device data.
3. Any and all standard operating procedures (SOP) used by (Agency or Expert) regarding audio evidence, to include but not limited to,
   a. The acquisition of audio evidence
   b. The preservation of audio evidence
   c. The storage of audio evidence
   d. The analysis and processing of audio evidence
   e. The production of audio evidence
4. A resume or curriculum vitae containing the qualifications and experience of any persons involved in the acquisition, preservation, storage, analysis, processing, or production of audio evidence.
5. A listing of all the tools used in the acquisition, preservation, analysis, and processing of audio evidence, to include both hardware and software tools. With software tools, the version of the software should be included. The tools should be listed as used in the examination of audio evidence in sequential order.
6. Any and all chain of custody records regarding the audio evidence.
7. Any and all reports and documentation concerning the methods used to preserve the audio evidence, to include but not limited to, reports and documentation pertaining to hardware or software forensic write-blocking, and reports or documentation pertaining to the hardware or software tools used to create any

duplicates of the original evidence and the method of storage for the original audio evidence.

8. A copy of any forensic reports that detail the work process used by the forensic examiner in the course of his or her examination for the audio evidence in this case, including any logs created by the analysis software used to examine the evidence.

SUMMARY

In this chapter we looked at some of the issues surrounding the discovery of audio evidence. We also discussed the different issues with audio media, such as magnetic tape. This chapter also covered why audio formats are important from a discovery standpoint and some of the various devices that can record audio. Audio metadata was also discussed, specifically the lack of metadata in analog recordings versus the presence of metadata in many types of digital recording devices.

Discovery of Social Media Evidence

INFORMATION IN THIS CHAPTER:

- Legal issues in social media discovery
- Finding custodian of records contact information
- Facebook example
- Google information
- Online e-mail accounts

INTRODUCTION

There are more ways for people to connect with one another than ever before. The widespread use of social media outlets such as Facebook, Twitter, MySpace, and LinkedIn ultimately means that evidence is being created, and is often available right in the open.

However, many cases will require that you obtain more information than is available in the open on public profiles, such as the Internet address of the computer that created or updated a web post, or a Facebook profile blog post. To get this information you will need to subpoena the custodian of the social media service.

In order to obtain information from social media services via a subpoena, you will need to gather and send to them the information they need to identify the information you are requesting. This chapter covers the types of information you will need to include in subpoenas to social media and free e-mail sites. Examples are included for Facebook, Google's Blogger service, and for free e-mail account services.

Social media evidence is covered in depth in Chapter 35. Online e-mail evidence is covered in Chapter 34.

20.1 LEGAL ISSUES IN SOCIAL MEDIA DISCOVERY

One of the primary barriers to getting information from social media sites is the Stored Communications Act,[1] which prevents disclosure of information or e-mail stored by an Internet service provider. While the social media site is not technically

139

an Internet service provider, they still fall under the same protection from disclosure in noncriminal actions.

The complete text of the Stored Communication Act can be accessed on the web at the U.S. Department of Justice, Computer Crime and Intellectual Property Section website at http://www.justice.gov/criminal/cybercrime/ssmanual/03ssma.html.

20.2 FINDING CUSTODIAN OF RECORDS CONTACT INFORMATION

One of the best sources for finding the custodian of records contact information for social media sites, Internet service providers, and phone companies is the website Search[2] at www.search.org. They maintain a listing of hundreds of addresses and phone numbers for custodians of records.

20.3 FACEBOOK EXAMPLE

In order for Facebook to comply with a subpoena request, they must have the information they need to identify the profile. Profile identification can be in either of two forms, either a numeric ID or an alpha ID chosen by the Facebook user.

The old ID system used automatically generated numbers for the profile ID, such as https://www.facebook.com/profile.php?id=1234567890. The group of numbers at the end of the web address or Uniform Resource Locator (URL) is the numerical profile ID. Bear in mind that the older numeric ID is an option for change by the user to the new ID. Not all users have made the change, so the numeric Facebook IDs are still very common.

The newer form looks like this: https://www.facebook.com/username. The part after the forward slash [/] at the end of the web address is the actual profile ID.

To locate these IDs, you only need to be able to find the user's profile on Facebook, or they can be gathered from the Internet cache on the user's hard drive during a forensic examination. Even if the person is not sharing their profile with the public, you can still see their profile ID in the web address in the browser if you can locate the profile on Facebook.

You will need to include the period of activity you are interested in having Facebook retrieve, as this will assist in getting back information more quickly. Also, any other identifying information you can supply can assist with locating and retrieving the online records, including birth date, e-mail addresses that may be associated with the account, and the person's name.

20.3.1 Sample language to include for Facebook

Included here is the technical language you would use in a subpoena to Facebook including the identifying information for the user's profile.

20.4 GOOGLE INFORMATION

Google is a massive presence on the Internet with a large number of services available to Internet users. In this example, we cover the Google Blogger service.

Some of the services they provide include: Search, Gmail, Talk, YouTube, Blogger, AdWords, AdSense, Checkout, Orkut, Picasa, Sites, Groups, Docs, Maps, Earth, Video, Android, and other Google Services. Google continues to expand their services by either introducing new services or purchasing existing services and rebranding them.

Here is the information you would want to use to subpoena Google for information about an online blog.

20.4.1 Google blogger example

In order for Google to comply with a request for information regarding a particular post from a user blog on the Blogger service, they need for you to supply specific information to identify the data you want them to retrieve. Getting all the information you need to get a proper response from Google on a blog post or blog site is somewhat technical. You may want to hire someone to assist you with gathering the information for your subpoena request.

- They will need the web address of the blog.
  - For example, www.blogspot.nameoftheblog.com
- They will need the internal ID of the blog.
  - This is found in the source content of the page from the blog.
- They will need for you to supply the date and time of the blog post and the individual post ID.
  - This information can also be found inside the page source by using the View Page Source feature in your Internet browser.

- They will also need the ID of the blog owner.
  - The blog owner ID can be found by clicking on the blogger's profile link, if it is shown on the blog.
- If you are interested in a single blog post, or several individual blog posts, the post ID for each one of them will be located and included in the subpoena.
- Also, for individual blog posts, they will want a copy of the content of the post as well.

20.4.2 Sample language for Google Blogger accounts and posts

Included here is a sample of the technical language you would use in your subpoena request to Google.

20.2

---

1. This is a request for historical records, including the originating Internet Protocol (IP) address for the creation of the blog, http://nameoftheblog.blogspot.com, identified by Google Blog ID: 1111111111111111111.
2. This request is for the timeframe beginning 1 June 2010 or beginning upon the creation date of the blog and continuing through 30 June 2010.
   a. We specifically request the dates, times, and originating IP addresses for any actions by the author of the blog, http://nameoftheblog.blogspot.com, identified by Google Blog ID: 1111111111111111111, further identified by Blogger Profile ID, http://www.blogger.com/profile/000000000000000, including the blog creation, any posting activity, any post editing activity, and/or any activity requiring that the blogger "log in" as the owner of the blog for any purpose.
   b. We specifically request the date, time, and originating IP address for the blog post identified as post ID=3333333333333333', including the original posting and the IP address of the connections for any subsequent edits of this post.
   c. We request any user-provided identification, such as the blog owner's e-mail address used when creating the blog http://nameoftheblog.blogspot.com, identified as Google blog ID=1111111111111111111 and Blogger Profile ID: 2222222222222222.
   d. Attached to this subpoena is a copy of the blog text as captured from the Google Blogger website for this blog.

20.5 ONLINE E-MAIL ACCOUNTS

The language included in the following example can be used generically for any of the online e-mail account services such as Hotmail, Yahoo Mail, Microsoft Live Mail, America Online, and Gmail by replacing the name of the service with the appropriate name for the information you are seeking. Bear in mind that you may need to tweak this as many of these services may not provide e-mail content, especially for free accounts.

20.3

---

1. Any and all subscriber records regarding (AOL, Hotmail, Yahoo mail, Ymail, Microsoft Live mail, Google Gmail) and/or (AIM, Google Instant, Yahoo Chat) records regarding the identification of (*e-mail address or chat handle*) to include real name, screen names, status of account, detailed billing logs, date account opened and closed, method of payment, and detailed billing records.
2. If a time period is required for compliance with this subpoena, then the time period shall be for the period beginning on January 1, 2009 and ending on January 1, 2011.
   a. Any and all connection logs to include the IP address, MAC address, and date and time of each connection.
   b. To the extent that it is available and allowable under applicable law, any e-mail content that is available including e-mail messages, mailboxes, and contact lists.
   c. A copy of your retention policies for the various types of content requested here.

SUMMARY

In this chapter we looked at some examples for requesting information from various online services including e-mail, chats, blog posts, and Facebook. Included is the information needed to properly create a subpoena for the services used in the examples shown for Facebook profiles, Google Blogger accounts, and free e-mail accounts. In some cases, the information you need to use to craft the subpoena is fairly simple such as what you need for a free e-mail account. In other cases where you need to gather specific information like that shown in the Google Blogger example, you may want to get assistance from an expert or other person who can properly ferret out the details required for the subpoena.

References

[1] U.S. Department of Justice, Computer Crime and Intellectual Property Section, *Searching and Seizing Computers and Obtaining Electronic Evidence in Criminal Investigations: Chapter 3, The Stored Communications Act.* <http://www.justice.gov/criminal/cybercrime/ssmanual/03ssma.html> (accessed 11.05.21).
[2] SEARCH: The Online Resource for Justice and Public Safety Decision Makers, High-Tech Crime, *ISP List.* <http://www.search.org/programs/hightech/isp/> (accessed 11.05.21).

Discovery in Child Pornography Cases

21

INFORMATION IN THIS CHAPTER:

- The Adam Walsh Child Protection and Safety Act of 2006
- The discovery process

INTRODUCTION

Internet predator and child pornography cases are among the fastest-growing number of cases we see. As a result of the efforts of the Internet Crimes Against Children (ICAC) task force, cases involving child pornography present challenges that other cases do not, specifically because the primary evidence in the case, the images or movies, cannot be given to the defense attorney or the defense attorney's expert. This means that any viewing of the items the client is charged with must be done at a law enforcement location. The same holds true for any examination of the evidence. Bear in mind that not every case that involves child pornography begins as a child pornography case. If you have a rape case or even a divorce case that involves some form of electronic evidence, there is potential for contraband to be found. When that happens, it changes the way all the electronic evidence must be handled and can pose significant cost and complexity issues. Also, if a non-law-enforcement examiner is analyzing evidence in any kind of case and finds child pornography, he or she is required to stop the examination and notify law enforcement so the evidence can be turned over to authorities.

In this chapter we will give you information on ways to deal with this special type of case.

21.1 THE ADAM WALSH CHILD PROTECTION AND SAFETY ACT OF 2006

It is important that you be aware of the language in the Adam Walsh Child Protection and Safety Act[1] regarding discovery in contraband cases. The full text of the bill is located at http://www.justice.gov/criminal/ceos/Adam%20Walsh.pdf. Section 501 provides the congressional findings cited in the bill.

145

21.1 LANGUAGE REGARDING CONTRABAND DISCOVERY

Sec. 501. Findings.

(2) The importance of protecting children from repeat exploitation in child pornography:
- **(A)** The vast majority of child pornography prosecutions today involve images contained on computer hard drives, computer disks, and related media.
- **(B)** Child pornography is not entitled to protection under the First Amendment and thus may be prohibited.
- **(C)** The government has a compelling State interest in protecting children from those who sexually exploit them, and this interest extends to stamping out the vice of child pornography at all levels in the distribution chain.
- **(D)** Every instance of viewing images of child pornography represents a renewed violation of the privacy of the victims and a repetition of their abuse.
- **(E)** Child pornography constitutes prima facie contraband, and as such should not be distributed to, or copied by, child pornography defendants or their attorneys.
- **(F)** It is imperative to prohibit the reproduction of child pornography in criminal cases so as to avoid repeated violation and abuse of victims, so long as the government makes reasonable accommodations for the inspection, viewing, and examination of such material for the purposes of mounting a criminal defense.

These findings form the basis for the discovery provisions codified in the U.S. Code as shown in 18 U.S.C. § 3509.[2]

21.2 (M) PROHIBITION ON REPRODUCTION OF CHILD PORNOGRAPHY.—

(1) In any criminal proceeding, any property or material that constitutes child pornography (as defined by section 2256 of this title) shall remain in the care, custody, and control of either the Government or the court.

(2)
- **(A)** Notwithstanding Rule 16 of the Federal Rules of Criminal Procedure, a court *shall deny*, in any criminal proceeding, any request by the defendant to copy, photograph, duplicate, or otherwise reproduce any property or material that constitutes child pornography (as defined by section 2256 of this title), so long as the Government makes the property or material reasonably available to the defendant.
- **(B)** For the purposes of subparagraph (A), property or material shall be deemed to be reasonably available to the defendant if the Government provides ample opportunity for inspection, viewing, and examination at a Government facility of the property or material by the defendant, his or her attorney, and any individual the defendant may seek to qualify to furnish expert testimony at trial.

In a federal case, there are no provisions for you or your expert to obtain a copy of the contraband materials, even under a protective order. In state cases, the rules may be different. For example, Virginia Code § 19.2-270.1:1[3] allows a court to release contraband data to counsel or a designated expert under the terms of a protective order.

21.2 THE DISCOVERY PROCESS

Having worked as defense experts on many contraband cases, we have learned that the discovery process must happen in two steps in order for the defense expert to have as much information as possible to help you and your client.

21.2.1 First round of discovery

The items that you and the expert need to begin the process of analyzing the case are listed below. These items should be included in any initial discovery request from the prosecution, with special care to ask for the forensic reports in a redacted form.

21.3

1. A copy of all police reports, witness statements, defendant statements, and any audio or video recordings made by police or other parties.
2. A copy of any computer forensic report completed by law enforcement experts with any contraband images redacted in accordance with the Adam Walsh Child Protection and Safety Act of 2006.
3. A copy of all search warrant affidavits, search warrant returns, item inventories, chain of custody reports, case reports, and field notes made by police.
4. A copy of any records obtained in the course of the investigation including but not limited to criminal histories, phone records, Internet service provider records, or other third-party records.
5. A copy of the resume or curriculum vitae of any prosecution or police expert who acquired, collected, copied, or examined any form of evidence.
6. A copy of any screenshots, photographs, or other images created by police during the course of the investigation. If such screenshots or other images contain contraband, the contraband images are to be redacted in accordance with the Adam Walsh Child Protection and Safety Act of 2006.
7. A copy of any subpoenas issued by police to third parties.
8. A copy of any dispatch records pertaining to the investigation.

21.2.2 The second round of discovery

The second step in a contraband case involves getting access to the evidence for examination by the defense expert. For this purpose the following language is provided as a guideline for use in cases as a method for setting up the ground rules for the expert to perform an examination of the evidence containing contraband. Whether or not the language in the following example is needed will depend on the law enforcement agency involved, the individual prosecutor, and the laws of the governing jurisdiction. Also, the guideline language provided should be modified to suit the individual case as needed.

21.4 ACCESS TO FORENSIC EVIDENCE

The Defendant moved the Court to compel the State of _____ to provide to the Defendant access to the physical evidence seized by the State in the course of its investigation. The Court considered this motion and arguments of counsel and for good cause shown allows the Defendant's motion under the following conditions:

1. The defense expert will supply in advance, an external hard drive, factory new, for the purpose of the forensic examination. If the evidence to be copied to the examination drive is in raw format, then the examination drive must first be forensically wiped to prevent contamination of the evidence.
2. The law enforcement agency shall copy to the provided hard drive any FTK, EnCase, or other type of forensic image files that are an exact copy of the hard drive(s), CD- or DVD-ROM media, flash cards, floppy disks, smart media cards, or any other digital evidence seized and copied by law enforcement.
3. The law enforcement agency shall provide to the defense expert an unredacted copy of any computer forensic reports for the purpose of the forensic examination. Such unredacted reports shall be returned to the law enforcement agent at the end of each day's examination period.
4. The expert will perform all of his work on the provided hard drive, using at his option, either his own forensic analysis equipment and software or forensic analysis equipment provided by the law enforcement agency.
5. At the end of the forensic examination session, the examination hard drive will be sealed in the presence of the defense expert and given to the law enforcement agent and kept in the custody of the police in case further review is needed at a future time.
6. When the expert sets up his case in his forensic analysis software, he will ensure that all temporary files, exports, and any other files that would normally be written out during the analysis will be written to the provided examination hard drive. The expert will show the law enforcement agent the setup of his analysis software for this case to support the above.
7. The law enforcement agency shall make such supervisory arrangements as deemed appropriate in accordance with the law enforcement agencies' policies and procedures for the forensic examination of contraband material by a defense expert.
8. The expert will show to the law enforcement agent any items he wishes to copy or print, to provide to defense counsel as part of his analysis reporting, to ensure that no contraband images are copied or transferred.
9. The expert will be given a minimum window of six hours per day, scheduled in advance, to perform the analysis, with further analysis time to be provided if needed at a future date.
10. All items and information discovered by the expert are to be treated as attorney work product, and protected as such even though the law enforcement agent will review said documents and information for the presence of contraband.

In many cases, this language has not been required to be put into a motion, but simply shared with the prosecution as a way to facilitate the examination of the evidence by the defense expert while complying with the requirements of the Adam Walsh Act.

SUMMARY

In this chapter we looked at the laws regarding discovery in cases containing contraband materials, specifically child pornography. We also looked at methods for obtaining the discovery items both in a pre-examination redacted form and for the examination of the evidence by a defense expert.

References

[1] GovTrack.us | Congress | Legislation | 2005–2006 (109th Congress) | H.R. 4472 [109th], *Adam Walsh Protection and Safety Act of 2006*. <http://www.govtrack.us/congress/bill-text.xpd?bill=h109-4472> 2006 (accessed 11.05.21).

[2] *Legal Information Institute at Cornell Law School*. U.S. Code: Title 18, Section 3509. Child victims' and child witnesses' rights. <http://www.law.cornell.edu/uscode/18/usc_sec_18_00003509----000-.html> 2010 (accessed 11.05.21).

[3] Legislative Information System>Code of Virginia>§ 19.2–270.1:1, *When Statement by Accused as Witness Not Received by Evidence*. <http://leg1.state.va.us/cgi-bin/legp504.exe?000+cod+19.2-270> 2011 (accessed 11.05.21).

Discovery of Internet Service Provider Records

INFORMATION IN THIS CHAPTER:

- Internet service provider records for IP addresses
- Example language for web-based e-mail addresses
- What to expect from an Internet service provider (ISP) subpoena

INTRODUCTION

The primary reasons for getting information from an Internet service provider are to obtain subscriber information and historical access information, or to find out who owns a website when the website is one of many connected to a single Internet address by a large corporation or by a shared hosting service.

Getting Internet service provider records is a reasonably straightforward process. To get the information you need, you will have to send the Internet service provider information that will assist them in locating the records you are after. Details on how to find the custodian of records for a web address are displayed through a step-by-step process you can perform using your Internet-connected computer.

In this chapter we will look at various types of record requests and include the technical language for those requests. Links to websites are provided where you can locate the custodian of records for nearly all of the Internet service providers. How to obtain subscriber information for web-based e-mail accounts is also discussed.

22.1 INTERNET SERVICE PROVIDER RECORDS OR IP ADDRESSES

In order to submit a subpoena for an IP address, you must first know who owns the IP address. All IP addresses are owned by someone. When we say "owned," we mean that in order for an IP address to be issued for use on the Internet, it must be either purchased from one of the suppliers of IP addresses, such as AT&T or UUNET, or it must be leased from someone who has the authority to provide the IP address to an individual or business.

22.1.1 How to find the Internet service provider for an IP address step by step

If you are starting from a Uniform Resource Locator (URL), which in people terms is an Internet address such as www.guardiandf.com, you can perform a lookup on the web address to determine the numerical IP address for that domain name.

The simplest way to get the numerical IP address is to run, from your computer, a command called *ping* that will attempt to locate the server for the web. The *ping* command does this by performing a Domain Name Server (DNS) lookup first to see if it can find the server for the web address. If it can, it will respond with the numerical IP address.

22.1.1.1 Using the ping command

First, you must be connected to the Internet on the computer you are using to perform this type of lookup.

In Windows Vista, you can run this command by first clicking on your Start button and going to Accessories and then to Run on the menu.

This will open a dialog box as shown in Fig. 22.1.

When you press Enter, you will be presented with a small window that is the command-line window. In this window, you enter the command *ping* followed by the Internet address you are interested in. This is demonstrated in Fig. 22.2.

When you press Enter, the *ping* command will attempt to locate the server for the web address you entered. If it can be located, the results of the command will tell you the numerical IP address, as shown in Fig. 22.3.

Now that you have the numerical IP address, you can take steps to determine who owns the IP address. One such service you can use for this, and there are a lot

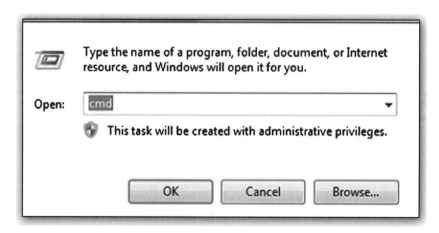

FIGURE 22.1

The Run feature in the Windows Accessories menu

of them, is www.domaintools.com. Figure 22.4 shows the screen where you enter the IP address of interest.

When you click on Search for Domain, the service will go out and locate the ownership records for the IP address. In Fig. 22.5 you can see that the owner of this IP address is Yahoo! Inc.

FIGURE 22.2

The command-line screen with the *ping* command entered for the web address www. yahoo.com

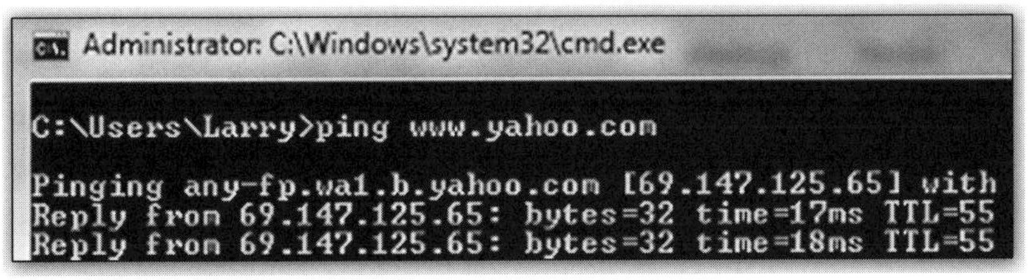

FIGURE 22.3

The results of running the *ping* command

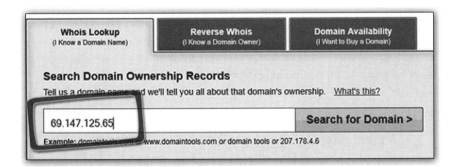

FIGURE 22.4

The IP address entry screen for www.domaintools.com

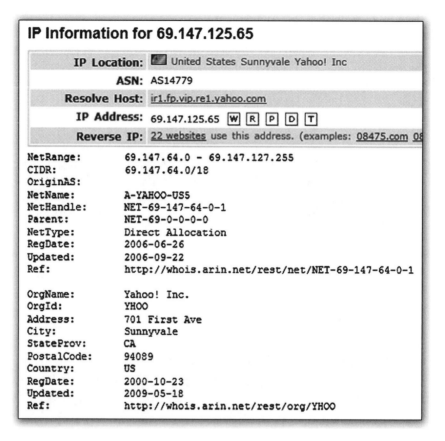

FIGURE 22.5

The domain owner information for the IP address you looked up on www.domaintools.com

Now that you know who owns the IP address, in this case Yahoo! Inc., you can take the steps you need to find the custodian of records for the subpoena.

Figure 22.6 shows the entry for Yahoo! Inc. from SEARCH, which is an excellent online resource for finding the custodian of records for Internet service providers, located at http://www.search.org/programs/hightech/isp/.

22.1.2 Motion language once you know the IP address

Your subpoena language should include all of the IP addresses of interest that belong to the individual service provider, as shown in the following example.

22.1

Any and all subscriber records pertaining to the following IP addresses. Also include any information about the computer or user for the date and time that they were issued.

IP Address	Date Range
123.123.123.111	June 1, 2009 to June 31, 2009
123.124.122.100	July 1, 2009 to August 31, 2009
123.122.123.111	July 1, 2010 to Present

Yahoo!
Contact Name: Yahoo! Custodian of Records
Online Service: Yahoo!
Online Service Address: 701 First Ave
                        Sunnyvale, California 94089
Phone Number: 408-349-3687
Fax Number: 408-349-7941
Note(s):   After-hours Emergencies:
                        Yahoo! Security at 408-349-5400
                        San Jose FBI

                        This is also the contact information for rocketmail.com

Last Updated: September, 2010

FIGURE 22.6

The entry for Yahoo! Inc. from the SEARCH site

22.2 EXAMPLE LANGUAGE FOR WEB-BASED E-MAIL ADDRESSES

Online or ISP-based e-mail addresses come up in cases so often that getting the subscriber information for them is another critical aspect of many legal matters.

The e-mail address itself will provide the information you need to locate the custodian of records. For instance, gmail.com is Google, while rocketmail.com, yahoo.com, and ymail.com are all Yahoo!, Inc. e-mail addresses. This same language can be used for paid e-mail accounts as well, such as America Online (aol.com), Road Runner (rr.com), and so forth.

The language for getting the information is short, but to the point:

22.2

Any and all subscriber records regarding the identification of Thisisanemailaddress@gmail.com to include real name, screen names, status of account, login log, IP address log, detailed billing logs, date account opened and closed, method of payment, and detailed billing records.

22.3 WHAT TO EXPECT FROM AN INTERNET SERVICE PROVIDER (ISP) SUBPOENA

Depending on the Internet service provider and how much information they capture and store, you can expect to get back, at a minimum, the name and address for the account holder, if it is a paid service. In some cases you will also get the credit card, checking account, or other payment information.

You can also expect to get the contact e-mail address for the account holder.

Finally, you will get back the dates and times along with the IP address that was assigned to the account for the dates requested in the subpoena. In a best-case scenario, you will get the MAC address of the computer that was actually connected to the Internet service provider.

SUMMARY

In this chapter we looked at examples of motion language for obtaining Internet service provider records. We found the owner of an IP address by following a step-by-step process using a Internet-connected computer. We looked at how to locate the custodian of records for an IP address as well. We also looked at how to determine the custodian of records for web-based e-mail addresses and the language to use for getting the subscriber information for a web-based e-mail account.

Discovery of Global Positioning System Evidence

INFORMATION IN THIS CHAPTER:

- GPS tracking evidence overview
- Discovery of GPS evidence

INTRODUCTION

Evidence in cases involving Global Positioning Systems (GPS) can be a vital factor in determining whether someone was in a particular place at a particular time, with the caveat that the information is coming from a device, not a person. Gathering GPS evidence can be a challenge as the data or evidence being sought can reside in several places: on physical devices, at third-party service providers, or as backups or data downloads on computers and smart phones.

When you begin to consider where GPS evidence may reside, the possibilities are on the GPS device itself, as a backup for data download on a computer, in place on a smart phone or pad computer, or as records collected by a third-party monitoring service.

The best-case scenario is to get the evidence from all applicable and available locations. In other words, if the only source is the GPS device itself, getting the device into custody for data collection and analysis is the only thing you can do.

However, if the device is part of a larger system, such as a monitoring system for house arrest, a monitoring system used to collect data in an investigation, or part of a system that is monitored by a third-party service, then getting the device and getting the records are equally important. How GPS works and the types of evidence that can be collected are covered in Chapter 42.

23.1 GPS TRACKING EVIDENCE OVERVIEW

The first thing to understand about GPS tracking as evidence is the wide variety of uses for GPS tracking today. As GPS devices have become available in smaller and more varied packages, they have been adapted to more uses in everyday life.

They are no longer only used by private investigators and trucking companies to track vehicles or law enforcement to track persons on house arrest. The following section provides some examples of how GPS tracking is used.

23.1.1 Categories of potential GPS tracking evidence

- Children and Teens
    - GPS devices in small packages are available for clipping to a child or teen's clothing for tracking of their whereabouts.
    - School buses in many localities are also being equipped with GPS tracking.
- Pets and Livestock
    - Devices are available that allow the owner to clip a GPS tracking device to a pet's collar or to a prize bull.
- Vehicles
    - Probably one of the most frequently used forms of fleet tracking. GPS devices in trucks and delivery vehicles allow the company to pinpoint the location of all the vehicles in their fleet.
- Employees
    - GPS tracking on service vehicles allows companies to determine where a service truck is for routing purposes from one call to the next and also to determine the whereabouts of employees who are on the job.
- Shipments and Packages
    - Small devices attached to packages and shipping containers can allow these items to be tracked worldwide.
- Persons (Electronic Monitoring)
    - Ankle bracelets are used in many jurisdictions as a form of house arrest, allowing police or the court to monitor the whereabouts of persons under supervision.
- Cell Phone Tracking
    - A number of applications are available for free on the Internet today that will allow tracking of a cell phone in near real time. They require that an application be installed on the phone. However, once the application is installed on the phone, the user can go to the service's website and turn on location services to track the phone on a map. One of these services is Mobile Defense, www.mobiledefense.com.
- Computer and Pad Tracking
    - Computers, especially pad computers, can be tracked via GPS in case the computer is lost or stolen. For instance, the iPad can be located using the Mobile Me service (www.mobileme.com) in conjunction with the iPad's onboard location awareness feature. Figure 23.1 shows this location method in action.

FIGURE 23.1

Find My iPad application showing the location of Larry's iPad on a map

23.2 DISCOVERY OF GPS EVIDENCE

Depending on where the evidence is located, on a GPS device, on a computer or smart phone, or at a third party, the approach to writing the technical language for inclusion in discovery motions varies. In the following sections, language examples are provided for getting evidence from devices and from third parties. In every case, as much information as possible about the device, records, or evidence needs to be requested in order to get a complete picture of the validity of the evidence. Also, when gathering devices for direct collection, requesting all of the pieces is important to avoid having to locate something as simple as a power supply that may prevent the device from being examined until a new power supply can be sourced.

23.2.1 Language for getting a GPS device for examination

A GPS device should be treated like any electronic device from a discovery standpoint. The important issues to address in a motion are in the language examples shown in the following box.

23.1

1. The device shall be made available for physical inspection and data extraction by a qualified forensic expert using tools specifically for the purpose of collecting and preserving GPS data.
2. Any reports or other information related to the chain of custody for the device, its storage and handling.
3. If the device was previously examined, any reports related to the examination shall be provided, including the methods used for the data collection, the name and version of any software used for the data collection, and a copy of the actual data files collected. Additionally, the resume or CV of the person or persons responsible for the handling, preservation, and forensic imaging and analysis of the device shall be provided.
4. Any photographs or screenshots made before, during, or after the collection of the device and its internal data.
5. Any manuals, accessories, or other items obtained and in custody related to the device, including but not limited to connection cables, power supplies, cases, carry bags, data disks, and media cards.

23.2.2 Language for getting information from a manufacturer about a device

If there are questions about the way a device functions, then the only real source is going to be the manufacturer of the device itself. The following language addresses getting device-specific information from a manufacturer.

23.2

1. This is a request for specific information about a GPS device manufactured by your company, specifically the device identified as **Make**, **Model Number**, **Series Name**, **Serial Number**, and **Software Version**.
2. Requested information to include specific details about the method of storage of data on the device, including but not limited to:
   a. How internal data is saved to the device
   b. How track logs are named
   c. What happens when new tracks are added to the device
   d. Whether or not date and time information is stored for track points, and when and if date and time information for individual track points is maintained or deleted
   e. How waypoints are handled when the user saves a waypoint using the menu for the current location and whether or not the waypoint receives an automatic time stamp
   f. How often track points are recorded in seconds
   g. How many track points are allowed in a track log before automatic rollover or creation of a new track log
   h. The maximum number of track points the device is capable of storing
3. Requested information to include hardware-specific information about the device, specifically but not limited to:
   a. The number of antennas in the device
   b. The power and signal ratings of the antennas on the device and the effect of same on the ability of the device to receive signals in normal conditions, overcast conditions, and in urban and rural settings
   c. The specified range of the device for receiving satellite signals for the purpose of geolocation, in meters or miles
   d. Any information regarding the ability of the device to receive assisted location services (ALS), including the type of ALS services, the accuracy enhancement of such services, and the conditions under which such services would be used by the device to assist in pinpointing its location
   e. Information about the specified engineered accuracy of the device as configured, including its specified accuracy rating for geolocation
   f. Any known conditions inherent to the device that can cause the device to incorrectly record its current location
   g. The method used to calculate velocity and direction
   h. Whether or not the unit has an internal compass
4. Information related to any known maintenance issues, failure rates, or software bugs in the device as specified herein.

23.2.3 **Language for getting GPS evidence from a third party**

Depending on the situation, evidence may also need to be collected from a third party, such as a monitoring service. The following language addresses the issues of importance in acquiring third-party GPS records.

23.3 _____

1. Any and all records related to the GPS records identified by serial number(s) _____ specifically for the period of time beginning on _____ and ending on _____.

2. All information related to GPS units identified by serial number(s) _____, to include but not limited to GPS activity such as powering up, powering down, distance traveled, mileage, latitude and longitude, location by address, speed of travel, distance traveled, long stop, short stop, and so forth.

3. Any information that is available regarding the physical GPS units that are the source of these records, identified by GPS unit serial number(s) _____. This is to include, but is not limited to: user manuals, installation manuals, owner manuals, manufacturer, make, model, dates units went into service, dates units went out of service, known issues or problems with the specific GPS models such as loss of signal, problems with calibration, pinging, areas of service, problems due to extraneous factors such as weather, and so forth.

4. Any information that is available regarding the software used by both (monitoring company) and their clients. This is to include, but is not limited to: user manuals, installation manuals, owner manuals, online documentation, known problems with the software used by either (monitoring company) or their clients, user errors that could have an effect on GPS records, and so forth.

5. Any and all maintenance records for the GPS units identified by serial number(s) _____.

6. A list of all GPS units supported by **MONITORING COMPANY NAME'S** tracking system up to **MONTH** of **20XX**.

7. Any and all information on the GPS units regarding their installation and operation. This information is to include, but is not limited to: how and where they are installed, possible errors in installation that could have an effect on GPS records, how the tracking ability of GPS units could be manipulated by being turned on and off by the user, otherwise disabling of the GPS unit, the use of software or hardware that could modify the unit, and other ways of intentionally causing a GPS unit to function in any way other than intended.

SUMMARY

In this chapter we looked at the various types of GPS tracking evidence. We also looked at discovery language that can be used to obtain evidentiary information from third-party monitoring services and device manufacturers. Discovery language for getting the devices for examination was also provided.

Discovery of Call Detail Records

INFORMATION IN THIS CHAPTER:

* Discovery issues in cellular evidence
* Example language for call detail records

INTRODUCTION

In order to properly analyze call detail records, a considerable amount of information should be gathered in addition to the cell tower locations and the call detail report. In this chapter we look at language for use in requesting this information in the most detailed manner possible. Bear in mind that all of the information you request may not be available because different cellular carrier companies' retention policies vary. Some carriers begin to purge records as early as 18 months after a call is recorded, while others may keep records for several years. The only way to know is to contact the custodian of records and inquire about the carrier's individual retention policy.

In any case where you are going to seek this information, even if it is a considerable amount of time after the date of the incident, it may be prudent to issue a preservation order to prevent the loss of any further stored data.

24.1 DISCOVERY ISSUES IN CELLULAR EVIDENCE

Call detail records in and of themselves provide minimal information. This is because the call detail records are used by the cellular carriers for the purpose of financial transactions such as generating bills to the subscriber and also for the purpose of settling accounts with other carriers.

However, when call detail records are needed for the purpose of evidence, additional information is needed to perform a comprehensive analysis. A standard call detail report will not contain any technical information about the individual cell towers or the health of the system at the time. If you only have a listing of calls made and the location of the various cell towers that were used in the transmission and reception of the calls, a lot can be left to interpretation. While locating a cell phone is not possible from historical records, many claims are made as to the location of a cell phone from these records.

163

In order for the analysis to be as complete as possible, information about the cell towers must also be gathered:

- Coverage maps for each cell tower,
- Whether or not cell towers were undergoing maintenance,
- The configuration of each of the cell towers

This information is needed so that the analyst can properly identify and map out the specific coverage area of a tower or tower sector.

The language that is included in the following section attempts to capture information about the configuration and health of the cellular system at the time of the incident. It also attempts to capture the history of any calls made, text messages, and data access for the phones in question.

Simply requesting the call detail records and cell tower locations for a cellular phone number will not compel the carrier to give you information that could be critical to your case. The cell phone system and how it works along with examples of the usage of the evidence you are asking for here is covered in Chapter 33.

24.2 EXAMPLE LANGUAGE FOR CALL DETAIL RECORDS

This example language includes all of the items that you would want to get when requesting cellular phone records in order for your expert to be able to provide the best analysis possible.

24.1

Defense or plaintiff requests the following information be provided regarding cell phone communications for cell phone number(s) **000-000-0000** for the period of time between **00-00-2000** and **00-00-2000**.

Any information including but not limited to:

1. Subscriber information for the above listed numbers, not limited to financially responsible party, social security number, billing address, features and services, and equipment
2. All call originations, call terminations, call attempts, voice and text message transactions, including push-to-talk, data communications, and voice communications
3. All stored SMS, MMS, or browser cache
4. Beginning and ending cell phone tower identifiers for each call cell phone tower/cell site location information including latitude and longitude for the coverage area, specifically for **City, State**, for the time period requested
5. Central office identifiers for the area of coverage for the time period requested
6. All connection attempts including completed and failed connections and call duration times to one one-hundredth of a second
7. A complete table of cell towers/cell site information for all cell towers/cell sites in the service area. This will include cell tower location information, cell tower/cell site designation information, and cell tower/cell site identification numbers and date of service origination for each tower/site, and date of service termination for each tower/site

8. A detail of the coverage radius and configuration of the cell towers/sites as of the time period requested
9. A Radio Frequency Plan map for the service area for the phone numbers for the time period requested
10. Originating and receiving phone numbers or network IDs for all incoming and outgoing call transactions, data transactions, and push-to-talk sessions
11. Date and time information for all transactions to one one-hundredth of a second
12. A legend and definition for any and all abbreviations used in the reports provided
13. Any information regarding roaming agreements with other carriers in the area that were in effect as of the time period requested
14. Any information regarding default or pushed to phone preferred roaming lists (PRLs) in effect for the time period request and for six months leading up to the time period requested
15. Any trouble tickets for towers within area designated herein for the dates and times designated herein
16. Any stored handset identification data for any cell phones related to the call detail records

Please indicate in your response to this subpoena if there is any data loss due to the time difference between the date of the receipt of this subpoena and the time period requested, and if so, a detailed description of what data is not recoverable versus what data would be recoverable based on the carrier's retention period for call detail records, cell tower/site records, and Radio Frequency Plan records.

SUMMARY

In this chapter we looked at some of the discovery issues relating to cellular evidence. We have also included sample language for obtaining as much information as possible for call detail records and supporting information that may be obtained in the course of discovery.

Obtaining Expert Funding in Indigent Cases

25

INFORMATION IN THIS CHAPTER:

- Justifying extraordinary expenses
- Example language for an ex parte motion for expert funds

INTRODUCTION

In cases involving indigent clients, you may have a need to get funding approved by a judge or other funding source. This varies by jurisdiction and other vagaries of the funding sources for indigent clients in federal and state cases. Essentially all power to fund defense experts flows from a statute, such as 18 U.S.C. § 3006A(e), or from the defendant's constitutional right to an expert as part of a fair trial first recognized in *Ake v. Oklahoma*, 470 U.S. 68 (1985).

Sometimes a barrier to obtaining funds is the lack of understanding by a judge as to why you need a digital forensics expert. Also, in some cases, you may need to engage an expert who is nonlocal, which will incur extra expenses for travel, or in cases where the expert is required to perform work at a law enforcement facility if the case is a contraband case covered by the Adam Walsh Child Protection and Safety Act. In this chapter some of the justification for extraordinary expenses in cases involving digital forensics will be covered and example language for an ex parte order for expert funds is included.

25.1 JUSTIFYING EXTRAORDINARY EXPENSES

In some cases, local experts are simply unavailable for various reasons:

- They don't handle criminal cases.
- They don't handle cases involving sex crimes.
- They don't handle cases involving child pornography.
- They lack the expertise in the specific technology in your case.
- They are simply too busy to take your case.

In a child pornography case in Alabama there was a request for the judge to approve funding for an out-of-state examiner to work as an expert. The judge wanted to better understand why the attorney needed to bring in an out-of-state expert instead of using someone who knew computer technology from a local university.

The following example includes the content of the order and the responses provided.

25.1 ORDER

This cause is before the court on the Defendant's Motion For Extraordinary Expenses For Expert. The court would be inclined to grant the motion upon a reasonable showing by the Defendant of the following:

1. The specific testimony from the State's experts for which rebuttal is necessary.

    The State's computer forensics experts will be expected to testify as to the dates and times that various files on the defendant's computer were created, opened, deleted, and/or accessed. Additionally, expert testimony as to the user's actions, ownership of the computer, forensic processes used to extract and verify data, the handling and collection of the digital evidence, specifics relating to software programs installed and used in the commission of the alleged offense, and other technical information regarding the specific evidence obtained from the computer or hard drives.

2. A more specific and detailed description of why a computer forensics expert is required for the Defendant.

    In order to assist the attorney in properly preparing a defense in matters involving electronic evidence, specifically from computers, hard drives, USB drives, and other digital media, the attorney must have the assistance of a person with the specific training and knowledge of computer forensics.

    A computer forensics expert will have knowledge of the proper collection and handling of electronic evidence that a computer expert would not.

    In order to prepare a proper defense, the State's expert's examination must be verified by an independent expert who has knowledge and training as well as access to the specific forensic software tools used by the State in preparing its case.

    Such software, knowledge, and training are not part of the background of computer experts, but are limited to the training and experience of experts in computer forensics.

    Additionally, a computer expert would not have the training and specific experience needed to assist the attorney with preparation for trial, including assisting the attorney in preparing for examination of the State's expert in relation to the forensic evidence that will be presented at trial, nor would a computer expert have the specific knowledge and experience to qualify and present expert witness testimony in the highly technical area of computer forensics.

3. A curriculum vitae and/or such information qualifying the requested expert to perform the services necessary.

    The expert's curriculum vitae is attached to this order.

4. A statement of the expert's rates for his services and a specific estimate, to the extent one can be given, for the services expected to be rendered.

    The expert charges $**150.00** per hour for work performed on behalf of the Client. The rate is the same for all activities, including time in court and court testimony.

    Based on the circumstances of the case, the expert estimates **10** hours on site for the computer examination, **10** hours for post-examination analysis of collected information, court preparation, and time in transit for a total of $**3,000.00**.

    If the defendant decides not to proceed to trial, then the case would require fewer hours than shown in the estimate above. However, if the defendant proceeds to trial and the expert is required to spend additional days in court, the estimated hours could be exceeded.

5. Where the requested expert resides and the estimated costs to be charged for his travel.

   The expert resides in **Raleigh, North Carolina**. The expected travel costs would be as follows:

   To perform the examination at the **State Forensics** Lab in **Montgomery**, **Alabama**, the estimated travel cost would be $**500.00**.

   If the expert is needed to return to testify in court, the estimated travel cost would be $**500.00**.

   The travel cost estimate includes airfare, rental car, hotel, and a per diem of $**25.00** per day.

   These estimates are based on airfares available at the time of this writing and are subject to change.

6. A statement from the requested expert setting out the services and testimony generally that he could provide that would be of assistance to the Defendant.

   The expert uses the same computer forensic software used by the **State's Expert** and has comparable training and experience. This will enable the expert to verify the examination performed by the State's expert to ensure that the evidence presented in the case is accurate and complete. The expert will be able to assist the attorney with court preparation, rebuttal of the State's expert's testimony, and advice as to the merits of the defense's case in regard to the computer forensic evidence.

   If the defendant decides to proceed to trial, the expert will be able to provide expert testimony about the forensic evidence in the case.

25.2 EXAMPLE LANGUAGE FOR AN EX PARTE MOTION FOR EXPERT FUNDS

The language and form that follow is an example of how an attorney might go about crafting a motion for expert funds. This is provided for convenience and should be crafted according to your needs by a licensed attorney in the appropriate jurisdiction.

25.2 SAMPLE EX PARTE MOTION FOR EXPERT FUNDS

STATE OF NORTH CAROLINA	IN THE GENERAL COURT OF JUSTICE
DURHAM COUNTY	DISCTRICT COURT DIVISION FILE NO. 11 CR **00000**

STATE OF NORTH CAROLINA
               Plaintiff.

  vs.

JOHN H. DOE
               Defendant.

On motion by the Defendant, by and through his attorney, ex parte pursuant to the Fifth, Sixth, Eighth, and Fourteenth Amendments to the United States Constitution, and Article

1, Sections 19, 23, and 27 of the North Carolina Constitution and *Ake v. Oklahoma*, 470 U.S. 68 (1985); *State v. Bates*, 333 N.C. 323 (1993); *State v. Parks*, 331 N.C. 649 (1992); *State v. Taylor*, 327 N.C. 147 (1990); *State v. Moore*, 3221 N.C. 327 (1988); and pursuant to N.C. Gen. Stat. § 7A-450(b); 7A-451, and 7A-545 to allow funds for the Defendant to hire a certified digital forensics expert, **Examiner**, to assist him in the evaluation and the preparation of his defense, the Court finds:

1. That Defendant has been charged with theft;
2. That Defendant was determined by the District Court to be indigent;
3. That counsel for Defendant has a reasonable belief that there exists information and data that is stored in electronic format on computers and or other electronic storage media, which information is necessary to ensure that Defendant receives a fair trial and the effective assistance of counsel and to adequately prepare a defense in this matter;
4. That the recovery of this information and data requires specific knowledge and expertise which counsel for the Defendant does not possess;
5. That **Examiner**, a certified Digital Forensics Consultant, has extensive experience in computer forensics and has provided these services in numerous criminal cases in North Carolina;
6. That the hourly rate charged by **Examiner** is **$250.00** per hour;
7. That Defendant has made a threshold and particularized showing that Defendant will be deprived of a fair trial without the expert assistance of **Examiner**, and that there is a reasonable likelihood that an expert such as **Examiner** would materially assist Defendant in the evaluation, preparation, and presentation of the Defense of his case.

THEREFORE, the Court HEREBY ORDERS:

1. That **Examiner** be appointed as an expert in digital forensics for the Defendant in order to assist Defendant in the evaluation, preparation, and presentation of his defense;
2. That the North Carolina Administrative Office of the Courts pay for **Examiner's** services and necessary expense related to said appointment pursuant to N.C. Gen. Stat. § 7A-454 and IDS rules and procedures, in the amounts and at the rates described herein, in an initial amount of **$2500.00**;
3. Counsel for the Defendant may seek leave of this Court if the need for further services of **Examiner** is demonstrated;
4. That this **ex parte** motion and order be sealed and held by the Johnston County Clerk of Court unless and until Defendant calls Mr. **Examiner** as a witness.

SUMMARY

In this chapter we looked at an example motion that used the language needed for obtaining expenses in indigent cases. We also looked at an example of how you can justify extraordinary expenses.

Common Types of Digital Evidence

4

Hash Values: The Verification Standard

26

INFORMATION IN THIS CHAPTER:

- Hash values
- How hash values are used in digital forensics

INTRODUCTION

When asked on the witness stand, any examiner should be able to show that he or she took the proper steps to verify the evidence collected using hash values for verification of the forensic copy against the original evidence.

In Chapter 4 (in the section "Acquisition Best Practices"), we saw that hash values play an important roles in forensics, especially in verifying that a forensic image of digital evidence is exactly the same as the original; a digital fingerprint, if you will.

Ignoring the benefit of using hash values in a case beyond simply verifying evidence does them a great disservice. If a particular file is of interest in your case, hash values can be used to find that file buried just about anywhere in a computer, even if the name of the file has been changed. Hash values can be used to link one device to another, such as a USB thumb drive to a computer, which can be particularly useful in cases that involve data theft or the distribution of contraband. Likewise, hash values can be used to help prove that something does not exist on a computer or other digital device. A good examiner knows the importance of hash values and how to use them. In this chapter we will highlight some of the more common uses of hash values and how you can put them to work in a case, and we will share some examples of how we have used them ourselves.

26.1 HASH VALUES

The process of *hashing*, as used in digital forensics, is a mathematical algorithm performed against a file, a group of files, or the contents of an entire hard drive. This hash value is the digital version of a thumbprint, allowing for that file or hard drive to be uniquely identified as it exists at the time it was hashed. Basically, you have a perfect snapshot in time of the data, which is an absolute must if the evidence itself, or any examination that is performed on the evidence, is going to be

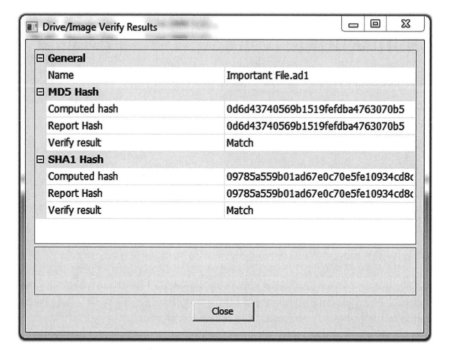

FIGURE 26.1

A hashed file, both in MD5 and SHA1

used in your case or the courtroom. The two types of hashes you will encounter in computer forensics are

- Message Digest 5 (MD5)
- Secure Hash Algorithm 1 (SHA1)

They both serve the same function in the verification of evidence and they aid in the examination of digital evidence.

The purpose of Fig. 26.1 is to familiarize legal professionals with what a hash value looks like so they can identify it when they see it in a warrant or forensic reports.

26.2 HOW HASH VALUES ARE USED IN DIGITAL FORENSICS

When a hard drive is hashed for verification purposes, the hashing process looks at all of the data on the hard drive and creates a "digital thumbprint" for it. At this point, the hashing process has performed its primary function, which is the verification of the data on the hard drive; the perfect snapshot in time of the data has been created. At this point, only the hard drive has a hash value. All of the files and documents that reside on the hard drive do not yet have a hash value. A forensic examiner can hash all of the files on the hard drive, giving each and every file a unique digital "thumbprint," or hash value.

Think of it like this: Imagine you are packing boxes in preparation to move. When packing your office, you clear off all the papers on your desk and put them in one box, and label it "Office Papers." This box of items now has a unique name, allowing you to identify it, so that it will be put in the correct room when you are unpacking. However, in the process of unpacking, you have to read each sheet of paper to know where it belongs since they are not labeled. This would be like hashing a hard drive for verification and preservation purposes. The hard drive has a unique hash value based on its data, which allows it to be identified, but the individual items inside the hard drive do not. Using the same scenario, let's imagine this time that before placing your papers in the box, you label each paper with a unique name. You labeled the box, so you know which room it belongs in, and since you also labeled each individual paper with a unique name, you are able to quickly organize and find a particular paper of interest. This is akin to the process of hashing the contents of a hard drive. Since all of the files and documents are hashed and now have their own "digital thumbprint," it is now possible to quickly and accurately locate a particular file of interest. The following sections show some of the ways in which hash values aid in digital forensics analysis.

26.2.1 Using hash values to find hidden files

One way to try and hide a file is to rename the file extension. For instance, let's imagine that an important picture is stolen from a server at a company and transferred to another computer. The stolen picture is named "evidence.jpg." Since the computer that has a copy of the stolen picture on the hard drive is running the Windows operating system, it would see the file extension (jpg) and recognize the file as a picture. If the file extension were changed to ".txt," Windows would not know it was a picture. The person who copied the stolen picture to the computer could go a step further in trying to hide the picture "evidence.jpg" by renaming the file to something innocuous, like "puppies.jpg," and then changing the file extension, giving us "puppies.txt." So now, when the nosy boss navigates through the files on the computer, he will not be clued in that there is a stolen picture that belongs to the company on the hard drive. In all probability it will seem to the boss, given the new name of the file and the file extension "txt," that it is a delightful short story about the joy of puppies.

While hiding a file in this method can fool a nosy boss, it will not hide it from a competent examiner who is using hash values as a way to locate a sensitive file. This type of file hiding is common in cases with a scenario like this. Hash values allow a forensic examiner to use the hash value from a known file (in this example, evidence.jpg), and search the suspect's computer for that sensitive file, looking for an exact match of that hash value. Since the hash value is created using the contents of the file and ignores the file name and file extension, it does not matter if someone

Filename	Size	Stored MD5 Hash	Stored SHA1 Hash
Important File.jpg	845941	ba45c8f60456a672e003a875e469d0eb	30420d1a9afb2bcb60335812569af4435a59ce17
Important File Renamed With Changed File Extension.doc	845941	ba45c8f60456a672e003a875e469d0eb	30420d1a9afb2bcb60335812569af4435a59ce17

FIGURE 26.2

An example of a hidden or renamed file, and how a hash value will find it despite efforts made to hide the file

tries to hide it using the aforementioned method, a hash value analysis will still find it, as shown in Fig. 26.2.

26.2.2 How to determine whether a file exists on a computer

Determining whether a file exists on a computer is a scenario in which hash values really shine. In forensics, when a group of files that are of particular interest is found, an examiner can run the hashing process on those files to generate the hash values for each of the files, and then put them together in what is called a hash set. That examiner can then use this hash to compare the hash values of the set against all the files on a hard drive to see if any of the files on the hard drive match any of the hash values for the files in the hash set.

26.2.3 De-duplicating data in e-discovery

Having to read the same e-mail or document multiple times is a real chore when reviewing discovery. In cases that involve electronic discovery (e-discovery), hash values allow data to be de-duplicated. After all the files are hashed in an e-discovery case, the de-duplication process finds files that have matching hash values. When multiple files with the same hash value are found, one of the files is kept, while the rest are removed from the discovery. The result is that you can still be assured you have the entirety of the discovery, since the de-duplication process only removes duplicate files that are exactly the same, so that you only have to read a particular e-mail or document once instead of multiple times.

26.2.4 The dangers of court testimony without verification

Failing to follow the basic steps of maintaining chain of custody for evidence by creating a verification hash of collected evidence leaves the question of the authenticity of the evidence open. The purpose of the hash value is to be able to, at any time, compare a file or an entire hard drive's worth of evidence to prove that the original is identical to the evidence being presented, without alteration.

It is this process of verification hashing for evidence that allows examiners to create and work from exact copies of original evidence.

When asked on the witness stand, any examiner should be able to show that he or she took the proper steps to verify the evidence collected using hash values for verification of the forensic copy against the original evidence.

26.2.5 What if an opposing expert did not verify evidence?

It is very common, especially in civil and domestic cases, to collect evidence as a "point-in-time" snapshot. In contrast to a criminal proceeding where computers and other evidence may be seized and held by a law enforcement agency for the duration, civil collections often require that the computer be taken out of service only long enough to make the forensic copy.

In a civil litigation, taking a production e-mail server out of a corporate office for an indefinite time would create an undue burden of discovery. To ensure that the producing party is not unduly burdened by disruption to their business, which would involve loss of business, employee costs, and so on, a server or computer must be forensically imaged quickly and put back into production.

Creating a verification hash of the collected evidence is a vital step in ensuring that the collected evidence matches the original evidence at the time it is collected. It also ensures that when produced, evidence can be verified against the collected "original," since the point-in-time snapshot in effect becomes the original evidence, even though the original media is no longer available for comparison.

In electronic discovery collections, it is common to collect a group of files, or a custodian's e-mail, without making a forensic image of the entire hard drive where those documents reside. However, even in a case where only a set of files is to be collected, they should be collected using forensic tools that provide a hash value in a defensibly sound manner.

SUMMARY

In this chapter we learned that hash values are used to verify that a forensic copy of a hard drive or electronic file is the same as the original, allowing the use of forensic copies for analysis and production of evidence. We also learned that hash values can be used to locate files that have been hidden by changing the file name and/or file extension to fool a computer user. Also covered in this chapter is the use of hash values in e-discovery for de-duplication where the same document or e-mail may occur multiple times in electronic discovery.

Metadata

INFORMATION IN THIS CHAPTER:

- The purpose of metadata
- Common types of metadata

INTRODUCTION

Metadata can be a veritable gold mine of useful information in a case. The prefix *meta* in English is used to express the idea that some information is about its own category. Hence the meaning of metadata is "data about data," just as metacognition means "knowing about knowing." While this might seem somewhat cryptic, when you get down to the nuts and bolts, metadata is not hard to understand in principle, but can be confusing in detail. Metadata can be found inside a file, kind of behind the scenes where an ordinary computer user will not see it, or in an external data store such as Internet history files that record information about files.

The information stored within metadata can be used to build timelines, establish alibis, and so much more. In the hands of a skilled digital forensics expert, metadata can shed light on a particular issue in a case, or it can be the turning point altogether. In many cases, tiny snippets of metadata can change how entire sequences of events are interpreted. However, a word of caution about metadata: Metadata alone, like any snippet of digital evidence, is rarely enough to "prove" something. Nearly all digital evidence requires some type of corroboration through a combination of evidence, electronic or otherwise. Relying on a single piece of electronic evidence can lead to misunderstandings without properly establishing a foundation for that evidence.

27.1 THE PURPOSE OF METADATA

The purpose of metadata is to store information about other data. This can help with the organization and retrieval of data. For instance, web pages on the Internet have metadata in such forms as meta-tags. A meta-tag is coded into a website where you do not see it, but it contains information about a website, such as keywords so that it can be easily found when those keywords match your Google search. Metadata can also be found inside many pictures and videos, containing copyright information if there is any, as well as information such as when the picture was taken and the make and model of the camera the picture was taken with. Or, as in the case of office documents, when searching for a document in Microsoft Windows, you can choose to search for documents by the author, the creation date, the last modified date, and so forth. All of this information is contained in the document's metadata.

27.2 COMMON TYPES OF METADATA

In the following sections, the more common types of metadata are discussed as well as where the metadata can be found and how it is used as evidence.

27.2.1 File system metadata

File system metadata includes the times recorded by the operating system when a file is modified, accessed, or created. File system metadata is easily misinterpreted and can be very difficult to understand. For this reason, file system metadata is covered in detail in Chapter 30.

27.2.2 Internet metadata

There are two types of Internet metadata:

1. Web page
2. Browser metadata

27.2.2.1 Web page metadata
Metadata for web pages is contained within the "code" of the web page and is in the form of meta-tags, page titles, page headers. and meta-descriptions. While this type of metadata can be interesting, it is almost entirely controlled by the user who creates the web page and rarely offers very much in the way of forensic value. The original purpose of web page metadata was to assist search engines such as Yahoo or Google in finding and indexing web pages. However, widespread abuse of meta-tags, keywords, and meta-descriptions has resulted in modern search engines largely ignoring this metadata in favor of actual page content.

If you examine the web page metadata in Fig. 27.1, you will notice that what the metadata does not contain is any information about when, where, or by whom the web page was created. This web page could have been created on a computer and never published to the web. If this is the only evidence you have, you have no evidence at all. This is why web page metadata is of limited value in a forensic examination.

27.2.2.2 Browser metadata
While it is not commonly referred to as metadata, the history stored by Internet browsing programs certainly qualifies as data about websites and pages that have

USER CREATED METADATA

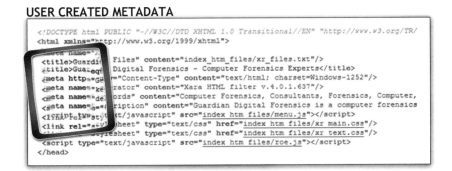

FIGURE 27.1

Example of metadata contained in a web page

Type	URL	Last Visited [Local]	User	Hits
https	https://channel.skype.com/facebook/ch...	4/21/2011 12:16:50 AM Thu	Larry	1
https	https://secure.skypeassets.com/channel...	4/21/2011 12:16:50 AM Thu	Larry	1
http	http://www.amazon.com/Digital-Forensic...	4/20/2011 10:11:18 PM Wed	Larry	11
http	http://d3l3kinz3f56t.cloudfront.net/pixel...	4/20/2011 10:11:18 PM Wed	Larry	2
http	http://www.amazon.com/aan/2009-09-0...	4/20/2011 10:11:18 PM Wed	Larry	2
http	http://www.amazon.com/Digital-Forensic...	4/20/2011 10:11:18 PM Wed	Larry	2
http	http://www.amazon.com/Digital-Forensic...	4/20/2011 10:11:12 PM Wed	Larry	1
http	http://office.microsoft.com/client/search...	4/17/2011 10:01:03 AM Sun	Larry	1
http	http://office.microsoft.com/client/search...	4/17/2011 10:01:03 AM Sun	Larry	1
http	http://office.microsoft.com/client/helpho...	4/17/2011 10:00:55 AM Sun	Larry	1
http	http://office.microsoft.com/client/helpho...	4/17/2011 10:00:55 AM Sun	Larry	1

FIGURE 27.2

An example of browser metadata extracted from Internet history files

been visited, and websites or pages marked as favorites by the user. Browser metadata is used extensively as forensic evidence in all kinds of cases. The screenshot in Fig. 27.2 is from the program NetAnalysis by Digital Detective (www.digitaldetective.co.uk) and shows the result of an Internet history analysis from a computer hard drive.

27.2.3 Document metadata

Document metadata is metadata stored inside a document that provides information about the authorship, editing time, and even the computer on which the document

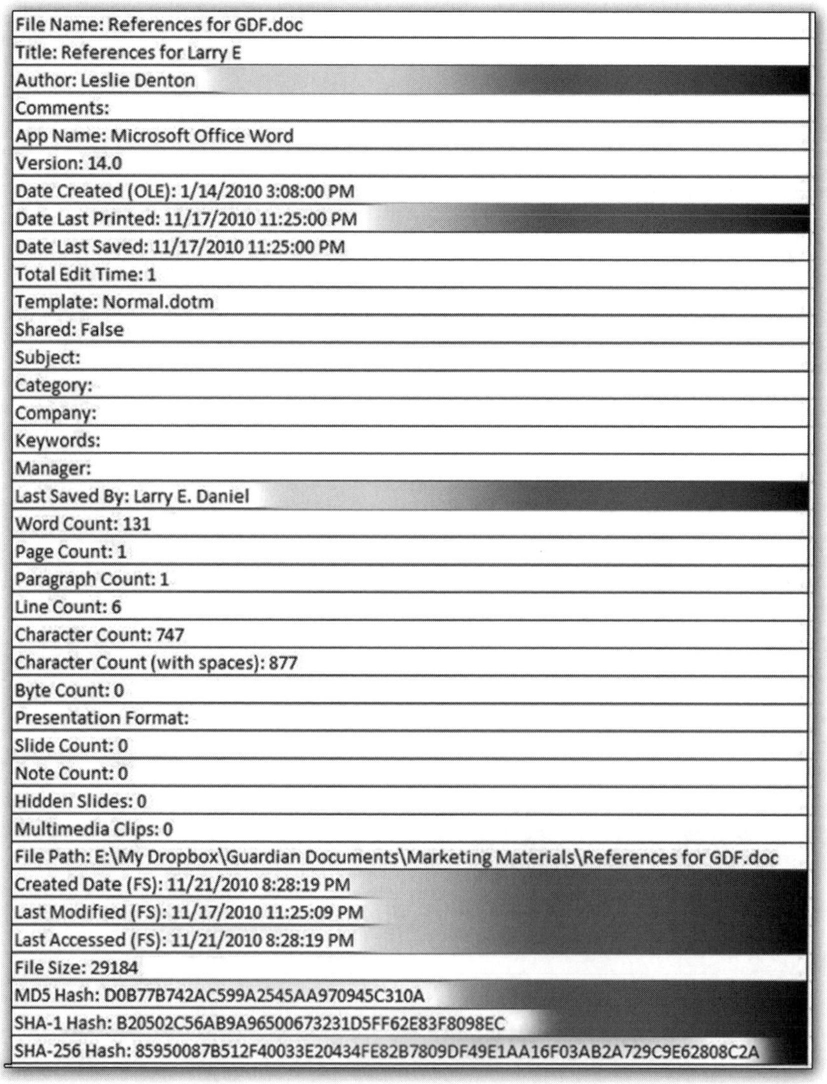

File Name: References for GDF.doc
Title: References for Larry E
Author: Leslie Denton
Comments:
App Name: Microsoft Office Word
Version: 14.0
Date Created (OLE): 1/14/2010 3:08:00 PM
Date Last Printed: 11/17/2010 11:25:00 PM
Date Last Saved: 11/17/2010 11:25:00 PM
Total Edit Time: 1
Template: Normal.dotm
Shared: False
Subject:
Category:
Company:
Keywords:
Manager:
Last Saved By: Larry E. Daniel
Word Count: 131
Page Count: 1
Paragraph Count: 1
Line Count: 6
Character Count: 747
Character Count (with spaces): 877
Byte Count: 0
Presentation Format:
Slide Count: 0
Note Count: 0
Hidden Slides: 0
Multimedia Clips: 0
File Path: E:\My Dropbox\Guardian Documents\Marketing Materials\References for GDF.doc
Created Date (FS): 11/21/2010 8:28:19 PM
Last Modified (FS): 11/17/2010 11:25:09 PM
Last Accessed (FS): 11/21/2010 8:28:19 PM
File Size: 29184
MD5 Hash: D0B77B742AC599A2545AA970945C310A
SHA-1 Hash: B20502C56AB9A96500673231D5FF62E83F8098EC
SHA-256 Hash: 85950087B512F40033E20434FE82B7809DF49E1AA16F03AB2A729C9E62808C2A

FIGURE 27.3

Example of metadata contained in a Microsoft Word document

was created. All of the major office suites such as Microsoft Office, WordPerfect Office, OpenOffice, and Star Office record metadata in some form inside the word processing documents, spreadsheets, and presentations created with the programs in these suites. Figure 27.3 is a screenshot of a Microsoft Word document as viewed in a metadata viewing program.

File Details	
Date	4/11/2011 6:26:59 PM
Is Read Only	No
Name	Larry E Daniel Curriculum Vitae.pdf
Path	E:\My Dropbox\Guardian Documents\Attorney Packets\Larry E Da
Size	38 KBytes
Metadata	
Author	**Larry**
Created On	D:20110411182659
Keywords	
Last Modified	D:20110411182659
PDF Creator	PScript5.dll Version 5.2.2
PDF Producer	**GPL Ghostscript 8.15**
Subject	
Title	**Microsoft Word – Curriculum Vitae – Larry E Daniel.doc**

FIGURE 27.4

Example of metadata contained in a PDF document

As you can see in the example shown in Fig. 27.3, office document metadata contains a wealth of information about the life of the document. In this example we see the name of the original author, who last saved the document, the original creation date, the date it was last printed, and the date it was last saved. Toward the bottom of the figure you can see the file system metadata also recorded inside the document including the file path, and the file system created, modified, and last accessed dates and times. You can also see the different hash values for the document. Hash values are covered in Chapters 4 and 26.

In addition to office documents, Adobe Portable Document Format (PDF) files also contain metadata. Figure 27.4 is an example of a Microsoft Word document after it has been saved as a PDF document and viewed in a PDF metadata viewer.

27.2.4 Picture metadata

Picture metadata can contain information about the make and model of the camera used to take the picture or about the software used to modify a picture. In the example in Fig. 27.5 you will see that the image was modified using Adobe Photoshop CS. When a photo has been modified using a program like Adobe Photoshop, the original camera information can be lost. However, the metadata will contain the name of the editing program that was used to modify the picture.

Figure 27.6 shows the metadata contained inside a picture taken with an Android phone. Instead of the camera make and model, in this instance you can see the make of the cell phone, a Motorola Droid, and the currently installed version of the phone's imaging application, 2.1-update 1.

/File/Main/FilePath	"E:\Documents\Pictures\toy-poodle-0075.jpg"
/File/Main/FileName	"toy-poodle-0075.jpg"
/File/Main/FileLocation	"E:\Documents\Pictures\"
/File/Main/FileExtension	"jpg"
/File/Main/FileSize	"30462"
/File/Main/DateCreation	"28.11.2010 17:39:57"
/File/Main/DateLastAccess	"28.11.2010 17:39:57"
/File/Main/DateLastWrite	"27.03.2010 11:20:31"
/Exif/Image/Orientation	"1"
/Exif/Image/XResolution	"150/1"
/Exif/Image/YResolution	"150/1"
/Exif/Image/ResolutionUnit	"2"
/Exif/Image/Software	"Adobe Photoshop CS Windows"
/Exif/Image/DateTime	"5/16/2005 9:31:30 PM"
/Exif/Photo/ColorSpace	"65535"
/Exif/Photo/PixelXDimension	"411"
/Exif/Photo/PixelYDimension	"437"
/Exif/Thumbnail/Compression	"6"
/Exif/Thumbnail/XResolution	"72/1"
/Exif/Thumbnail/YResolution	"72/1"
/Exif/Thumbnail/ResolutionUnit	"2"
/Xmp/Exif/ColorSpace	"4294967295"
/Xmp/Exif/PixelXDimension	"411"
/Xmp/Exif/PixelYDimension	"437"
/Xmp/Tiff/Orientation	"1"
/Xmp/Tiff/XResolution	"150/1"
/Xmp/Tiff/YResolution	"150/1"
/Xmp/Tiff/ResolutionUnit	"2"
/Xmp/Xmp/CreateDate	"2005-05-16T20:29:47-07:00"
/Xmp/Xmp/ModifyDate	"2005-05-16T21:31:30-07:00"
/Xmp/Xmp/MetadataDate	"2005-05-16T21:31:30-07:00"
/Xmp/Xmp/CreatorTool	"Adobe Photoshop CS Windows"
/Xmp/MediaManagement/DocumentID	"adobe:docid:photoshop:4cfe8c92-c683-11d9-9ba0-b6b7cfe3a29d"
/Xmp/MediaManagement/InstanceID	"uuid:4cfe8c93-c683-11d9-9ba0-b6b7cfe3a29d"
/Xmp/DublinCoreSchema/Format	"uuid:4cfe8c93-c683-11d9-9ba0-b6b7cfe3a29d"

FIGURE 27.5

Example of metadata contained in a picture modified using Adobe Photoshop CS

27.1 CASE EXAMPLES: METADATA AS EVIDENCE

Metadata and Timelines

There was a case where a man was accused of molesting a girl while taking pictures of her using a camera. The pictures were innocent in content. While this girl and her family were visiting his home, she asked the accused to take pictures of her for her MySpace page. In the girl's recount of the events, the molestation was said to have happened over a 30-minute period, where the accused was supposedly taking pictures of her, and in between taking the pictures was molesting her. A review of the metadata in the pictures showed that the entire picture-taking session lasted a total of four minutes and forty-six seconds. By examining the metadata of the first and last picture, the entire time period of the picture-taking session could be shown, and by looking at all metadata for all the pictures, it was revealed that no two pictures were taken more than 30 seconds apart. This information was critical in refuting the charges, as the picture metadata painted an entirely different picture than the girl's story. What she claimed to have happened would have been physically impossible to have occurred in a timeframe of four minutes and forty-six seconds.

/File/Main/FilePath	"H:\DCIM\Camera\2010-06-19 08.02.00.jpg"
/File/Main/FileName	"2010-06-19 08.02.00.jpg"
/File/Main/FileLocation	"H:\DCIM\Camera\"
/File/Main/FileExtension	"jpg"
/File/Main/FileSize	"1021353"
/File/Main/DateCreation	"19.06.2010 08:02:00"
/File/Main/DateLastAccess	"21.04.2011 00:00:00"
/File/Main/DateLastWrite	"19.06.2010 08:02:00"
/Exif/Image/Make	"Motorola"
/Exif/Image/Model	"Droid"
/Exif/Image/Orientation	"1"
/Exif/Image/XResolution	"300/1"
/Exif/Image/YResolution	"300/1"
/Exif/Image/ResolutionUnit	"2"
/Exif/Image/Software	"2.1-update1"
/Exif/Image/DateTime	"6/19/2010 8:01:58 AM"
/Exif/Image/YCbCrPositioning	"1"
/Exif/Photo/ExposureTime	"33333/1000000"
/Exif/Photo/FNumber	"14/5"
/Exif/Photo/ExposureProgram	"2"
/Exif/Photo/ISOSpeedRatings	"68"
/Exif/Photo/ExifVersion	"0220"
/Exif/Photo/DateTimeOriginal	"6/19/2010 8:01:58 AM"
/Exif/Photo/DateTimeDigitized	"6/19/2010 8:01:58 AM"

FIGURE 27.6

Example of metadata contained in a picture taken with a Motorola Android cell phone

27.2 CASE EXAMPLES: DOCUMENT METADATA

A good example of document metadata as evidence is not from the biggest or most complicated case. In fact, it is from a rather simple case, but it does highlight the usefulness of document metadata in an exemplary way. The case involved a student who submitted a paper from one of his classes at a university. The professor, upon reading the paper, did not believe that the student was smart enough to have written it. The student was accused of cheating, and subsequently kicked out of school. The professor claimed that the student must have plagiarized the paper from sources on the Internet.

The document metadata revealed that the paper was written over a period of several days, included 33 separate editing sessions and a total writing time of over 800 minutes. This indicates that the student did actually compose the paper on the computer on which it was found. However, that alone is not enough. Using key phrases and terms from inside the paper to perform a search of the student's hard drive, it could be shown that no other references were on the computer hard drive that could have been copied and pasted into the paper.

The results of this investigation showed that the paper did not indicate any plagiarism from Internet sources or other documents on the computer.

SUMMARY

In this chapter we looked at what metadata is, what it looks like, and how it can be used in cases. We also learned that the use of metadata should be tempered with caution as to corroborating the evidence with other evidence. Many cases will contain a combination of metadata from different sources; for example, picture metadata may be used in conjunction with document metadata to show that pictures contained inside a document or e-mail were taken using a camera model that is also in evidence.

Thumbnails and the Thumbnail Cache

28

INFORMATION IN THIS CHAPTER:

- Thumbnails and the thumbnail cache
- How thumbnails and the thumbnail cache work
- Thumbnails and the thumbnail cache as evidence

INTRODUCTION

The typical computer today stores tens of thousands of images. These images can come from activities the user is aware of, such as transferring pictures from a digital camera to a computer. The images are also saved to the computer without any input from the computer user. For example, when you browse the Internet, many of the pictures and graphics you see can be saved to your computer automatically. When you open a folder like your My Pictures folder, you can view the files in a thumbnail format, like a bunch of small pictures. These small pictures or thumbnails are stored in a special file called a thumbnail cache database. These thumbnail databases can be read using special software and used as evidence in both civil and criminal cases.

28.1 THUMBNAILS AND THE THUMBNAIL CACHE

Starting with the Windows 2000 operating system,[1] Microsoft introduced the thumbnail cache. The thumbnail cache assists the computer user in reviewing a large number of images at once by taking the full-sized images and making miniature representations of them. Instead of having to look at each image individually within a folder to find a particular picture you are looking for, the thumbnail cache will display all of the images at once as "thumbnail"-sized pictures. The thumbnail cache also speeds up how quickly pictures will display; it reduces the load time of images because the smaller thumbnail images no longer have to be recalculated every time they are accessed by a user, unlike the original images.

Figure 28.1 illustrates the difficulty in navigating a large set of pictures without thumbnails. Figure 28.2 shows the same set of pictures in thumbnail view.

As you can see from the two illustrations in Figs 28.1 and 28.2, if you want to be able to easily find a picture, thumbnail view is much easier to deal with since you can see the image and not have to rely on remembering the file name.

FIGURE 28.1

A list of files of original images

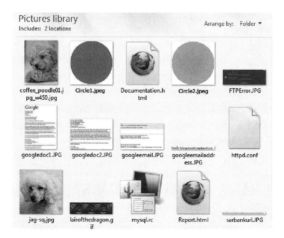

FIGURE 28.2

A list of files of original images in thumbnail view

28.2 HOW THUMBNAILS AND THE THUMBNAIL CACHE WORK

When you are looking in a folder that contains images and even documents, remember that the computer may store smaller versions of the images in a thumbnail cache. The thumbnail cache is a database of multiple images inside the cache file. In Windows 2000 and Windows XP, these databases were named thumbs.db and stored in the same folder that contained the image files. These files are hidden from the computer user by default. If you want to see the actual thumbs.db file in a folder, you must change your folder settings to show hidden files.

28.2.1 When are these thumbs.db cache files created?

Thumbs.db files are not created automatically unless you open the folder containing the pictures or images and change the view to thumbnail view.

In Fig. 28.3 you can see a listing of picture files. Note that there is no thumbs.db file in this folder because it has not been created yet.

Now if you look at Figure 28.4, you will see that the thumbs.db has been created once the view is changed to the thumbnail view.

Name ▲	Size	Type	Date Modified
Blue hills.jpg	28 KB	JPEG Image	4/14/2008 8:00 AM
Sunset.jpg	70 KB	JPEG Image	4/14/2008 8:00 AM
Water lilies.jpg	82 KB	JPEG Image	4/14/2008 8:00 AM
Winter.jpg	104 KB	JPEG Image	4/14/2008 8:00 AM

Address: ll Users\Documents\My Pictures\Sample Pictures\New Folder   Go

LIST VIEW

FIGURE 28.3

Files shown in list view

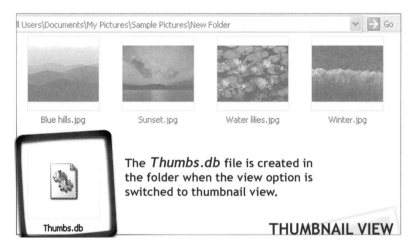

Address: ll Users\Documents\My Pictures\Sample Pictures\New Folder   Go

Blue hills.jpg   Sunset.jpg   Water lilies.jpg   Winter.jpg

The *Thumbs.db* file is created in the folder when the view option is switched to thumbnail view.

Thumbs.db

THUMBNAIL VIEW

FIGURE 28.4

Files shown in thumbnail view

However, in order for a thumbs.db thumbnail cache to be created at all, the user of the computer must have write access to the folder; or in other words, you must be able to create new files in the folder. If the folder contains images, you can still view them as thumbnails; however, a thumbs.db file will not be created.

Another anomaly of the thumbs.db cache is that when you have a very large number of pictures in a folder and you view them in one of the thumbnail views, Windows will not automatically add all of them to the thumbs.db cache. The reason is that Windows will only add thumbnails to the database cache that it actually renders into thumbnail view. If you notice, when you open a folder with a lot of images in thumbnail view for the first time, there is a noticeable pause when you scroll down, before the thumbnails appear. This is because Windows has not created the thumbnail yet. If the thumbnail has not been created, it will not appear in the database. What does this mean? Someone with a lot of pictures in a folder may never have seen the pictures at the bottom of the folder, if they did not bother to scroll down all the way, forcing Windows to render the thumbnail images. This can be especially important in a contraband image case where the defendant denies knowledge of the images. Being able to show that the images were never opened can help to show that intent was not present in possessing the images.

28.2.2 Changes in Windows Vista and Windows 7

When Windows Vista was released, the thumbnail database was no longer stored in each folder as it was in the earlier Windows operating systems. Now the thumbnail database is stored in a central location for each user account, referred to as the thumbnail cache. These files are located in the AppData\Local\Microsoft\ Windows\Explorer folder for each user account on the computer. For example, if the computer has two user accounts, Bob and Sue, when Bob is logged on to the computer, the thumbnail cache will be saved to his private user area. If Bob logs off the computer and Sue logs in, the thumbnail database will be saved to her private user area. Note that if Bob is logged in and Sue starts using the computer without logging him out, any thumbnail database changes will still be saved in Bob's private area.

28.2.3 Thumbs.db and networked drives

An odd issue is that in Windows Vista and Windows 7, if the user is looking at pictures in thumbnail view on a shared network hard drive where the user is allowed to create files, a thumbs.db file will be created in that shared folder when someone views the pictures in thumbnail view. There will not be a record of this in the thumbnail cache in the user's private area on the local computer that is accessing the shared network drive. This is shown in Fig. 28.5.

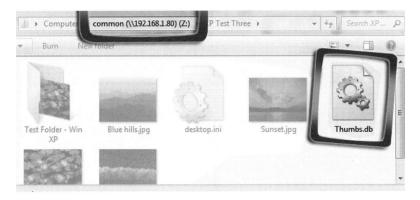

FIGURE 28.5

A thumbs.db file created on a networked drive

28.3 THUMBNAILS AND THE THUMBNAIL CACHE AS EVIDENCE

Thumbnail caches are used in a wide variety of cases, mostly to attempt to establish whether or not an image file existed on the computer at some point in the past. The reason is that even if you delete all the pictures from a folder, the thumbs.db cache will retain the little thumbnail pictures.

The presence of a thumbs.db file can also reveal the last time the thumbs.db was updated to show that a folder was accessed at a certain time.

28.1 CONTRABAND IMAGES

An examiner is presented with a computer to analyze that contains suspected child pornography. Upon review of the hard drive, no contraband images are present. However, a review of the thumbs.db cache shows thumbnail pictures of child pornography.

There are several things to consider in this scenario:

1. The images were on the hard drive and were deleted, leaving behind the thumbs.db file with the smaller images. However, without having something more to present, that is not a lot of evidence by itself.
2. The examiner is also presented with a USB stick containing contraband images. Can you prove whether or not those images have been on the computer in the past? Lo and behold, on the USB stick is a thumbs.db file that contains thumbnail images that match the thumbnail images from the computer hard drive. Case solved! Well, maybe not completely, but that is stronger evidence than in the first part of this scenario. The examiner would need to match the files using hash values of the thumbnails from inside the two thumbs.db caches to make a stronger case. For information on hash values, see Chapters 4 and 26.
3. The thumbs.db cache file did not originate on the computer being examined. Consider that someone handed you a USB stick containing files for work. You open the USB

stick on your computer, select all the files, and start the copy process. A window pops up telling you that there are two hidden files that will be copied; do you want to copy them, yes or no? Not knowing exactly what that means, you select "Yes." Unbeknownst to you, you just copied a thumbs.db file to your computer containing contraband images of child pornography.

Figure 28.6 is a screenshot of what the contents of a thumbs.db file looks like. What you see in the figure are the small thumbnails of all of the pictures viewed in the folder.

Figure 28.7 shows the same thumbs.db as in Fig. 28.6 in EnCase forensic software, with the details of the internal database shown.

What you can see in Fig. 28.7 is the file detail information from inside the thumbs.db file. The Last Written date is carried over from the file system date stamp.

The Root Entry at the bottom of the screenshot shows an Entry Modified date of when the thumbs.db file was last updated. The Root Entry date and time will update whenever the contents of the folder change.

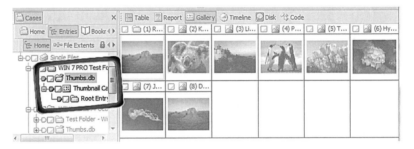

FIGURE 28.6

A screenshot of the contents of a thumbs.db file

FIGURE 28.7

A view of the data inside the thumbs.db file

28.2 FILE DELETION CLAIM AFTER A COURT ORDER TO PRESERVE EVIDENCE

You are embroiled in a civil case and the Plaintiff has hired a computer expert to examine your client's computer. When the Plaintiff's computer expert examines the computer, he sees a folder that is named the same as a file eraser program that is used to clean up computer files.

Your client says that he has used the program in the past to remove confidential files from the computer and also to clean up old junk as part of his normal business practices to prevent confidential information from falling into the wrong hands in case the laptop computer is lost or stolen. He also states that right after the court hearing, he removed the file-wiping program from his computer.

The Plaintiff's expert concludes that the file-wiping program was run after the court hearing on the same date that the client claims he removed the program from his hard drive.

You hire your own expert to examine your client's computer. Your expert reviews the hard drive and notes that the only file left in the hard drive–wiping program folder is the thumbs.db file. He also notes that the Entry Modified date and time match the date and time your client says he removed the software from his computer.

Since your expert knows that deleting the image files from a folder will cause the Root Entry time stamp to update in the thumbs.db file, he concludes that your client is accurate and that the file-wiping program was removed and not run the day after the court hearing.

In Fig. 28.8, you can see that the Root Entry date and time have changed after several pictures were deleted from the folder.

		Name	Last Written	Entry Modified	Filter	In Repo
☐	1	Root				
☐	2	Big Block FAT				
☐	3	Small Block FAT				
☐	4	MFT				
☐	5	{A42CD7B6-E9B9-4...	04/25/11 01:53:03PM			
☐	6	Winter.jpg	04/14/08 08:00:00AM			
☐	7	Catalog				
☐	8	256_74857036800...				
☐	9	256_fad75331839e...				
☐	10	256_c979b1c71d42...				
☐	11	256_479e07fb057e...				
☐	12	Sunset.jpg	04/14/08 08:00:00AM			
☐	13	Water lilies.jpg	04/14/08 08:00:00AM			
☐	14	Blue hills.jpg	04/14/08 08:00:00AM			
☐	15	Unallocated Cluster				
☐	16	Root Entry		04/28/11 02:10:59PM		

FIGURE 28.8

A view of the data inside the thumbs.db file after files were deleted

SUMMARY

In this chapter we learned about the thumbnail databases that Windows uses to make viewing a large number of pictures in a folder faster and easier. We also looked at how and when those databases are created. We also learned what dates and times are updated when the contents of the folder changes. Finally, we looked at the thumbnail databases as evidence in a couple of case scenarios.

Reference

[1] D. Hurlbut, Thumbs db files forensic issues. *Access Data Training*. <http://accessdata. com/media/en_us/print/papers/wp.Thumbs_DB_Files.en_us.pdf>, 2005.

Deleted Data

INFORMATION IN THIS CHAPTER:

- How data is stored on a hard drive
- Deleted file recovery
- Evidence of data destruction

INTRODUCTION

One of the foundations of digital forensics is data recovery. Truly deleting data from a computer hard drive so that nothing is recoverable is quite hard to do. This chapter explains the ins and outs of how a computer stores data and what it does when it deletes data.

In digital forensics, it is rarely a case of whether some form of deleted data still exists; it is a matter of locating and recovering deleted data. This chapter will explain the different levels of deletion, such as the Recycle Bin and unallocated space, and how this data is recovered and used.

29.1 HOW DATA IS STORED ON A HARD DRIVE

Think of a hard drive as a filing cabinet, with drawers, folders, and files. The cabinet itself would be the hard drive; and each of the drawers in the cabinet would be a partition or volume, with each partition containing folders and the folders containing files. Figure 29.1 is a visual representation of the filing cabinet paradigm.

Before a hard drive or any other data storage device can be used, it must prepared for use in a format that the operating system can recognize. In Microsoft Windows, the most common formats are FAT, FAT32, and NTFS. The Apple Mac file format and the Linux file formats are different from Windows, and Windows cannot read a disk formatted for a Mac or a Linux computer unless there is a special portion of the disk formatted in one of the Windows formats. However, the Mac operating system and the Linux operating system can read some or all of the Windows formats.

However, before a hard drive can be formatted, it must first be prepared at an even lower level by creating partitions on the hard drive or other media. A partition is a way of dividing up a hard drive or storage media so you can either apply

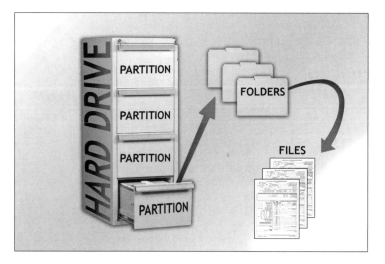

FIGURE 29.1

How a hard drive is like a filing cabinet

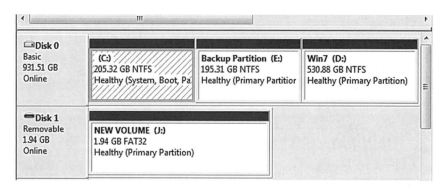

FIGURE 29.2

Two physical hard drives, Disk 0 and Disk 1 and the partitions on the two drives

different formats to each of the partitions, or use them for different purposes. Figure 29.1 shows this in a visual way, while Fig. 29.2 shows it in the way you would view this in Windows.

Figure 29.2 is a screenshot of the Microsoft Windows Disk Management application. This application allows the user to view the details of the hard drives installed in the computer. It also provides a simple and easy way to create partitions and format volumes. Disk 0 in this example is a 1-terabyte hard drive, divided into three partitions or volumes. Disk 1 is a 2-gigabyte USB stick with a single partition or volume.

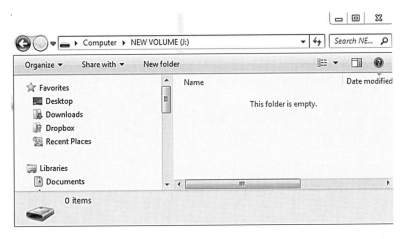

FIGURE 29.3

How Microsoft Windows sees the empty USB drive before files are written to it

You can also see in Fig. 29.2 that the two disks are formatted using different file systems. Disk 0 is formatted using the NTFS file system and Disk 1 is formatted using the FAT32 file system. By default, USB storage devices, smart cards, and other small-scale storage devices are formatted as FAT32 at the factory.

This USB drive will be used for our illustrations in this chapter by writing files to the drive, deleting the files on the drive, and then showing the recovery of those files.

The point of showing the screenshots in Figs 29.3 through 29.5 is to illustrate that Windows cannot see deleted files. There is no special command or different view the user can switch to that will show deleted files on a drive. However, be aware that all of the data from the files deleted in this example is still present on the hard drive.

Figure 29.3 shows the empty USB drive as a user would see it in Windows.

In Fig. 29.4 we see how Windows sees the drive after we have copied files to it.

And lastly, Fig. 29.5 shows the same drive after all of the files were deleted, as viewed in the Microsoft Windows Explorer program.

29.1.1 **Hard drive data storage structure**

On a hard drive, the sectors are always the same size of 512 bytes. Depending on the file system used to format the hard drive, the sectors will be clumped together into clusters. For instance, in Windows NTFS, the standard size for a cluster is four sectors. This means that a cluster is $(4 \times 1024 = 4096)$ bytes. A cluster is the smallest unit the file system can use for saving data. Each of the clusters can be completely filled by the data from a file or only partially filled, leaving a little bit of space called file slack space.

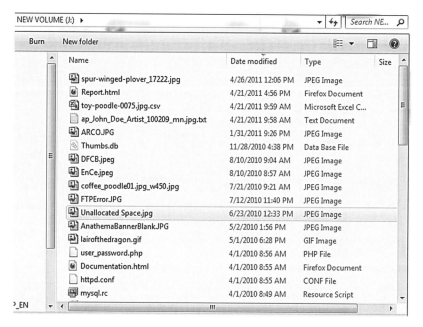

FIGURE 29.4

View of the USB drive after writing files to it from another drive

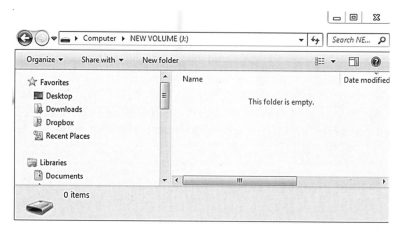

FIGURE 29.5

The USB drive after all the files that were just added to it were deleted

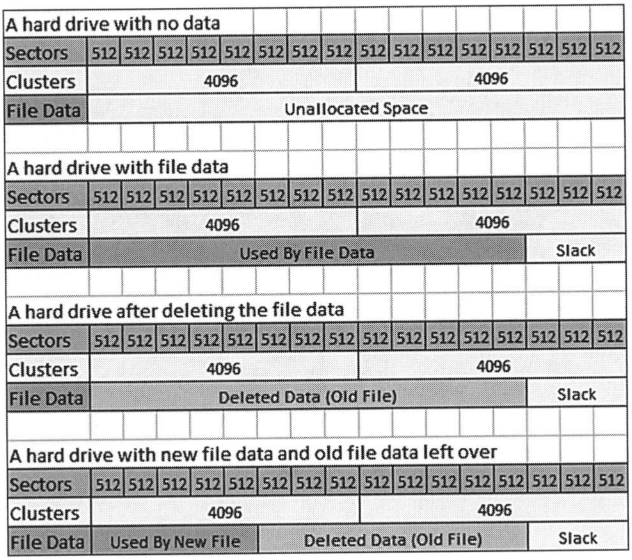

FIGURE 29.6

A graphical view of the layout of the NTFS file system

29.1.1.1 A little computer storage math

Let's say you have a file that is 4608 bytes in size. In order for the operating system to save the file, it will use one cluster for the first 4096 bytes and a second whole cluster of 4096 bytes for the last 2560 bytes.

Figure 29.6 shows a graphical illustration of this storage layout.

In Fig. 29.6 the first grid is an empty formatted hard drive. In the second grid, a file has been saved to the hard drive, filling one whole cluster and part of a second cluster. In the third grid, the file has been deleted, but the data is still present on the hard drive, but no longer viewable in Windows.

In the fourth grid, a new smaller file has been written to the same place as the old file. This leaves the data from the original file still on the hard drive in the area called slack space. The data in the slack space can be recovered by file carving. File carving is covered in the sections that follow.

29.2 DELETED FILE RECOVERY

Recovering files or data from hard drives and other media that have been deleted is part and parcel of a forensic examination. Even if you are not interested in the contents of a particular file, it is sometimes critical to simply know that it was deleted. This can be used in a civil case to show spoliation if the file was deleted after a preservation order was issued.

FIGURE 29.7

The Windows Recycle Bin icon before and after emptying by the user

29.2.1 Simple file recovery

The simplest method of file recovery is simply to open the Recycle Bin on the computer and restore the files. This is something any user can do.

However, if the user has emptied the Recycle Bin, Windows does not offer the user any other method for recovering their files. In Fig. 29.7 you see two views of a Recycle Bin, one with files still present and recoverable by the user and one of the Recycle Bin after the user empties it.

29.2.1.1 Simple file recovery using forensic software

The first method for recovering files uses information stored in the file system itself to locate deleted files. This will find files that have been recently deleted and that have not been damaged in some way by being partially overwritten by other files.

Figure 29.8 is a view of the drive in EnCase forensic software showing the file entries along with one of the pictures on the drive. This is an example of simple file recovery.

Figure 29.8 gives a listing of all of the deleted files that the forensic software can see without having to perform any special recovery operations, along with the dates and times that the files were written to the drive, when they were created or first appeared on the drive, and when they were last accessed. Since this USB stick is formatted as FAT32, you can only get the date it was last accessed, not the time. What is important to note from the screenshot in Fig. 29.8 is the Last Accessed time column. A file must be accessed to be deleted, and this will update the last accessed date.

Also, as shown in Fig. 29.8, if the files on the hard drive have only been recently deleted and removed from the Recycle Bin, forensic software can easily find deleted files.

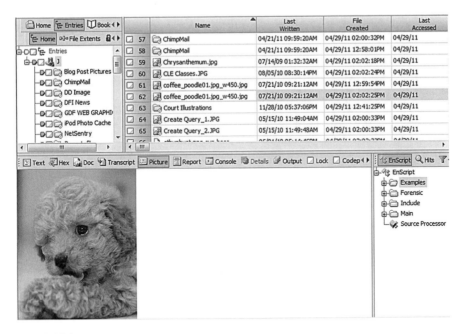

FIGURE 29.8

A view in Encase forensic software of the USB drive showing the deleted files

29.2.2 Advanced file recovery: file carving

When an examiner is presented with a hard drive that does not reveal data of inter-est, there are several possible reasons for this. If the data was deleted at some time in the past and the files are partially overwritten, they will only exist in the area of the drive that is unallocated. If the drive has been reformatted to get rid of the data, then the data will only be in the unallocated space.

This is the part of the hard drive that the operating system considers available for use by any new data it needs to save to the hard drive.

In Fig. 29.7 we see a view of the USB hard drive in EnCase Forensic software showing the unallocated space. In the figure, the unallocated space is seen as the part of the image that has nothing in it except for the little bump in the center of the square. Each of the little squares shown in the upper-right panel of Fig. 29.9 is a sector. Sectors are covered later in this chapter.

29.2.2.1 File carving

A better view of how this works on a conceptual level is shown in Fig. 29.10. Think of the files in unallocated space as just like files that have been run through the office shredder.

What file carving does is to find the pieces of the deleted files in unallocated space and electronically tape them back together, in the same way you could try

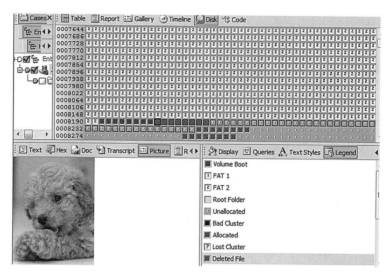

FIGURE 29.9

A view of the USB hard drive showing the unallocated space

FIGURE 29.10

File carving is like electronically taping pieces of a document back together from the office shredder

to find all the pieces of a paper document in a shredder bin and tape them back together.

Figure 29.11 shows what a file carved from unallocated space looks like in EnCase forensic software. The important take-away from this is that, as you will notice, all of the date and time information is missing. This is because files carved

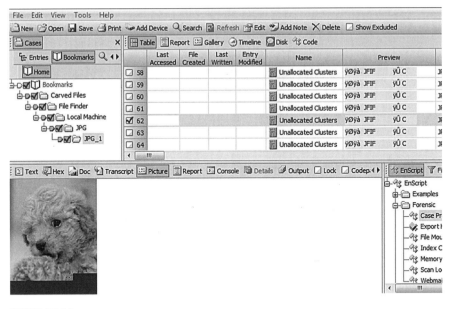

FIGURE 29.11

A view of a file carved from unallocated space using EnCase forensic software

from unallocated space are not known in any way by the file system and no longer contain the file system metadata.

We can also see in Fig. 29.11 that while about 90 percent of the picture is back from the unallocated space, the software could not get all of it. This is very common when doing file carving because the operating system will eventually use the space on the hard drive for new files and overwrite all or part of any file that was previously deleted. However, it is typically enough to be used as evidence. All kinds of files can be recovered from unallocated space, not just pictures. Files such as e-mail, web pages, documents, and databases can all be recovered using file carving.

In a case where a husband suspected his wife of having an affair, he asked that the hard drive be examined for any evidence of e-mails, chat logs, or other documents that could confirm his suspicions. Initial examination of the hard drive did not reveal any information that would show that his wife was involved with anyone, at least based on the computer evidence. However, by carving files out of unallocated space from the hard drive using the suspected paramour's e-mail address, web-based e-mails were located and produced that showed conversations between the wife and the suspected paramour of a very graphic nature along with planning to leave their current spouses to be together. This also led to locating the real name of the paramour and the location of her Facebook page showing her real information and pictures of her and her family.

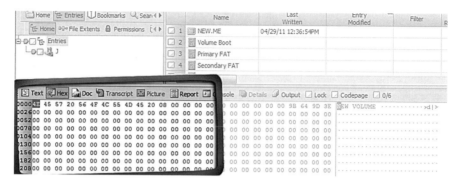

FIGURE 29.12

Evidence of a wiped hard drive

29.3 EVIDENCE OF DATA DESTRUCTION

In some cases, the lack of recoverable data is just as much evidence as having the data. However, to be cautious, it is very hard to prove a negative. A person can destroy data in many ways without physically destroying the storage device.

Data-wiping software is used to destroy data so that it cannot be recovered using forensic methods. This is accomplished by overwriting the sectors with ones, zeroes, or random data. Figure 29.12 shows the USB stick that has been used in these examples after it has been wiped using a disk-wiping program. The area in the bottom left of the pane is a view of the hard drive in hexadecimal. Notice that there is a continuous set of zeroes. To a forensic examiner, this is clear evidence that the drive has been wiped with disk-wiping software.

On the other hand, if someone on one side of a case is claiming that a person intentionally wiped a hard drive using disk-wiping software and the forensic examination does not show evidence of such, that is, the examiner does not find repeated patterns of ones, zeroes, or random data, then that is evidence of the opposite situation and can be used to dispute such a claim.

29.3.1 Physical destruction

Even when someone does attempt to destroy a physical storage device, the data may still be recovered in whole or in part. Physical destruction can happen intentionally or unintentionally. Simple hardware failure would be a good example of unintentional data destruction. However, hardware failure, fires, floods, and even intentional attempts to destroy data are not always the end of the story.

One case involved a client who brought a hard drive that had been sitting in a bucket of water in the backyard for over two years. Allowing the hard drive to dry out for a few days was all that was necessary to bring the drive into working order. Examination of the drive revealed evidence of an affair that the husband had thought was long gone and unrecoverable. This is because hard drives are completely sealed to keep out even the tiniest speck of dust. Unless the seals on the hard drive are broken, fresh water will not damage the drive in such a short period of time.

If the electronics board on the bottom of the hard drive is broken, there is a good chance that the data can still be recovered by replacing the electronic board with one from an identical hard drive. In many instances drives have been brought in that had a bad electronic board due to cracking or physical damage. Replacing the board from an identical hard drive allowed full recovery of the data.

Even in the case of small devices like USB sticks that have the metal end that goes into the USB port on the computer snapped off, the data may possibly be recovered if both pieces are available or a compatible USB stick can be found for parts.

In one data recovery case, a doctoral student had all of his research and dissertation on a USB thumb drive. When the drive stopped working, he thought he had lost two years of work. Examination of the USB drive showed that the connection was cracked and had separated from the data store chip. Some delicate soldering allowed all of the data to be recovered.

It is never safe to assume that data cannot be recovered by a forensic examiner or a data recovery lab, even in extreme circumstances. Even in the case of a cell phone where the phone itself may have a cracked screen or other damage, if the phone will still power up, there is a possibility of getting the data from the phone.

SUMMARY

In this chapter we looked at data storage and recovery in detail. We learned about both simple recovery of files that the user can perform by restoring files from the Recycle Bin and how forensic software can easily locate and recover files that have been recently deleted from a hard drive or other storage device. Advanced data recovery was also covered including how forensic software can "carve" files from the unallocated space on a computer hard drive or other storage device. How file destruction software works and how evidence of that kind of destruction can be detected was also covered. We also discussed physical damage to hard drives and storage devices and how, even in those circumstances, data can be recovered.

Computer Time Artifacts (MAC Times)

30

INFORMATION IN THIS CHAPTER:

- Computer file system time stamps
- Fundamental Issues in forensic analysis of timeline
- Created, modified, accessed
- The bottom line

INTRODUCTION

Computer time artifacts are undoubtedly one of the most important forms of digital evidence. They play a critical role when establishing a timeline for a body of evidence for any case where time is important. If the case involves an alibi, computer time artifacts can be used as part of a body of evidence to negate or validate the alibi claims. If the case involves data theft, computer time artifacts can be used to help determine when the alleged theft occurred. Furthermore, computer time artifacts are used extensively when attempting to prove or disprove user attribution. This form of evidence is arguably the most important when it comes to placing someone at a computer at a given time. While computer time artifacts are extremely valuable as evidence, they are also very complicated. There are numerous exceptions and variables when it comes to interpreting this type of evidence, and incorrect interpretations can lead to serious mistakes when coming to a conclusion based on computer time artifacts. These artifacts are most commonly called MAC times, which stands for Modified, Accessed, and Created. However, some file systems record four dates including the additional last written date. E-mail time stamps can also be confusing unless you are careful in the interpretation of the method of recording the time and the correct time zone of the time stamp record.

The purpose of this chapter is to familiarize you with the complexity of interpreting the date and time stamps recorded by computer operating systems and applications. To completely cover the subject of computer time stamps would require an entire technical book.

30.1 COMPUTER FILE SYSTEM TIME STAMPS

While you would think it would be a straightforward process to look at the dates and times recorded for a file and to know that those date and times accurately reflect when the file was created, modified, or accessed, that just simply is not the case. The reason for this dilemma is that different operating systems record these dates and times in different ways. For instance, older operating systems like Windows 98 and Windows XP record dates differently than Windows 7.

30.2 FUNDAMENTAL ISSUES IN FORENSIC ANALYSIS OF TIMELINE

One of the easiest and most common mistakes that is made in the forensic analysis of computer-generated time stamps is either not checking to see if the computer clock that is creating the time stamps is accurate or not properly identifying the offset of the time local to the computer clock to the time zone format of the time stamp.

Depending on the device, be it a GPS unit, a computer, an e-mail server, a digital camera, or a web server at an Internet Service provider, the way that the date and time is recorded can be in different formats and different default time zones.

- Time Zones and Time Formats
  - The most fundamental mistake an examiner can make is to forget to check the clock setting on a computer or other device he is examining to see what time zone it is set for and how accurate the current time on the computer clock is at the time of the examination. This is a simple task of recording the time the computer or device thinks it is by checking the real time clock (RTC) of the device and comparing that time to a reliable outside time source such as a cell phone. Computer or device clocks can be off by minutes to months, and failing to perform this basic test can lead to incorrect interpretation of any timeline that depends on a device's clock to be accurate.
  - When an examiner receives records from a third-party source for analysis, the time zone of the recording party must be taken into account. For instance, many record keepers do all of their time stamps in their local time zone, independent of the time zone of where the record was created, or in Greenwich Mean Time (GMT). In a case from many years ago, analysis of the account creation time from Microsoft's Hotmail service was a factor in determining premeditation in a death penalty case. At the time, Microsoft recorded the creation time of Hotmail accounts in GMT. The task at hand was to determine the exact creation date and time for an e-mail account. On the one hand, the date and time was from Microsoft in GMT. On the other hand, the account creation happened three years prior to the trial, so the second task was to determine the correct time offset from GMT on that particular date, which included determining if the date was in Eastern Standard or Eastern Daylight Time.

- In another case, there was a dispute as to when an e-mail originated. What the previous examiner failed to note was that the e-mail server where the e-mail was processed and stamped was located in Arizona, where they do not change over to Daylight Savings Time. This made the e-mail appear to have been sent an hour earlier when in fact it was not.
- The Energy Policy Act of 2005 changed Daylight Savings Time in the United States, extending the time four weeks beginning in 2007. For devices operating prior to the change in 2007, care must be taken to make sure that the device understands the new extended time zone change and that it was properly set.
- In international cases, the examiner must be aware that other areas of the world have their own savings time zones and dates. In 1996, the European Union standardized European Summer Time.
- Different operating systems and devices will record time in different formats, making the correct calculation of the time difficult in some instances.
- Epoch Time Format: Epoch or UNIX/POSIX time format is based on the number of seconds since January, 1, 1970, not counting leap seconds. If a device or program is using epoch time for recording time stamps, the examiner must calculate the correct local time in human readable format. This format is found in some GPS devices and also on devices that use the UNIX or Linux operating system.
- Zulu Time: Many devices record time stamps in Zulu time, which refers to the time at the prime meridian. Zulu time is also known as GMT. However, GMT has been replaced by Coordinated Universal Time (UTC), which takes into account the variations in the rotation of the earth. When a time is recorded in Zulu, the examiner must make certain that the correct local time is calculated based on the current state of Standard or Daylight Savings Time to determine the correct offset from UTC. For instance, Eastern Daylight Time is UTC minus 4 hours.

30.3 CREATED, MODIFIED, ACCESSED

The most relied upon and most misunderstood part of many forensic examinations is the time stamps associated with the created, modified, and last accessed date recorded for files and folders on a computer hard drive. The following sections discuss these time stamps and how the interpretation of the time stamp is dependent on many factors. Simply pointing at a particular time stamp and making a claim about its connection to a timeline for a piece of evidence would be a mistake without properly interpreting how the time stamp was created.

- **Created Time Stamp.** The created date for a file is recorded when a file is first created locally on a file system. However, the created date for that same file can be changed by different operations performed on the file. Here are some examples:

- If the file is copied to a new hard drive or storage device like a USB stick, the creation date on the new location will change to the current date and time that the file was copied.
- If the file is downloaded from a peer-to-peer networking service such as LimeWire or FrostWire, the created date will be the date and time the file started to download.
- In Windows 7, if a file is copied from one folder to another on the same hard drive, the created date in the folder will be the date the file was copied.
- However, if the operating system is Windows XP, the created date for the file in the new folder will be the same as the original created date and time. In Windows XP, the folder itself will have a created date and time of when the folder was created.
- In both Windows 7 and Windows XP, if you burn a file to a CD, the created date will be retained in its original state.

- **Modified Time Stamp.** The modified time stamp indicates when a file is changed in some manner and records the date and time of that change when the file is saved to a device or hard drive. Here are some examples:
  - In Windows 7, if a file is modified and saved, the entry modified date will change to the current date and time of the local computer.
  - In Windows 7, accessing a file will change the entry modified date if the file is viewed in EnCase forensic software. However, the last accessed date will not be changed.
  - If a CD-ROM is viewed in EnCase forensic software, the time stamps for the last modified date would not be apparent. However, if in EnCase, the file is added to a case by dragging it from the CD-ROM to the EnCase software, the last modified date will appear and will match the actual date and time the file was burned to the CD-ROM, provided that the CD-ROM was burned using Windows 7. If the file was burned in Windows XP, this will not occur.

- **Last Accessed Time Stamp.** In theory, the last accessed time stamp should be an indication of when the file was last viewed. However, in many cases, this time stamp will not change if a file is opened and then closed without making any changes to the file. This is due to the fact that when Windows is using the NTFS file system, it does not immediately write changes in file system time stamps to the disk. In the NTFS file system, Windows will write the last accessed time to disk when the current recorded time on disk is one hour or more different from the current last accessed time in memory. If the computer is shut down within the one-hour time delay, the last accessed date will not be updated on the hard drive. Another way this time stamp can be misinterpreted is making the assumption that the last accessed time stamp is an indication of the last time a person opened the file.
  - When a file is deleted, it is accessed by the file system to perform the deletion and the last accessed time stamp is updated.

- Some types of antivirus programs will access a file in the process of scanning the file for viruses. They can change the last accessed time stamp to the date of the last virus scan.
- Creating a backup of a file using some backup software programs can change the last accessed time stamp.
- When a file is printed, the last accessed time stamp can be updated.

30.4 **THE BOTTOM LINE**

Time stamps are not the end all of authority as to when something occurred. However, they can be critical if correctly interpreted by the examiner. In order to do so, the examiner must understand the different ways that time stamps are recorded by different computer operating systems, file systems, and various devices. The examiner must also understand what operation was being performed that may have changed the time stamp and in what way that operation would affect the recording of the time stamp. To simply say that the time stamp on a file or in a record is present is not sufficient; failing to analyze it completely can lead to incorrect analysis of the timeline in a case.

It is critically important that the examiner be well versed in how time stamps are modified and under what circumstances if the interpretation of the data is to be of any value. Also, the examiner must understand the nuances of the different operating systems and file systems and how each of them handles time stamps; otherwise, their interpretation could be completely wrong.

SUMMARY

In this chapter we looked at the value of time stamps in the analysis of electronic evidence. We also looked at some of the many ways a time stamp can be affected by different operating systems, file systems, and devices. We learned that while time stamps are a critical part of the forensic analysis of electronic evidence, proper interpretation of time stamps is more complex than simply taking the time stamp at face value.

Internet History (Web and Browser Caching) 31

INFORMATION IN THIS CHAPTER:

- What is web caching?
- How Internet browser (web) caching works
- Internet (web) caching as evidence
- What if the Internet cache is cleared by the user?

INTRODUCTION

As you surf the Internet, the web browser you are using saves information to your computer in temporary storage. This process of saving web pages and documents in temporary storage is called Internet browser caching or web caching. The purpose of web caching is to improve the experience of the computer user as he or she browses the Internet. When you visit a website, your web browser will begin to save the information that you are viewing to your computer, and also parts of a website that you are not viewing. So while you are at the home page of a website, your browser might be temporarily saving the other pages also. The browser is anticipating that you will look at the other pages and images on the website, and it saves this information so that it will load faster when you navigate to them. With Internet Explorer, the website information is saved into what is known as Temporary Internet Files. However, the "Temporary" part of that is a bit of a misnomer, as these files are not truly temporary. They will remain saved to the hard drive until the user manually clears the browser cache. Even if these files are deleted by the user, they can still be recovered using forensic tools, or carved out of unallocated space. All of the various browsers such as Mozilla Firefox, Opera, Google Chrome, and Apple Safari cache web pages in much the same way as Microsoft Internet Explorer. However, where these various web browsers store their web cache data is dependent on the browsing program. Only Internet Explorer stores its cache data in the Temporary Internet Files location on the hard drive.

31.1 WHAT IS WEB CACHING?

Web caching was developed for two primary reasons: to reduce load on web servers and to improve the Internet user's experience while browsing the web. Back in the early days of the Internet, nearly everyone accessed the Internet via dial-up modem service. This type of Internet access is very slow compared to the high-speed Internet services available today. The speed difference in the connections is orders of magnitude:

- The fastest single-channel dial-up modem is rated at 56KB or 56,000 bits per second, although the modem cannot actually achieve that speed.
- The typical high-speed Internet connection today is 3 to 6 megabits per second or 6,000,000 bits per second.
- New services are currently coming on line at 50 megabits per second or 50,000,000 bits per second.

To quantify those numbers, consider that at 56KB/Sec a 10MB file would take approximately 24 minutes to download. At 5MB/Sec, the same file would take approximately 10 seconds to download. At 50MB/Sec it would take less than a second.

For that reason, Internet caching on the local computer has been around a long time to improve the browsing experience for the Internet user.

On the other hand, the web server that supplies web pages for viewing by Internet users is also limited in the number of requests the server can handle at any given time due to server loads and bandwidth available to the web server. Bandwidth is the speed of the Internet connection from the server to the Internet. To support websites that handle millions of users, multiple servers provide web pages to users, balancing the total load on the servers by splitting up the users each server is handling. However, it is in the interest of the web server administrator to reduce the number of items the server has to send to the Internet user, for both practical and economic reasons; bandwidth and servers cost money to maintain.

Whenever you connect to a website, the web server sends something called a Hypertext Transfer Protocol (HTTP) header to your local computer. This header contains information about the last time the web page was updated. This information is stored on your local computer for the web server to access when you next browse that particular page. What the HTTP header does is allow the web server to know that you already have part of the web page on your computer so it does not have to send it to you again; it can load that part of the web page from your local hard drive, both speeding the page rendering for you and reducing the load on the server.

31.2 HOW INTERNET BROWSER (WEB) CACHING WORKS

When you connect to a web page for the very first time, or after you have cleared the Internet cache on your computer, the web server sends everything that makes up the web page to your computer over the Internet. Your Internet browser, whether it is Internet Explorer, Mozilla Firefox, Apple Safari, or Google Chrome, to name the more popular Internet browsers, receives the web page in the form of a programming language called Hyper Text Markup Language (HTML). The web page can

```
File Edit View Help
<!DOCTYPE html PUBLIC "-//W3C//DTD XHTML 1.0 Transitional//EN" "http://www.w3.org/TR/xhtml1/DTD/xhtml
<html xmlns="http://www.w3.org/1999/xhtml">
<head>
 <meta name="XAR Files" content="index_htm_files/xr_files.txt"/>
 <title>Guardian Digital Forensics - Computer Forensics Experts</title>
 <meta http-equiv="Content-Type" content="text/html; charset=Windows-1252"/>
 <meta name="Generator" content="Xara HTML filter v.4.0.1.637"/>
 <meta name="keywords" content="Computer Forensics, Consultants, Forensics, Computer, murder, cell ph
 <meta name="description" content="Guardian Digital Forensics is a computer forensics  company.  We p
 <script type="text/javascript" src="index_htm_files/menu.js"></script>
 <link rel="stylesheet" type="text/css" href="index_htm_files/xr_main.css"/>
 <link rel="stylesheet" type="text/css" href="index_htm_files/xr_text.css"/>
 <script type="text/javascript" src="index_htm_files/roe.js"></script>
</head>
<body>
<div class="xr_ap" id="xr_xr" style="width: 955px; height: 700px; top:0px; left:50%; margin-left: -47
 <script type="text/javascript">var xr_xr=document.getElementById("xr_xr")</script>
 <img class="xr_ap" src="index_htm_files/0.png" alt="" title="" style="left: -37px; top: -37px; width
<!--[if IE]><div class="xr_ap" id="xr_xri" style="width: 955px; height: 700px; clip: rect(0px 955px 7
<!--[if !IE]>--><div class="xr_ap" id="xr_xri" style="width: 955px; height: 700px; clip: rect(0px, 95
<div class="xr_ap" style="left:14px; top:151px; width:929px; height:195px;">
```

FIGURE 31.1

A web page showing the code that is sent to your browser for rendering

contain additional programming languages buried inside that HTML file, such as Java code, Adobe Flash elements, and other programming bits. What the browser does when it receives this file is to render the page into a readable form for the user.

Figure 31.1 shows the web page code sent to your browser for rendering in the form the that the browser program receives it.

In Fig. 31.2, the program code shown in Fig. 31.1 is rendered or drawn by the browser program into an attractive web page.

31.3 INTERNET (WEB) CACHING AS EVIDENCE

Data saved to a hard drive, phone, or tablet such as an iPad can be used as evidence in legal matters. Figure 31.3 shows what happens when you visit a web page. While your monitor may only let you see part of the web page, all of it is immediately downloaded to your computer.

For instance, mapping web pages such as Google Maps pages are used in many murder cases to show that the accused had been looking for a dump site for a body or a likely place to commit the crime. This was a factor in the trial of Scott Peterson in the murder of Laci Peterson where the prosecution introduced Google Maps pages recovered from Scott Peterson's computer to allegedly show that he had been looking at areas that could become a possible disposal site.

The wide variety of uses for the Internet today has made the Internet cache and history on local computers an extremely valuable repository of evidence. Consider that your computer tracks every page you visit, including the time you visit and the user account that was logged in at the time of the web page visit. Also consider that the entire web page is downloaded and saved on your local computer hard drive.

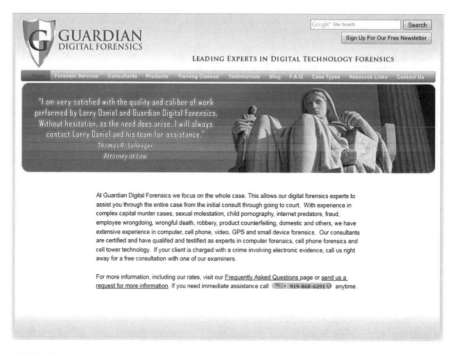

FIGURE 31.2

A web page rendered in Mozilla Firefox

Figure 31.4 shows part of an Internet history file viewed in forensic software. You can see that the Last Accessed date and time are recorded. This is the last time the user visited the web page. The Last Modification Time is the last time the web page noted that it was updated. The Expiration field records the time when the page will expire and be reloaded by the user's browser if he or she visits the page again after that time. The Profile Name is the name of the user account that is logged in at the time the web page was visited. The URL Name is the actual Internet address of the page that was visited. The URL Host is the name of the website, in this case "office.microsoft.com."

In a recent case in Cary, North Carolina, Brad Cooper was tried for the murder of his wife, Nancy Cooper. It was widely reported in the news that the prosecution produced a Google map web page from one of Brad Cooper's computers showing the site where Nancy Cooper's body was found. The date and time of the web page's origination was used by the prosecution to show that the map page was visited prior to the murder. The prosecution argued that this was proof that Brad Cooper was scouting out a place to commit the murder of his wife.

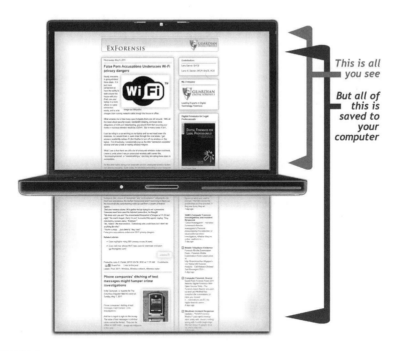

FIGURE 31.3

The user may not see all of the web page that is saved to the computer

Url Name	Url Host
https://liteapps.mcafee.com/apps/mss/2.0/default.asp?auto=1&cver=2.0.181.2&lan...	liteapps.mcafee.com/
https://liteapps.mcafee.com/apps/mss/2.0/affid/0/en-us/lang_urls.asp?sb=3.0	liteapps.mcafee.com/
https://liteapps.mcafee.com/apps/mss/2.0/affid/0/en-us/lang_strings.asp?sb=3.0	liteapps.mcafee.com/
http://office.microsoft.com/client/helphome14.aspx?NS=POWERPNT&VERSION=14&...	office.microsoft.com/

Name	Last Accessed	Last Modification Time	Expiration	Profile Name
default[1].htm	12/03/10 08:16:11AM		12/03/10 12:16:12PM	larry
lang_urls[1].htm	12/03/10 08:16:11AM			larry
lang_strings[1].htm	12/03/10 08:16:12AM			larry
helphome14[1].htm	04/17/11 10:00:54AM	04/17/11 10:01:02AM	04/17/11 01:00:56PM	larry

FIGURE 31.4

Internet history as viewed in EnCase forensic software

31.1 INTERNET HISTORY AS A BASIS FOR INTENT

In a child pornography case, the defendant was claiming that the images found on his computer were put there by a disgruntled employee from a USB drive. A forensic examination of his computer was performed and the prosecution used his Internet history to show that he regularly visited websites with web addresses that suggested they contained images of young girls. While the case did not turn on this evidence, it certainly did not help his argument that he was not interested in obtaining or viewing child pornography and had never searched for or looked at child pornography in the past.

31.4 WHAT IF THE INTERNET CACHE IS CLEARED BY THE USER?

All Internet browsers provide a way for the user to clear the Internet history and cache. However, that does not mean that the history and web pages are gone from the computer. In fact, when you delete something in Microsoft Windows, no data is actually removed from the hard drive. This means that a forensic examiner can very likely recover not only the Internet history records, but also the web pages themselves. The factor that is most common in not getting back Internet history or web pages is the length of time between the clearing of the cache and the examiner processing the hard drive. Once something is deleted, there is the possibility that the space being used by the deleted data will be used for some other data as the computer is used. Even if the data is partially destroyed in this manner, it may still be possible to recover some web pages from a computer hard drive. How deleted data can be recovered is discussed in Chapter 29.

31.2 INTERNET HISTORY AS SUPPORTING EVIDENCE

In a murder case, recovery of web pages and web-based e-mail was a factor in establishing that the two persons charged with the murder of the wife's husband were having many conversations regarding future plans to be together, planning for moving to a new location, and also applying for new jobs at the new location. While no direct evidence of any conspiracy to commit the murder was found in the web cache, this type of circumstantial evidence was very damaging to the defendant's case.

SUMMARY

This chapter covered what Internet caching is, how it works, and how it is used as evidence. It was also shown that clearing the Internet cache does not actually remove the evidence from the computer hard drive, leaving the possibility that deleted Internet history can still be recovered.

Windows Shortcut Files (Link Files)

INFORMATION IN THIS CHAPTER:

- The purpose of link files, how they are created, and how they work
- How link files can be of evidentiary value
- Link files as evidence

INTRODUCTION

Before the digital age, when library books had checkout cards in the back, those paper cards were used to keep track of certain information about the book they were associated with. When a book was checked out, the checkout card would be filed away so that the library could know who checked that book out, and when they did so.

The purpose of the checkout card is to store information about something else. You can think of a link file in much the same way. A library card is used to store information about where the book is located, who is in possession of the book, when the book was checked out, and other information. A link file is the digital equivalent to a library card, storing information such as the location of the file it is associated with, the time that file was created, when it was last accessed, when it was last modified, and to which user account that file belongs.

32.1 THE PURPOSE OF LINK FILES, HOW THEY ARE CREATED, AND HOW THEY WORK

A Windows shortcut, or link file, is a pointer file to a file in a different location, which is called the target file. Using our analogy, the library card would be the pointer, and the book itself the target file. Figure 32.1 shows this using the library card file as a paradigm for link files. For example, when you install a program on your computer, a shortcut icon is created on your desktop, which is a link file. When you double-click this shortcut icon on your desktop, it opens a program associated with it. If you uninstall a program, but the shortcut icon was left on your desktop, when you double-click that shortcut now, nothing will happen except that

FIGURE 32.1

A card catalog paradigm for link files on a computer

you would see an error message letting you know that the program cannot be found. This is because that shortcut icon (link file), now points nowhere since the target file it was associated with is now gone. This would be like trying to use a checkout card to find a book that the library no longer has. The checkout card would know where the book used to be, but when you went to that section of the library where the book is supposed to be located, the book itself would be missing. The converse is also true; deleting the shortcut icon on your desktop does not uninstall the program it is associated with. Destroying a library card does not also destroy the book it is associated with.

Link files are used liberally by the Windows operating system, and they can be created in numerous ways. A user can create a link file intentionally, for example, by placing a shortcut on the desktop, or they can also be created by Windows, without the user's knowledge.

The overall purpose of a link file is to enhance the user's experience as he or she navigates a computer. A link file can help you find documents you recently opened, quickly open a program on a computer via a shortcut, or access a device such as a printer or network hard drive that is not directly connected to your computer. Link files are created in numerous ways and used liberally by the Windows operating system; they can be useful as evidence in many ways.

32.2 HOW LINK FILES CAN BE OF EVIDENTIARY VALUE

Link files contain useful information within themselves about the target file they are associated with. A link file can tell you what Windows account, or username, the target file was opened with. It can also potentially contain information on when that target file was created, last accessed, or last modified. Link files can show that a file previously existed on a computer, and can also be useful in determining if a file was opened from a device connected to a computer, such as a USB thumb drive or external hard drive.

While link files can be useful as a part of a body of evidence, digital or otherwise, using them to come to any conclusion without other corroborating evidence can be precarious. Link files alone can be used as solid evidence in some case situations; in others they cannot, since the interpretation of link file evidence can vary given the knowledge and capability of the examiner and their intended use in a case.

32.3 LINK FILES AS EVIDENCE

As data is moved from one device to another, it can leave a trail of digital bread crumbs that can be useful as evidence. Data today travels more easily, more discretely, and in greater quantity than ever before. A USB thumb drive of today, while physically very small, can easily hold hundreds or thousands of documents, pictures, movies, or music files.

Link files can be used as part of an investigation to determine if a device, such as a USB thumb drive, has been connected to a computer, and also what files were moved to that device, when they were moved, and where they were moved from. This scenario is most promising when you access all the digital evidence in question. In this case that would be the thumb drive and the computer. By having both devices, it is possible to use link files that exist on both devices to conclusively show that a file was moved or copied from one device to another, even if the file does not exist on either device anymore.

Often there are cases where data theft or employee wrongdoing involving a particular file is of concern. In these situations, the computer is usually owned by the company and it is provided for examination. However, the USB thumb drive might be personally owned by the suspected employee, making it more difficult to get. The information gathered from the examination of link files on a computer can help determine information about the USB thumb drive, such as the make and model, and even the volume serial number of the USB thumb drive. Every USB thumb drive has a unique volume serial number. This information can then in turn be used to provide sufficient proof of the need to get the USB thumb drive for examination. Figure 32.2 shows a screenshot in EnCase forensics software of a link file's volume serial number.

Name   SomeFile.lnk
File Ext   lnk
File Type   Windows File Shortcut
File Category   Windows\Shortcut
Description   File, Archive
Last Accessed   05/26/11 09:56:49AM
File Created   05/26/11 09:56:49AM
Last Written   05/26/11 09:56:49AM
Entry Modified   05/26/11 09:56:49AM
File Acquired   05/26/11 05:20:38PM
Logical Size   342
Initialized Size 342
Physical Size   342
Starting Extent   0D-C801610,296
File Extents   1
Permissions   •
References   0
Physical Location 56,978,876,712
Physical Sector   111,286,868
Evidence File   2
File Identifier   60714
Code Page   0
Full Path   ThumbDrive\2\D\Users\Jason\AppData\Roaming\Microsoft\Windows\Recent\SomeFile.lnk
Symbolic Link   I:\SomeFile.txt
Sequence ID   140

Link Data
Volume Name   TOOLS
Serial Number   B0CE-F0C7
Link Type   2
Base Name   I:\SomeFile.txt
Working directory I:\

FIGURE 32.2

The volume serial number for a USB device as contained within a link file

32.3.1 Using link files to show that a file was accessed by the user

Sometimes it is important to establish whether a particular file or files were accessed by a user on a computer. In many situations, when a file is created, copied, or downloaded, a link file is created. The presence of a link file associated with the file in question can help to establish whether or not a user accessed a particular file and also when he or she did so.

For example, when you open a file in Windows, it creates a link file in your Recent Items folder. This allows you to quickly access the file again later by clicking the Start button and selecting the Recent Items button from the menu. While the Recent Items button on the Start menu may only show a handful of files, the Recent Items folder, which is buried in the Windows file structure, can contain hundreds of link files that point to files that were accessed by a user on the computer, and it can retain several months of history.

32.3.2 Using link files to show that a deleted file once existed on a computer

Windows operating systems do not always clean up after themselves very well. Just because a file has been deleted from a computer, it does not mean that the link file has also been deleted. In fact, it is highly probable that the link file will remain on the computer for a very long time. By locating the link file that was associated with a deleted file, you can show that the file did exist on the computer at one time.

However, one of the questions that often arise in cases involving deleted files is where the file came from in the first place. While a link file can show where a file was when it was accessed, it cannot show where the file came from. For example, if someone is accused of taking documents from a file server, and link files on the suspected employee's computer are found showing that the documents were last accessed from a USB drive, the link file information can only show where the file was last accessed from, not where it was copied from. In other words, it cannot be determined from the link file itself whether the file was put on the USB stick from the file server, from an e-mail attachment, or even another USB stick.

32.3.3 Using link files to show that a contraband image was saved to a computer but never opened again

Determining whether a computer user ever viewed an image after saving it to his or her computer when surfing the Internet can be of importance, especially in cases involving child pornography. By using the temporary Internet file associated with the image, the image file itself, and link file associated with the image, it can be determined whether or not the image was ever viewed after being saved to the computer by comparing the MAC (modified, accessed, and created) times of these three files.

32.3.4 Connecting a deleted file on a computer to a USB device using link file evidence

One of the properties of link files is the volume serial number. When a USB device is examined in forensic software like EnCase, the volume serial number of the device can be seen. If a link file for a deleted file is located on a computer hard drive and the volume serial number matches that of a USB device that is in evidence, a clear connection can be made between the USB device and the file that once existed on the hard drive, even if the file is no longer present on the USB device or the hard drive.

SUMMARY

In this chapter we learned the purpose of link files, which are created by the Windows operating system to make a computer user's experience more enjoyable by making files easier to access with features like desktop shortcuts and recent items. We learned that link files point to other files in different locations. We also learned that link files can be valuable as evidence in a case to build timelines, find out how a file has traveled from one device to another, determine if a file has ever been opened, or see if a deleted file existed on a computer at one point in time.

Cellular System Evidence and Call Detail Records

33

INFORMATION IN THIS CHAPTER:

- An overview of the cellular phone system
- How cell phones work
- Call detail records
- Call detail records as evidence of cell phone location
- Enhanced 911 wireless location services
- The E911 system overview
- Emergency situations: Real-time cell phone tracking

INTRODUCTION

Call detail records are coming into play more often in cases every day. The purpose of the call detail records is to bill customers for cellular usage. However, they are also being used in court to attempt to place the cell phone user in a geographical location based on the tower used by the cell phone to send or receive a phone call, text message, or Internet data connection. This kind of evidence is fraught with potential misunderstanding by courts and juries alike and should be treated accordingly.

The purpose of the cellular network is to allow cellular phone companies to provide wireless phone calls and data transfer at the least expensive cost in terms of infrastructure, power usage, and coverage area. The cellular system was not designed to locate cellular phones beyond simply knowing if a cell phone can be reached to connect a call. In other words, cellular mobile phone networks are optimized for capacity and call handling, not for location of cellular phones.

33.1 AN OVERVIEW OF THE CELLULAR PHONE SYSTEM

The cellular phone system is part of the regular telephone system or Plain Old Telephone System (POTS), which provides the public telephone system we all use every day.

The cellular system is equipment that has been added to the POTS network to accommodate wireless voice and data calls.

FIGURE 33.1

A picture of a cell tower showing the antennas in a three-sector configuration

The system is made up of cell towers, base transceiver stations (BTS), Mobile Switching Centers (MSC), radio network controllers (RNC), and the home and visitors (roamers) location register. Figure 33.1 shows a cell tower with antennas in a three-sector configuration.

A cell tower normally covers an area that is roughly circular in shape and can be divided up into sectors. Figure 33.2 shows a top-down view of a cell tower divided into three sectors. In a call detail record, each sector will be numbered so the sector can be identified. The sector number will be the first number in the cell tower ID.

At the base of every cell tower there is a base transceiver station (BTS) that processes and handles local radio communications with cellular phones and facilitates communication between the wireless network and the landline network. The

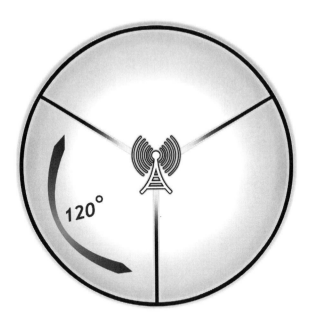

FIGURE 33.2

A top-down view of a cell tower with three sectors

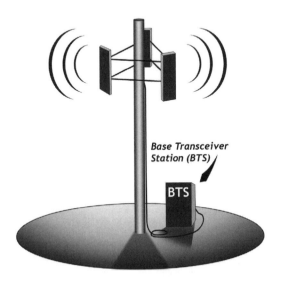

FIGURE 33.3

A cell tower with the base transceiver station

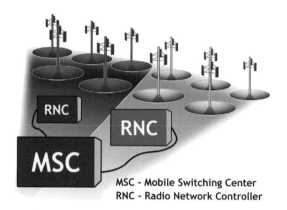

MSC - Mobile Switching Center
RNC - Radio Network Controller

FIGURE 33.4

Multiple cell sites connected to radio network controllers (RNC) and a Mobile Switching Center (MSC)

tower, antennas, and base transceiver station make up a cell site. Figure 33.3 shows a cell tower and BTS that make up a cell site.

The base transceiver station (BTS) is connected via landline to a radio network controller (RNC). The RNC manages several base transceiver stations. The radio network controller is connected to a Mobile Switching Center. Each Mobile Switching Center (MSC) manages the cell towers in a single coverage area. One or more Mobile Switching Centers make up a location or market area.

Figure 33.4 shows all of the pieces connected together into a functional wireless network.

The Home Location Register (HLR) is a large database that permanently stores data about subscribers. The HLR maintains subscriber-specific information such as the individual cell phone, and the SIM card identifies the current location of the cell phone, roaming restrictions, and subscriber-supplemental features for each phone that belongs to the wireless carrier. There is logically only one HLR in any given network, meaning that there is only one master HLR database, but generally speaking, each network has multiple physical HLRs spread out across its network to account for hardware failures.

The visitor location register (VLR) is a database that contains the same type of information located on the HLR, but only for subscribers currently in its Location Area. There is a VLR for every system to store the information about a mobile phone that is roaming in the system.

Figure 33.5 shows the cellular systems for two wireless carriers side by side. If a subscriber of Carrier 1 calls a subscriber on Carrier 2's system, the call must go first to the home location register for Carrier 1. Carrier 1 will recognize that the subscriber belongs to Carrier 2 and will contact Carrier 2's HLR to locate the phone to make the call.

Figure 33.6 shows a cellular system with all the parts in place.

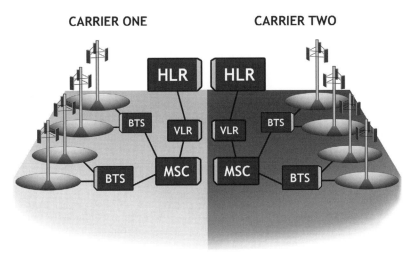

FIGURE 33.5

Two wireless carrier systems

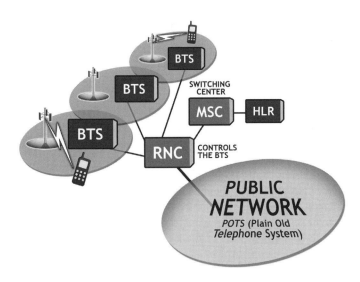

FIGURE 33.6

A diagram of a cellular system showing all the parts

33.2 HOW CELL PHONES WORK

A cell phone is basically a two-way radio and communicates with cell towers via radio signals. When a cell phone is turned on, it registers with the cellular system by contacting the cell tower with the strongest signal, which may or may not be the closest tower. This allows the cellular system to know how to find the cell phone in case the system needs to route a call to the phone. Records of this process are not part of a call detail record since this is not a billable transaction. In most cases, these registration pings are only present for a few hours and are not recoverable after the fact.

At this point, the cellular system knows the tower location of the phone, which market it is in, and whether or not the phone is a "registered" phone. In other words, a registered phone is one that has an active account and can receive calls or make calls.

Once the phone is turned on and operating, it will periodically "ping" the tower with the strongest signal to maintain its registration so the system can locate it for incoming calls.

These registration pings are recorded in the equipment located at the individual cell towers and are maintained for a very short length of time, normally less than 48 hours.

33.2.1 Anatomy of a Cell Phone Call

This is a simplified description of how cell phones communicate using the cellular system.

When a person dials a number on his or her cell phone and presses the "Send" button, the phone will attempt to place the call via the cell tower with the strongest signal at that point in time, and the cellular system equipment will begin call processing.

Every cell tower is connected to the phone system via landlines. The call is actually sent along these landlines to the local market Mobile Switching Center and then via landline to the central telephone switching center where the number is looked up using the home location registration database.

If the number dialed is a landline phone, then the call will traverse the landline telephone system and ring at the landline address.

If the phone is another cellular phone, then the call will still traverse the phone system via landlines to the local market Mobile Switching Center, to the central market switching center, and then to the local market Mobile Switching Center of the dialed phone, and finally to the cell tower that the phone has registered with, and finally to the phone itself.

Figure 33.7 shows this process in diagram form.

Once the call is attempted, one of several things can happen:

1. The person answers the cell phone using the cell phone handset that was dialed. This is a completed call. The dialed digits and the phone number on the call detail record will match.
2. The person does not answer the cell phone. This is a call attempt.
3. The phone is a valid number but cannot be reached by any cell tower at that moment in time. This is a call attempt.

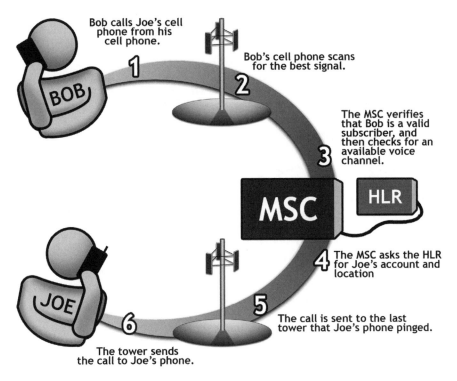

Bob calls Joe's cell phone from his cell phone.

1

Bob's cell phone scans for the best signal.

2

The MSC verifies that Bob is a valid subscriber, and then checks for an available voice channel.

3

MSC

HLR

The MSC asks the HLR for Joe's account and location

4

The call is sent to the last tower that Joe's phone pinged.

5

The tower sends the call to Joe's phone.

6

JOE

BOB

FIGURE 33.7

What happens when a cell phone call is made

4. The cellular number dialed has been forwarded to another number, which can be another cell phone or a landline, and the forwarded number is answered; however, the dialed digits and the answered phone number will not match since the dial phone was answered by a different number. This is a completed call.

33.3 CALL DETAIL RECORDS

It is important to remember that cellular service providers use derived information in call detail records for use in their billing, coverage, and analytics.

Call detail records are a potential form of evidence, but the claims made based on them are often overstated when they are used as evidence. Knowing the merits and limitations of call detail records is critical when bringing them to bear in a case. Call detail records need a significant amount of supplementary information to be of most use, such as the maintenance records or trouble tickets of the cell towers referenced in the call detail records, information about the configuration of cell towers of interest, and the radio frequency maps, if available, for the cell towers.

These and other factors must be taken into consideration and dealt with if an examination of call detail records is to be performed comprehensively and correctly.

33.4 CALL DETAIL RECORDS AS EVIDENCE OF CELL PHONE LOCATION

One of the most important things to remember is that a cell phone *cannot* be located from a historical call detail record. The best that can be done is that the phone can be placed in a general area corresponding to a cell tower that was connected to the phone at a particular time when a call was made or attempted.

What the call detail record report contains varies by carrier; however, they will usually supply the following information for each call attempt:

- Date: The date the call was attempted or received
- Time: The time the call was attempted or received
- Number called: The number called or calling depending on the direction of the call
- Usage type: Voice, Data, SMS, MMS
- Call duration: In minutes or seconds

Figure 33.8 shows the portion of a call detail record containing the date, time, and number called. This kind of information is part of what is used to perform an analysis of call detail records by providing the timeline information for an incident.

Once it is established that the date and times of phone calls in the call detail record correspond with the timeline in a case, the next step is to get the cell tower identifier from the call detail record.

Figure 33.9 shows the part of the call detail record that contains the cell tower identification number or CID. Note that carriers use different abbreviations for the cell tower ID. Some use terms like SZR or other designations for the tower IDs.

The cell tower ID (CID) in this case is a five-digit number. The first number is the sector of the cell tower and the last four digits are the cell tower ID number.

Using this information, a call can be associated with a particular cell tower and sector of a cell tower. This is done by matching the cell tower ID from the call detail record with the cell tower ID on the list of tower locations that should always

Date	Time	Number Called	Calls To	Mins Used
07/24/2008	03:15	(555)132-1234	AIKEN SC	2

FIGURE 33.8

A portion of a call detail record showing dates, times, and phone numbers called

be supplied with any subpoena request for call detail records. Requesting call detail records is covered in Chapter 24. Figure 33.10 shows a portion of a cell tower location report with the geolocation information for the towers. By matching the cell tower IDs from the call detail records with the tower IDs in the cell tower location report, you can determine the geolocation of the tower using the latitude and longitude for the tower.

33.4.1 A Cell Tower Location Example

The coverage of a cell tower is normally discussed in terms of its radius. A cell tower with a 1-mile coverage radius is equal to 3.14 square miles or 2010 acres.

If a cell phone is connected to one of the three sectors, the area that the cell phone can be in is one-third of the total coverage area, or in this case, 670 acres.

One way to think of this is to imagine a subdivision with houses on one-acre lots covered by one sector of the cell tower. If a cell phone is "located" in that sector, it could be in any of the 670 houses. Or if the cell phone is traveling on a road adjacent to the subdivision, it could be in none of the houses at any time. At best, this kind of evidence is circumstantial as to the location of a cell phone at any particular time.

That would be the closest you can get in locating the cell phone in that subdivision. Figure 33.11 shows a diagram of a cell tower coverage area. You'll notice that the diagram is divided into three sectors, with the top pie slice at the top. This would be a tower with a northern orientation. In this case, the sectors would be numbered starting at the top and going clockwise. This means that the north sector would be identified as 1, the southeast sector as 2, and the southwest sector as 3.

Servicing Area	LAC	CID
CHARLOTTE	08415	24252

FIGURE 33.9

Portion of a call detail record showing the cell tower ID (CID)

LAC	CID	Street Address	Latitute	Longitude
08414	12332	9874 DAWN ROAD / FORT MILL/ SOUTH CAROLINA/ 98464	35.98745	62.98764

FIGURE 33.10

A cell tower location report

FIGURE 33.11

A diagram of a three-sector tower with a 1-mile radius

If the cell tower has a three-mile radius, then you can triple the numbers above. Now the subdivision would contain 6030 houses. The cell phone could be in any of them or none of them at all. Figure 33.12 shows a cell tower plot over a Google Earth Pro map. This is one common method that is used in court to show that a cell phone is in an area. If you study the map in Fig. 33.12, it is not hard to see that the best location you can get in this case is somewhere in one of the very large sectors drawn on the map.

33.5 ENHANCED 911 WIRELESS LOCATION SERVICES

With the development of the Enhanced 911 system (E911), it is possible to locate a cell phone with varying degrees of accuracy and success depending on the level of E911 services available in the locality.

By the end of 2005, wireless telephone carriers were required to comply with the Federal Communications Commission regulations for the E911 system.

However, even at this late date, the FCC continues to issue waivers to telephone companies for areas where full implementation of the E911 system has not been fully implemented for technical or geographic reasons.

FIGURE 33.12

A three-sector tower coverage map using Google Earth Pro

33.6 THE E911 SYSTEM OVERVIEW

With the advent of wireless technology, a system had to be implemented that could handle the location of a wireless caller when he or she dialed 911.

The purpose of the E911 system is to provide enhanced information to emergency services personnel when a caller dials 911. These enhancements include the number calling, the address of the caller, and the ability to call the caller back if they should hang up.

Figure 33.13 gives a visual overview of the E911 system. The PSAP operator *may* update the location on demand. It is not automatic.

However, the reality of it is that the E911 system is not fully implemented in all areas due to several factors, including geographic considerations and lack of cell towers that would make accurate location of a cell phone impossible. If the E911 call is a Phase 1 call, all the wireless carrier is required to provide is the *calling number*, and the *location of the cell tower.* This means that the call location can be anywhere in the overall sector of the cell tower coverage area. As shown earlier, a single sector of a cell tower coverage area can be very large, especially in rural areas.

If the E911 call is a Phase 2 call, then there is a good likelihood that the cell phone location will be accurate to several hundred feet.

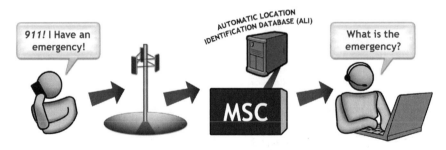

FIGURE 33.13

An overview of the E911 system

Even though the Public Safety Answering Point (PSAP) may be able to receive location information, the ability to handle the information is not consistent throughout the system. In one case in Tennessee, Germantown dispatchers were unable to locate a cell phone from the location information even though the information was transmitted to the PASP dispatcher.

*Neither a veteran Germantown (Tenn.) public safety dispatcher or her supervising lieutenant followed up on a 911 call where at least 10 **gunshots** were audible because they had no way to look up the latitude and longitude of the call, and both believed—mistakenly—that department policy did not require them to dispatch an officer to a call with no location and no person's name. The 911 call received by dispatcher **Claudia Woods** on July 19th was later linked to the murder of former NBA player **Lorenzen Wright**, whose body was found a week later about a mile and one-half from the coordinates displayed on Woods' ANI/ALI screen. In transcripts of interviews with Woods, Lt. Donald Taylor, and dispatchers Richard Frederick Jr. and Chris Rowlson, the communication center personnel told investigators they followed departmental policy, and believe they did everything they could, given their training and the availability of computer systems. Woods was interviewed by Germantown police Insp. Danny Payne as part of an internal investigation, and said the location of the cellular phone wasn't plotted on her computer mapping screen. Sources say she heard gunfire, but that detail was redacted from the transcript. Woods said the call ended and she dialed the number back and heard only a generic voicemail greeting. The latitude and longitude of the call was displayed, but Woods told Payne, "We didn't have the equipment to plot it." Even though she heard gunfire and a latitude and longitude was displayed, no officers investigated the call. It was forgotten until 10 days later when investigators linked the call and Wright's disappearance. Police reportedly used the cell phone signal to find Wright's body in a field 10 days after the 911 call.[1] (Emphasis by author)*

33.7 EMERGENCY SITUATIONS: REAL-TIME CELL PHONE TRACKING

In an emergency situation where a person is in immediate danger, the E911 system can be activated to locate the phone, providing that the phone is turned on and in an area where the phone can receive a cellular signal.

SUMMARY

In this chapter we looked at how call detail records and cell phone location works, both as historical data analysis and via the E911 system. We discussed the makeup of the wireless phone system and how cell phones work within the wireless system.

We also discussed the content of call detail records and the methods used to attempt to provide location information for a cell phone from those records. The reality of attempting to locate cell phones via historical call detail records is suspect at best and highly inaccurate in worst-case scenarios. Beware of this type of evidence being used to pinpoint the location of a person via these records unless they dialed 911 from the cell phone and the local E911 system is fully implemented for accurate location services.

Reference

[1] G. Allen, Murder Revelation: No 911 Call Follow-Up | Dispatch Magazine On-Line. *Dispatch Magazine On-Line | news and information about public safety communications.* <http://www.911dispatch.com/2010/08/murder-revelation-no-911-call-follow-up/>, (2010, August 3). (accessed 11.04.30).

E-mail Evidence

INTRODUCTION

E-mail is probably one of the most prolific forms of evidence available today. It seems that everyone has an e-mail account, from children to octogenarians. With the availability of free e-mail accounts that can be set up in a matter of minutes, the number of e-mail accounts exploded in the late 1990s. Today the big three e-mail hosting providers are

1. Yahoo Mail
2. Microsoft Hotmail / Live Mail
3. Google Mail

In September of 2010, Microsoft stated in a Windows Live Hotmail fact sheet, "Windows Live Hotmail is one of the world's largest e-mail providers with more than 355 million active accounts, providing features for an efficient and clutter-free inbox whether via the Web, a mobile phone or a PC."[1]

The way the world of electronic communications works today has made getting e-mail evidence more important and more likely than ever due to the increasing number of people who send and receive e-mail on multiple devices.

34.1 E-MAIL AS EVIDENCE

With e-mail evidence there are normally four things that someone wants to know:

1. The content of the e-mail
2. Who sent it
3. When was it sent
4. Where was it sent from

While getting the content is dependent on getting the actual e-mail, the origination of an e-mail can be quite a bit more complex. The evidence of the origination of an e-mail is embedded in the e-mail itself in the form of an e-mail header. However, note that portions of an e-mail header are easily faked by inserting false records. Spammers often fake the sent from e-mail address as well as the Internet address of the sending server to attempt to fool antispam software.

34.1 A CASE OF A MYSTERY SENDER

In a case where a woman was receiving e-mails from an unknown person using a Yahoo mail account, the person seemed to know a lot about her and her relationship with her husband. The content of the e-mails included a lot of personal information that a stranger would not know. She questioned her husband about the e-mails and he denied knowing who it was. She wanted to see if it could be determined who the sender really was.

After examination of the e-mail headers, the location of the origination of the e-mails was determined, geographically placing the sender in a particular city. When the city name was disclosed to the woman, she recognized it as a place where her husband routinely traveled on business. When she confronted him with the originating city, he confessed to having an affair with another woman on his travels.

34.2 E-MAIL STORAGE AND ACCESS: WHERE IS IT?

Depending on the type of e-mail account and how "connected" the user is, e-mail can be stored for a single account in several places. Just because an e-mail is deleted in one place, it does not mean that the e-mail cannot be retrieved from somewhere else. Many people today access their e-mail on multiple devices creating duplicates on mail servers, phones, and computers.

34.2.1 Server-based storage

In this section the various places that e-mail may be stored are covered. Since e-mail is so ubiquitous, the places that e-mails can be found and collected for evidence abound, providing multiple opportunities in many cases to recover e-mail that may be thought lost.

- Mail Servers
    - Corporate e-mail accounts are typically hosted on a mail server that is either owned or leased by the company. These mail servers can be Microsoft Exchange, Lotus Notes, Novell GroupWise, or some other mail type of server. Corporate mail servers are typically backed up on a regular basis and those backups may be stored on site on tape or disk. Additional backups may

be available at remote locations via off-site storage applications. In the case of older backups where the physical server is no longer available, it is still possible to retrieve the e-mail from the backups by duplicating the missing server on a new computer or entirely in software in a virtual environment. A virtual environment is a method for creating the equivalent of a physical computer entirely in software by using a "host" computer to contain the virtual computer. Using this method, a single computer can take the place of several physical computers at once. Depending on what type of backups were made, the type of e-mail server, the size of the e-mail store, and the backup media, restoring e-mail ranges in cost from a couple of thousand dollars to hundreds of thousands of dollars.

- Free e-mail accounts are hosted by companies who are in the business of marketing via the Internet, with Microsoft, Yahoo, and Google dominating the free e-mail marketplace. There are many other free e-mail account providers out there. Depending on the free e-mail account provider, e-mails may be stored for only a short time if an account goes inactive; in some cases e-mail is purged from a free account if it is not accessed for a 30-day period. However, the record of the account creation can be stored for a very long time.

- Internet Service Providers (ISPs) also provide e-mail accounts as part of the service when you sign up for an account. These range from local ISPs who provide dial-up services in rural areas to high-speed Internet providers via DSL, cable, or satellite.

34.2 CREATING AN E-MAIL ACCOUNT TO COVER UP A CRIME

In a case from several years ago, a client was facing the death penalty for murdering his girlfriend. While he admitted that he had killed her, he maintained that it was in a fit of rage and not a premeditated plan. Part of the penalty phase hearing was to show that he had created an e-mail account to send e-mails found on their home computer from his deceased girlfriend to himself after the murder occurred. In this case, the retention window at the free e-mail service had lapsed for inactive accounts and the e-mails were no longer available from the service provider. However, they did keep account creation records for several years. Using the account creation record, it was shown that the account was created after the murder occurred, which helped to show that the murder was not premeditated. Information on how to subpoena e-mail information is covered in Chapter 22.

34.2.2 User-based E-mail Storage

Computers are still the primary way that people send and receive e-mail. However, that dominance is quickly being challenged by e-mail on mobile devices such as cell phones and pad computers.

This means that when you approach e-mail as evidence today, you must consider that the user may have e-mail stored in multiple locations on multiple devices. For instance, a person may have e-mail stored on his or her work computer, home computer, cell phone, and pad computer such as an iPad or one of the many competitors to the iPad entering the market.

- User-based E-mail Storage
  - Computers
    - E-mails on computers can be stored in different formats depending on the type of e-mail program the person uses to access their e-mail account. Here is a short list of some of the common formats:
      - Microsoft Outlook e-mail is stored in a personal folder file or Personal Storage Table (.PST file). An Outlook installation that is set up for disconnected syncing with a corporate mail server may also have e-mail stored in an Offline folder file or Offline Storage Table (.OST file).
      - Microsoft Outlook 2011 for MAC stores e-mail as individual messages in folders for each user identity.
      - Apple Mac OS X mail uses the mbox format.
      - GroupWise uses the .MLM format for saving messages to a local computer. However, this file is not typically created unless the e-mail user sets it up to store messages locally on their hard drive.
      - Lotus Notes e-mail files are stored in the .NSF format.
      - Outlook Express stores e-mail in a .DBX file for each user on a local computer.
  - Phone Storage
    - Smart phones that have e-mail capability store e-mail messages in their own format that is compatible with the phone operating system. The interesting thing about e-mail stored on phones is that it can be hard to manage due to the quirks of the individual device. For instance, on an Android phone, you have your inbox as the main e-mail window. To get to your sent items or deleted items, you have to go through the menu system when you are looking at your inbox. The sent items folder and deleted items folders can grow to enormous size depending on the amount of storage the phone has on board. Since the phone e-mail program does not have a convenient way to bulk delete items, nor is there a function to empty the deleted items folder, these messages can accumulate without the user being aware that they are even on the phone. And if they are, then there is a good chance they have not gone through the painful process of deleting the messages manually one by one.
    - iPhones store e-mail on the device as well. If the owner of the phone connects the iPhone to a computer running iTunes, the phone will want to perform an automatic backup of the phone's contents. This will back up all of the user's e-mail currently on the phone to the computer and these backups can be found in the iTunes backup folder for the phone.

34.3 IS IT REALLY GONE? AN ATTEMPT TO DESTROY EVIDENCE OF AN E-MAIL

In a case where a large company wanted to know if an employee had sent an e-mail containing a nude picture to the board of directors, the employee's iPhone and company laptop computer were submitted for examination. When the phone was examined, it was discovered that it had been factory reset, wiping all data from the phone. This ruled out checking the phone itself for evidence. Next the computer was examined and it did not have any pictures or e-mails of interest. However, there was also evidence that the computer had been cleaned up using a file-wiping program. In some instances, this would have been the end of any possibility of discovering what really happened. However, what the clever employee missed was the backups of his iPhone that were still on the computer in his iTunes directory. The picture was recovered from the iTunes backup folder to prove that the picture originated from his iPhone and his e-mail.

- Pad Computers
    - Pad computers such as the Apple iPad, Motorola XOOM, and the Blackberry Playbook are very popular as replacements for a bulkier laptop computer for people who need e-mail access on the road. For example, the iPad stores e-mail on the device, and also makes a backup of any e-mail to iTunes when the unit is plugged into a computer running iTunes that recognizes the iPad as having been synced with the computer.

34.3 WEB MAIL

Free web mail is by far the most commonly used e-mail service overall. It is also one of the most common types of e-mail evidence that people want to recover in all types of cases. Many people believe that because they are using a web-based e-mail account that they only access through the Internet browser, there will be no record stored on the local computer. However, in many cases, web-based e-mail is cached to the local hard drive as a web page. These web pages can be recovered like any other web page by either locating the web page in the Internet cache or by carving the web pages from unallocated space. Web page caching is covered in Chapter 31.

Not only can the individual messages composed or read be retrieved this way, but the main mail page listing the messages in the user's mailbox can be recovered showing that an e-mail was sent or received, even if the e-mail itself cannot be recovered.

In addition to the pages cached on the local computer, it is possible to get e-mail directly from the provider via subpoena. However, if the e-mail was deleted from the user's account, there is little likelihood of retrieving it from the provider if any significant time has passed. Most free e-mail services purge deleted e-mails on a regular basis, normally within 30 days for inactive accounts. However, this varies by service provider, so the best solution is to always check with the custodian of records to find out the retention policy of the individual service. How to subpoena free e-mail accounts is covered in Chapter 22.

SUMMARY

This chapter covered e-mail as evidence and where this evidence might be found. The different types and places for e-mail storage were covered along with the various methods that can be used to collected e-mail as evidence. Case studies were included that showed how e-mail evidence was used in some criminal and civil cases.

Reference

[1] Microsoft News, *Microsoft Corporation.* <http://www.microsoft.com/presspass/presskits/windowslive/materials.aspx>, 2010 (accessed 11.04.30).

Social Media

INFORMATION IN THIS CHAPTER:

- Common forms of social networking (social media)
- Evidence out in the open
- Convenience versus security
- The allure of anonymity
- Social media as evidence
- Getting information from online services

INTRODUCTION

There are more ways for people to connect with one another than ever before. For example, Facebook reports that they have over 500 million active users.[1] The widespread use of social media outlets such as Facebook, Twitter, MySpace, and LinkedIn ultimately means that evidence is being continually created, and is often available right in the public domain. The usage of social media does not require that someone be tethered to a computer anymore. Almost all social media outlets can be accessed using phones, iPads, and other mobile devices. Facebook alone reports that more than 250 million users are accessing Facebook through their cell phones or other mobile devices.[2]

35.1 COMMON FORMS OF SOCIAL NETWORKING (SOCIAL MEDIA)

The number of social networking websites and applications available today is staggering. If there is a common interest among a group of people, no matter how obscure, there is almost certainly a website or online organization where they can communicate and collaborate. To cover individual social networking websites and applications in any sort of detail would be outside the scope of this book. In the following section, in broad strokes, are examples of the most common forms of social networking, how people interact with them, and how they can be used as evidence.

35.2 EVIDENCE OUT IN THE OPEN

A great deal of evidence can be collected from information that is available in the public domain. Examiners should not impersonate someone else, or engage in any activity that might become an invasion of privacy. Creating fake profiles for the purpose of accessing someone's private profile can raise ethical questions and perhaps even legal questions about such a practice. This is also not necessary because in many cases there are other ways to gather the information without sending a friend request to the person in the first place. This is a limitation in some sense, but working with information available in the public domain can produce a significant amount of evidence that could be of interest in a case.

Most social networking sites have available options to increase the amount of privacy the user has. However, when an account is created with Facebook or MySpace, the default security settings allow other users to see a great deal of information about your profile without having to be your friend or connected to you in any way. This makes sense from the perspective of the companies and organizations that create and supply social media outlets, as it is in their best interest to do everything they can to draw people to their websites. For example, websites geared toward facilitating sexual encounters between people make some of the user profiles viewable for non-members of the website. For someone seeking to engage in such an activity, seeing other's profiles, which could contain such information as location, age, pictures, and sexual interest, would have a greater appeal than a website that would not allow that person to see the information unless they signed up or paid a subscription fee. The purpose in giving some random member information for free is to get the visitor to pay a fee to be able to search for and connect with others in these types of paid sites.

With some websites, such as MySpace, the default privacy settings limit the viewability of a profile by a nonmember to some degree. To see more information, all that is required is to create a dummy profile to make the hidden information available. You would not have to engage the person in any way, either through messaging her or adding her as a friend.

The revenue for social media websites and applications usually comes from advertising. If the websites were locked down with privacy and security as their main objective, it would inhibit their ability to have maximum user traffic. While enhanced privacy options are available with these websites, for the users there is always a trade-off when these security measures are employed. Usually, when a user places enhanced privacy or security on their information, the convenience of using the social media outlets can be decreased. With almost all forms of digital information and devices, people tend to err on the side of convenience. Typically, the more security that is in place, the harder it is to share your information with others, which makes it more difficult to connect with people in social media websites and applications. Since the primary purpose of social networking is in fact to network with others, it is not difficult to understand why someone might risk their information for the sake of convenience, if they even consider privacy to be a priority in the first place.

35.3 CONVENIENCE VERSUS SECURITY

The choices made by people for convenience over security when using social media extend beyond the privacy settings on their profile or account. Imagine that you had an account with ten different social media websites. One of the most efficient ways to increase your security would be to isolate them from one another by using different e-mail addresses, passwords, and usernames for each of these websites. This would dramatically reduce the likelihood that if someone found one of your online profiles, they would be able to track them all down. However, this would also be extremely inconvenient, as you would have to manage ten e-mail accounts, and remember ten different passwords and usernames. While behavior such as described here is not unheard of, it is rare. When it comes to usernames and e-mail addresses used to create accounts with social media networking websites and applications, people tend to be predictable. If someone has a username they prefer, they will use it whenever they possibly can (if it is not already taken by someone else), and the same is true with e-mail addresses. If a person creates an e-mail address for the sole purpose of engaging in activity that they would not want others to find out about, it is common for them to use that same e-mail address or username for all the social media websites and applications. So if an examiner is able to discover that e-mail address on one social media website, or on a computer or cell phone, it is probable that they will find more if they exist. There are websites available for doing social media searches that can be of great assistance in locating information about a person's online presence, such as Spokeo (www.spokeo.com). You can check your exposure on Spokeo's site for free. If you are concerned about what is revealed, you can follow these steps to have Spokeo remove your information from their database:

1. Search for your profile information.
2. Once you find it, copy the entire link in the web browser.
3. Click on the tiny "privacy" link at the very bottom of the page.
4. Paste the profile link into the box provided.
5. Enter your e-mail address.
6. Enter the letters in the box.

35.4 THE ALLURE OF ANONYMITY

Imagine that you could say whatever you wanted without any repercussions or consequences. This is how many people function in online environments. Much of the realm of social media allows for anonymity, and when people believe that their identity cannot be tied to their comments or actions online, they are much less inhibited with what they say or post.

Evidence of how anonymity affects the way people communicate can be seen all over the web. All you have to do to see this is go and read the comments posted by people on websites and message forums. People say hateful things about and to people that you must believe is not the way they are in real life, unless of course they want to spend most of their time in interactions with others getting punched in the nose. The beauty of the Internet is you can say something that would in many cases cause a physical altercation, but since the other person can't reach through your monitor and grab you, you are safe to say anything you want.

It is doubtful that someone would say in a post on a news site comment that the best situation for handling a person accused of a crime is to skip a trial and just kill them. Yet you can see these kinds of posts on nearly any news site that allows comments on their news stories.

35.4.1 **Hobby or obsession?**

If you go and look at the comments posted by people who follow some of the high-profile criminal cases seen on national news, you will see people who become obsessed with these cases, posting all hours of the day and night for months, even years at a time. They become involved in these virtual communities, sometimes to the point that the virtual community is more important than real-life friends and families. They rush back to their computers to get back into the conversation, lamenting even a few hours away from the group they have attached themselves to.

Chat rooms where people gather to socialize are particularly attractive to the person who wants the freedom of anonymity provided by the Internet. By creating a profile that can represent anything or anyone, people log into chat rooms to play out fantasies online, argue with people over religion or politics, and chat about their favorite media personality or sports team and any number of other subjects. The same people may stay in the same chat room for weeks and even years; people who in real life may be a pillar of the community or a shy wallflower can turn into an entirely different person in their online persona, acting out online what they cannot do in the real world.

One of the dangers is that people seem to forget that while they know their online persona may be a complete fabrication, they can begin to believe that the persona of others is representative of the real person. That person you are chatting with and think is a gorgeous lingerie model could just as easily be a guy.

The Internet lets people pretend to be something they are not and never can be, and chances are, they probably will not be exposed for who they really are. This can be very alluring to people who are or believe they are unattractive or unpopular in the real world, but on the Internet they are exactly the opposite: beautiful, handsome, witty, strong, accomplished, smart, and so on. This is because people are responding to a persona, not a person. It is the persona that becomes the online personality, not the poor schlep behind the keyboard.

On the Internet a person can be anything they make up; an adult can be a child, a child can be an adult, and who would be the wiser unless they reveal themselves?

It is human nature to gravitate to groups and places where a person feels accepted and liked. The Internet provides such a place via thousands of chat rooms, discussion forums, virtual online communities, and multiplayer games.

And all of these can leave some type of evidence on a computer, on a phone, and at a third-party service provider.

While this anonymity might seem foolproof to someone unfamiliar with social media examinations, it is not. In some cases, all it takes is a single lead like an e-mail address or a chat handle to bring this anonymous information into the light of day.

35.5 SOCIAL MEDIA AS EVIDENCE

Social media evidence works best when it is a part of a body of evidence, meaning that it is usually optimal to use that information in conjunction with evidence gathered from other sources, such as cell phones and computers. However, an examination can be performed successfully with only the information available from social networking sites and other information available online.

35.5.1 Connecting evidence from a device to social media evidence

During the process of a computer or cell phone examination, it is common to find information pertaining to the social media activity of a person. For example, a computer can store information about social media websites in Internet history and unallocated space. While only a limited amount of information might be available on the computer regarding social media activity, if pertinent information is found, such as usernames or an e-mail address, that information can in turn be used in the process of a social media examination to find information about the person online.

For example, in a civil case a company was in the position of being sued for wrongfully terminating an employee. The employee's computer was examined and numerous e-mail addresses belonging to him that were previously unknown were found. These e-mail addresses were used to find usernames belonging to him. The usernames were associated with social media accounts. This led the examiner to locate his activity on message boards where he posted questionable content. The forum posts led to an e-mail address registered to him from the forum information. Following the lead of this particular e-mail address resulted in locating the registration information for a website domain name he was using to operate a business in competition with his employer, which was a point of contention in the case. The collection of the online information was a direct result of information located on the person's computer.

In another case involving the murder of a young woman, MySpace messaging was a factor. In many criminal cases, the online information will be quickly deleted by persons who are contacted by police for many reasons. Being able to connect the MySpace accounts from information retrieved from the defendant's and victim's computers resulted in the creation of a timeline of messaging among the victim, the victim's friends, and the defendant. To do this, the examiner must understand how the messaging system works and how MySpace or other media sites record identifying account information inside the web pages and or messages.

35.6 GETTING INFORMATION FROM ONLINE SERVICES

Online services like Facebook, MySpace, and others resist giving user profile content in cases unless they are served with a criminal subpoena. Citing the Stored Communications Act, Facebook has successfully resisted complying with civil subpoenas for user content. However, in a recent decision by the Supreme Court, Suffolk County, New York, Judge Jeffrey Arlen Spinner[3] ruled that Facebook and MySpace would in fact have to turn over private information. Included here is an excerpt from the ruling:

> Ordered, that defendant Steelcase's motion is hereby granted as set forth herein below.
>
> Defendant Steelcase moves this court for an order granting said defendant access to plaintiff's current and historical Facebook and MySpace pages and accounts, including all deleted pages and related information upon the grounds that plaintiff has placed certain information on these social networking sites which is believed to be inconsistent with her claims in this action concerning the extent and nature of her injuries, especially her claims for loss of enjoyment of life.
>
> The present application was brought on by order to show cause. The court has reviewed the submissions both in favor of and in opposition to the relief sought, as well as the applicable federal statutory law, specifically the Stored [*2]Communications Act (18 USC § 2701 et seq.), which prohibits an entity such as Facebook and MySpace from disclosing such information without the consent of the owner of the account (see 18 USC § 2702 [b][3]; Flagg v City of Detroit, 252 FRD 346, 352 [ED Mich 2008]).

Information on how to subpoena records from social media sites is covered in Chapter 20.

SUMMARY

In this chapter we looked at the widespread use of social media outlets such as Facebook, Twitter, MySpace, and LinkedIn. We also covered the privacy and security issues connected to social media. We discussed the anonymity factor, and some of the different ways to collect social media evidence with some examples of how this evidence can be used in cases. We also looked at the issues with getting information from online services in civil cases and cited a recent case that may open the door to making this information easier to obtain.

References

[1] Facebook | Company, Statistics, *Statistics*. <http://www.facebook.com/press/info. php?statistics>

[2] Facebook | Company, Statistics, *Statistics*. <http://www.facebook.com/press/info. php?statistics>

[3] Romano v. Steelcase Inc. (2010 NY Slip Op 20388) *available at* <http://www.courts. state.ny.us/Reporter/3dseries/2010/2010_20388.htm>

Peer-to-Peer Networks and File Sharing

36

INFORMATION IN THIS CHAPTER:

- What is peer-to-peer file sharing?
- How it works
- Privacy and security issues with peer-to-peer file sharing
- Peer-to-peer network evidence

INTRODUCTION

There is no "server" needed for peer-to-peer file sharing. Every computer connected to the network is both a server and a workstation. As of this writing, one of the largest of the file-sharing companies, LimeWire, has been ordered to cease operations as the result of a civil lawsuit. The official notice they have placed on their website can be seen in Fig. 36.1. However, the file-sharing community is still alive and well thanks to the many other providers of this type of software and services, such as FrostWire, BearShare, BitTorrent, and dozens of others.

36.1 WHAT IS PEER-TO-PEER FILE SHARING?

The basic premise of peer-to-peer file-sharing networks is to allow people who want to share files on their computer to freely connect with other persons of like mind without having to know anything about how the network operates or anything about other computers on the network.

Every computer in a file-sharing network can be both a client and a server, and the methods for connecting them together into one huge network are all handled by the file-sharing software. Figure 36.2 shows an example of what a file-sharing network looks like.

36.2 HOW IT WORKS

The first part of this chapter contains examples of file-sharing programs for the purpose of providing some background in this type of software. From a user's standpoint, peer-to-peer file sharing is no more complicated than finding and installing a software application. In this section two popular file-sharing programs are

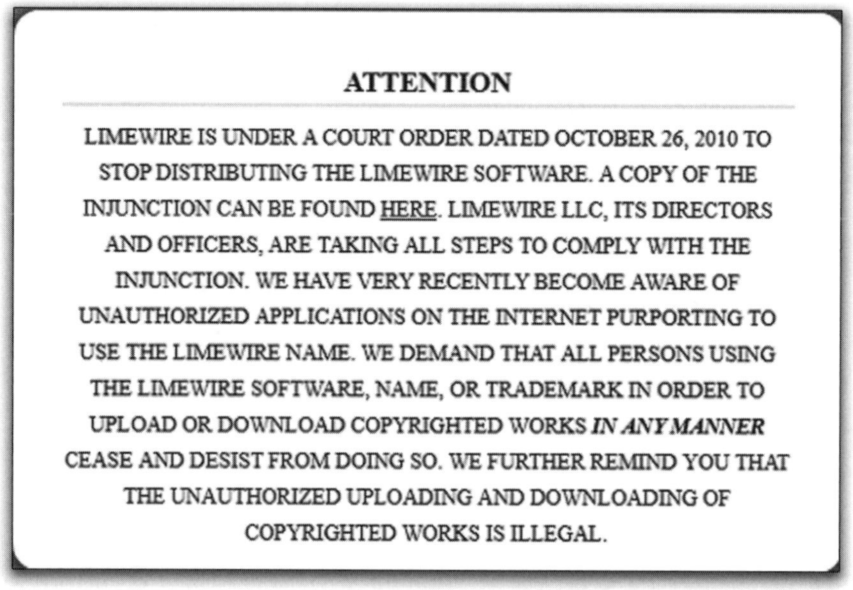

> ## ATTENTION
>
> LIMEWIRE IS UNDER A COURT ORDER DATED OCTOBER 26, 2010 TO STOP DISTRIBUTING THE LIMEWIRE SOFTWARE. A COPY OF THE INJUNCTION CAN BE FOUND HERE. LIMEWIRE LLC, ITS DIRECTORS AND OFFICERS, ARE TAKING ALL STEPS TO COMPLY WITH THE INJUNCTION. WE HAVE VERY RECENTLY BECOME AWARE OF UNAUTHORIZED APPLICATIONS ON THE INTERNET PURPORTING TO USE THE LIMEWIRE NAME. WE DEMAND THAT ALL PERSONS USING THE LIMEWIRE SOFTWARE, NAME, OR TRADEMARK IN ORDER TO UPLOAD OR DOWNLOAD COPYRIGHTED WORKS *IN ANY MANNER* CEASE AND DESIST FROM DOING SO. WE FURTHER REMIND YOU THAT THE UNAUTHORIZED UPLOADING AND DOWNLOADING OF COPYRIGHTED WORKS IS ILLEGAL.

FIGURE 36.1

When you visit the LimeWire home page, you see this notice

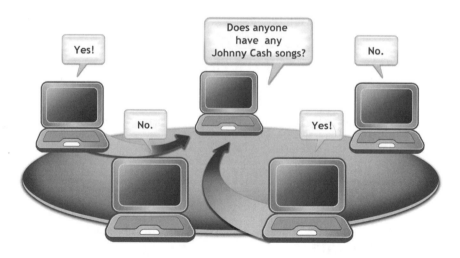

FIGURE 36.2

An example of a peer-to-peer network

FIGURE 36.3

The BearShare installation screen

examined, FrostWire and BearShare. One of the most simplistic of these programs is BearShare. The opening installation screen for BearShare is shown in Fig. 36.3.

During the installation process, the user is not asked much of anything. It does require that you create an account, but in testing, fake e-mail addresses (that do not exist) were found to work just fine. BearShare does not attempt to authenticate the e-mail address, or require that you respond to an e-mail to confirm that you are a real person using a valid e-mail address. Once the program installs, it will start automatically and the user can start downloading right away. The BearShare program is shown in Fig. 36.4.

36.2.1 It's all about sharing!

Since the whole purpose of file sharing is to share, BearShare does not ask the user if they want to share their files. It just assumes that to be the case. Also, these programs can make it very hard for a user to turn off file sharing by hiding the settings for file sharing deep in their menu systems, if the program allows file sharing to be turned off at all.

36.2.2 Using a file-sharing program

These programs are centered on searching for keywords for the content the user wants. For instance, a search for the keyword Johnny Cash is used in all of the programs selected for examples in this chapter.

FIGURE 36.4

The BearShare program screen showing search results

Name	Quality	#
Johnny Cash & Willie Nelson - Vh1 Storytellers	★★★★	18
Johnny Cash (Bootleg Volume 1 Personal File)Mp3	★★★★	26
Johnny Cash (Bootleg Volume 2) From Memphis To	★★★★	38
Johnny Cash - At Folsom Prison	★★★★	3
Johnny Cash - 1932-2003 Memorial Songbook.pdf	★★★★	7
Johnny Cash - 1969 - More of Old Golden Throat	★★★★	7
Johnny Cash - 2010 Icon.www.lokotorrents.com	★★★★	15
Johnny Cash - A Boy Named Sue (Beat	★★★★	5
Johnny Cash - Ain't No Grave.avi	★★★★	3
Johnny Cash - American III Solitary Man	★★★★	7

Johnny Cash (3083)

FIGURE 36.5

Search results in FrostWire

In this example all the user has to do is enter the keywords Johnny Cash and click on the search button to get a screen full of files that can be downloaded. Figures 36.4 and 36.5 show the results of the keyword search in BearShare and in FrostWire.

FIGURE 36.6

Selecting multiple files for download in FrostWire

What is interesting about both of these programs is the ability of the user to select multiple files at once and start downloading them all. This can lead to a user carelessly selecting files he doesn't really want to download, resulting in the possibility of unintentionally receiving contraband files, copyrighted music, and software on their computer. Since a user does not have to actively click on each download, the likelihood of that user carefully reading the file description information is decreased. When downloading from peer-to-peer networks like FrostWire, it is common for many of the downloads to be fake or low quality, or for the download process not to work at all.

This can encourage a user to select multiple files at once, as in the example shown in Fig. 36.6, where they could select dozens of Johnny Cash songs at once to increase their chances of getting the music they want.

36.3 PRIVACY AND SECURITY ISSUES WITH PEER-TO-PEER FILE SHARING

When a user is connected to a file-sharing network with this type of software, the program can share information without the user's knowledge, such as the files they are sharing and the Internet protocol address of the computer's Internet connection.

Many users do not understand that careless installation of file-sharing software can put their personal information at risk. While doing the research for this chapter, personal tax returns, personal and business financial statements, tax ID numbers, contracts, legal settlement offers, and other personal documents that people are sharing on the peer-to-peer network were downloaded. This illustrates that using this kind of software can expose a user's personal information to the world even when they do not intend to share anything at all.

36.4 PEER-TO-PEER NETWORK EVIDENCE

A great many cases involving child pornography stem from law enforcement personnel gathering evidence via the peer-to-peer networks. The Internet Crimes Against Children (ICAC) task force is aggressively funding federal, state, and local law enforcement agencies to enable them to perform investigations of child abuse including peer-to-peer network investigations of the distribution and receipt of child pornography.

In the fiscal year of 2008 and the first three quarters of fiscal year 2009, the ICAC trained 58,000 law enforcement personnel and 4,032 prosecutors. During that same time period ICAC investigations led to over 6,400 arrests. The ICAC program today is a national network of more than 3,000 federal, state, and local law enforcement agencies.[1]

In addition to contraband material investigations, the Recording Industry Association of America (RIAA) has been aggressively pursuing persons sharing copyrighted music via the peer-to-peer networks for several years now and has filed thousands of lawsuits against file sharers.

Investigators and law enforcement agencies collect evidence during peer-to-peer investigations using various tools and techniques, some designed specifically for the purpose of locating files and gathering evidence about sharing computers.

36.4.1 Investigating file-sharing networks

Suppose you were interested in locating people who are sharing particular files. How would you go about finding out if those files were present on the peer-to-peer network and then how would you go about locating the source of those files?

If you wanted to find a particular file on the peer-to-peer network, you would develop a special software application that could search for files, not just by keyword, but also by the SHA1 hash. Hash values are covered in Chapters 4 and 26.

The SHA1 hash is like a fingerprint for a file. If you find a file on the network with a SHA1 hash matching your file of interest, you could be confident that the file had been present on the network at some point.

Another file-sharing program, Phex, shows how easy it is to find information about someone's file sharing. In Fig. 36.7, the search results window in Phex is

FIGURE 36.7

A view of the Phex peer-to-peer software showing the SHA1 value of the file and the Sharing Host IP address

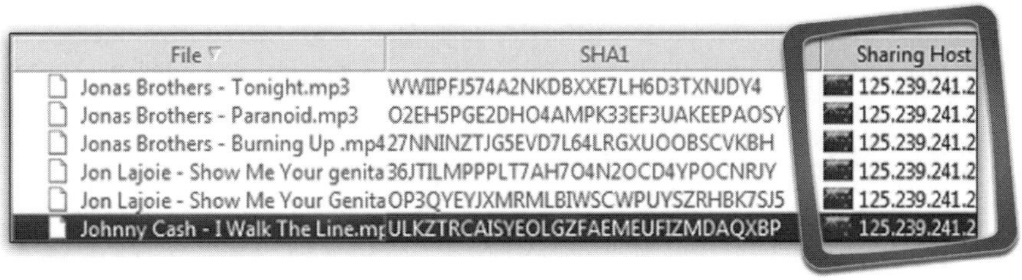

FIGURE 36.8

A view of the Phex peer-to-peer software after executing the *Browse Host* command to see other files being advertised for sharing

shown for the keyword Johnny Cash. The sharing host gives the IP address of the Internet connection in use by the computer sharing the files. The SHA1 column gives the hash value of the file being shared.

The highlighted file matches (in this imaginary scenario) the SHA1 you are looking for.

Now that you have located a matching file, your next step is to see if the computer sharing the file is in an area of interest to you.

The Sharing Host IP address here is the key. You can find out who owns the IP address by using tools available for looking up this information, such as the lookup tools provided by websites like DNS Stuff (www.dnsstuff.com). This will typically lead to an Internet service provider like Time Warner, Verizon, or some other company that provides Internet access to consumers.

Meanwhile you might want to see if the computer sharing the one file has other files you are interested in. In Phex and many other file-sharing programs you can request that the program perform a *Browse Host* to see what other files that particular computer is sharing. However, bear in mind that even performing a *Browse Host* on a particular IP address is not a guarantee that the files listed are actually available to be downloaded. The results of a *Browse Host* command executed using the Phex file-sharing program are shown in Fig. 36.8.

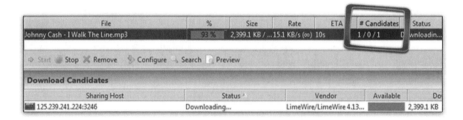

FIGURE 36.9

A view of the Phex peer-to-peer software downloading a file of interest from a single host

In order to verify that the file of interest really is on the computer, a step that can be taken is to perform a direct download of a file from a particular sharing computer. Care must be taken to ensure that the file is downloaded only from the single host to verify that the file actually came from that host IP address. Figure 36.9 shows a file being downloaded only from the host computer of interest.

In Fig. 36.9, note that the # Candidates is shown as one / zero / one, meaning that the file is being downloaded from the single host and is not being assisted by other sharing computers.

However, it is important to remember that all of the evidence you have gathered in this scenario does not lead necessarily to an individual person, even if you can locate the physical address of the Internet subscriber assigned to the IP address at the time of the investigation. You would still need to locate the individual computer and perform a forensic examination to verify that the files are on the hard drive and that the files were in fact downloaded by the individual of interest.

36.1 SOME OTHER DUDE DID IT

A man was arrested for downloading child pornography on his girlfriend's laptop computer using LimeWire. The computer was examined by law enforcement personnel and subsequently by the defense expert. The defense expert examined the hard drive and located the child pornography files along with the timeline of when the files were downloaded. He also examined the user profile information under which the downloads were made. It was discovered that the defendant did not have a password to access the profile that was logged in during the downloading and that the file-sharing program was installed under this password-protected user profile. The accused did have a user profile on the computer that was not password protected. However, the accused's profile had not been logged on for some months prior to the downloading of the child pornography. Based on other evidence, it was learned that the accused did not have possession of the computer during the time in which the downloads occurred. This was a clear-cut case of a revenge setup, and all of the child pornography charges against the defendant were dropped.

> **WARNING**
>
> We want to emphasize that the example scenario in this chapter is oversimplified and that the actual investigation of a peer-to-peer file-sharing case is complicated and must be analyzed on both sides with care to ensure that the evidence is authentic and verifiable.
>
> Cases like the one shown in the case study tend to be the exception rather than the rule in file-sharing cases involving contraband files. And in many cases the evidence seems insurmountable when someone is arrested for downloading contraband files via the file-sharing networks. Even though evidence presented by a law enforcement examiner might seem cut and dried to someone not familiar with how peer-to-peer networking operates, depending on the claims made, the interpretation of peer-to-peer evidence in a case can have a significant impact on the outcome of the case. As with any form of digital evidence being presented, the evidence should be properly verified and not viewed in isolation without considering all of the facts that may come to light if the evidence is reviewed by another examiner. Based on experience as examiners in hundreds of cases, we have found that proper interpretation of evidence in light of the totality of the circumstances is a critical aspect of handling cases involving electronic evidence.

SUMMARY

In this chapter we looked at peer-to-peer networking and how it works. We discussed some of the privacy issues related to peer-to-peer file sharing and how evidence is gathered using information revealed to the public by file-sharing software.

Reference

[1] Criminal Justice Collaboration Portal, *Internet Crimes Against Children Task Force*. <https://www.thecjportal.org/ICAC/Pages/ICACTFP.aspx>, 2011 (accessed 11.04.30).

Cell Phones

37

INFORMATION IN THIS CHAPTER:

- The fragile nature of cellular evidence
- Forensic acquisition methods for cellular phones
- Subscriber identity module (SIM) cards
- Cell phone backup files
- Advanced cell phone data analytics
- The future of cell phone forensics

INTRODUCTION

The 2010 United States Census reported that the population of the United States was 308,745,538.[1] The CIA *World Factbook* reported that in 2009 there were approximately 286,000,000 cell phone subscriptions in the United States alone. That is getting close to one cell phone for every man, woman, and child in the United States. The *World Factbook* also reports that there are over 4.8 billion cell phone subscriptions worldwide.[2] With numbers like these, it is no surprise that cell phones have become a common form of evidence in cases.

In addition to their sheer numbers, cell phones have become progressively more complex with the passage of time. Cell phones can store more data and perform more functions than ever before. Today's smart phones can perform functionalities that were only possible with a computer a handful of years ago. Ultimately, this increase in complexity means that people tend to use their cell phones for more and more functions. In many ways, the cell phone, once a luxury, is quickly becoming the communications hub and mobile office for people all over the world. In turn, the more functions someone can perform with a phone, the more data that phone stores.

Cell phones are made by numerous manufacturers, and come in thousands of different models. Between the different cables used to connect cell phones to chargers and computers, different file systems, device-specific applications and services, and proprietary operating systems, the forensic examination of cell phones becomes reliant on the use of an entire toolbox of examination methods, forensic software, and forensic hardware. There is no one-size-fits-all method for handling cell phones when it comes to forensic acquisitions and examinations of the data stored on these devices.

37.1 **THE FRAGILE NATURE OF CELLULAR EVIDENCE**

It is important to remember that cell phones do not operate in the same way as computers do. When your cell phone is powered on and has service, it is constantly receiving new data. On modern cell phones, there is a constant stream of data such as phone calls, text messages, e-mail, Twitter updates, and Facebook updates, along with pushed data from various other applications the user may have installed on the handset.

Depending on the make and model of the phone and whether or not supplemental storage is installed on the phone, many cell phones can store only a limited amount of information, which means that as new data is received on your phone, the oldest data is being deleted. This is true whenever the phone reaches the limit on a particular storage area. For instance, many phones limit the number of text messages to a fixed amount. If the phone can store a maximum of 100 text messages, when the 101st message comes in, the oldest message is automatically deleted. This works a lot like a conveyor belt that can only hold a limited number of items, as shown in Fig. 37.1.

If there is a possibility of data being deleted as new data is coming into the phone, the evidence on that cell phone is not being preserved. This is why the first and most important step in the acquisition and examination of cell phones is to isolate the cell phone from any networks it might connect to. This includes the cellular network, Bluetooth, wireless networks (WiFi), and infrared connections. By isolating the phone from all networks, the cell phone is prevented from receiving any new data that would cause other data to be deleted. This illustrates how the data on cell phones is fragile due to the nature of the way cell phones operate. Even if the cell phone is isolated from the networks correctly, the data can still be damaged or lost through an improper examination of the cell phone. The following section covers how a cell phone is isolated from networks, the different methods of cell phone data acquisition and examination, and some of the ways we have seen acquisitions performed incorrectly.

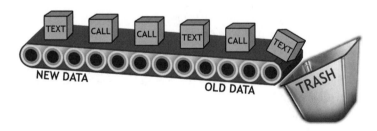

FIGURE 37.1

A conveyor belt showing new information coming on the conveyor, with the oldest information falling off

37.1.1 **Protecting cell phone evidence**

Like all digital evidence, the data on cell phones must be protected from being changed or destroyed during the examination process that can occur if the cell phone is allowed to connect to a cellular network. To do this, a cell phone must be isolated from all networks to prevent the phone from sending or receiving. This is usually handled by using a Faraday bag to block radio signals to or from the phone. Figure 37.2 shows a phone inside a Faraday bag for isolation during an exam.

A Faraday bag blocks any signals that a cell phone might pick up by blocking electrical fields and radio frequencies. A microwave uses this same technology, utilizing a Faraday cage to contain the radio frequency generated by the magnetron within the cooking chamber. A cell phone can also be isolated from any networks by wrapping the phone in radio frequency shielding cloth and placing the phone into Airplane mode. These are the most common methods of isolating a cell phone from any networks it might connect to. There are others, but whatever methods are used to block the cell phone's signal, they need to comply with best forensic practices and be recognized as a viable solution by the digital forensics community.

37.2 **FORENSIC ACQUISITION METHODS FOR CELLULAR PHONES**

There are three types of forensic acquisition or collection methods for cellular phones: logical, physical, and/or manual. Depending on the type of acquisition

FIGURE 37.2

A phone being examined while inside a Faraday bag

performed on a cell phone, the amount and type of evidence that can be collected will vary due to the limitations that may be imposed by the method being used.

37.2.1 Logical acquisitions

Logical acquisitions of cell phones are performed using cell phone forensic software. A logical acquisition typically only recovers data on a cell phone that is not deleted. Depending on the phone and the forensic tools used, some or all of the data might be able to be acquired. For instance, where only some of the data can be acquired, this means that the text messages, contact list, and call history might be acquirable using the cell phone forensics tools, but the images and ringtones are not. Even if only existing data can be captured from a cell phone, there are good reasons for performing a logical acquisition instead of simply taking pictures of the information on the phone from the device itself. When a logical acquisition is performed, the data can be preserved in stasis and the phone returned to the custodian to which it belongs. You would then have a snapshot in time of the cell phone evidence as it existed when the acquisition was performed, which preserves that evidence and also allows for verification. Some cell phone forensic tools allow multiple phones to be added to one case, which allows the data from multiple phones to be compared using graphs and diagrams. Examples of this are included later in this chapter. If a logical acquisition is not performed, then the possibility of performing these analysis functions is off the table.

Although it is uncommon, it is possible to get deleted data when performing a logical acquisition. This only applies to phones where the unallocated space on the phone can be acquired as if it were a logical file. This allows an examiner to carve out information from the unallocated space that might be of interest in a case.

37.2.2 Physical acquisitions

Physical acquisitions of cell phones are also performed using cell phone forensic software. A physical acquisition of a cell phone is the acquisition of the data at the hardware level. In other words, a physical acquisition is able to acquire all of the data present on a device, regardless of the file system, operating system, or other factors that act as limitations when performing a logical acquisition. If a physical acquisition is possible, this is almost always the best option when acquiring cell phone evidence. Physical acquisitions are able, in almost every situation, to get all the types of data from a cell phone, and also the unallocated space. An examiner can then carve out deleted information from the unallocated space. An example of this is shown in Fig. 37.3. For more information on unallocated space and deleted data carving, see Chapter 29.

37.2.3 Manual examinations

With cell phones, a physical acquisition is usually the best option, and logical acquisitions are the second best option. Manual examinations should be the last

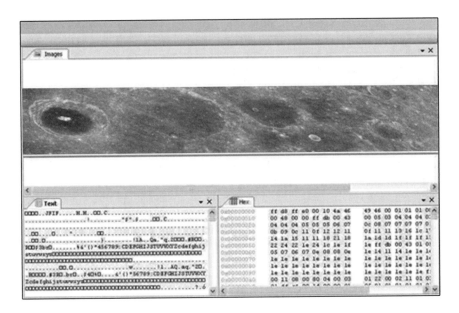

FIGURE 37.3

Carving an image file out of unallocated space on a cell phone, from a physical acquisition evidence file

option when performing a forensic acquisition of a cell phone. A manual examination introduces a greater degree of risk than the previous acquisition methods in the form of human error. With physical and logical acquisitions, the manipulation of the actual cell phone from the keypad and menu on the device is minimal. With a manual acquisition, the entire process must be performed using the keypad and menu to navigate through the cell phone.

When you get a new cell phone, it can be difficult to operate at first since there is a learning curve associated with getting familiar with the keypad, menu, and other ways to manipulate the controls of the phone. The chance of you accidentally creating evidence, such as accidentally hitting a speed dial button and creating a call attempt, is greater. The chance of deleting evidence is also greater; for example, you might accidentally delete a text message instead of just viewing the next one as you intended.

A correctly performed manual examination will reduce the risks of modifying the original evidence. With correct procedures and thorough documentation, a manual examination is a viable option when acquiring cell phone evidence. The quality of a manual cell phone examination really depends on the competency of the examiner; if correct procedures and thorough documentation are not part of the manual examination, it can call into question whether or not the evidence was actually preserved, or if any tampering, intended or otherwise, occurred during the examination of the cell phone.

A manual examination of a cell phone typically involves an examiner manipulating the cell phone to the different areas of information, such as text messages or call history, and taking pictures of the screen with a camera. While this is viewed as acceptable by some members of the digital forensics community, to others this is not enough.

Pictures only tell part of the story; what could have happened during the time between the individual pictures being taken? Pictures alone do not provide any real verification that the phone evidence has not been modified or tampered with. The only way to make a truly verifiable manual examination of a cell phone is to also record the process using a digital video camera running continuously throughout the process with no breaks, pauses, or edits. The video should begin before the phone is taken out of the secure evidence container and should be powered on in view of the camera. At the end of the examination, the phone should be powered down in view of the camera and placed back into a secure evidence container.

37.3 SUBSCRIBER IDENTITY MODULE (SIM) CARDS

Some phones have Subscriber Identity Module (SIM) cards in them. SIM cards can contain a significant amount of data, such as text messages and contact lists, as well as the last numbers dialed on the cell phone. A SIM card should be examined using a SIM card reader that meets forensic standards in conjunction with forensics software that is capable of acquiring data from a SIM card. Figure 37.4 is a view of a SIM card.

37.3.1 Media cards (removable storage cards)

Many cell phones today have expansion slots in them designed to accommodate a Secure Digital card (SD Card) as shown in Fig. 37.5. Usually they accommodate a small version of a SD card, called a microSD card. Users would purchase one of these cards and place it in their phones if they wanted to be able to store additional data. SD cards can be examined as if they were a tiny hard drive. They need to be write-protected just like a hard drive during the acquisition process for evidence preservation. If an SD card is present, it is possible to recover any form of deleted data that might have been saved to the SD card. Media cards are formatted and act just like computer hard drives when storing data. The presence of a media card almost guarantees that some level of deleted data recovery is possible. Figure 37.5 shows some of the different types of storage cards available.

37.4 CELL PHONE BACKUP FILES

Many cell phones can interface with a computer in order to transfer data and create backup files. Backup files can be an excellent source of evidence. For instance, backup files for a Blackberry or iPhone can contain almost all of the data that exists

FIGURE 37.4

A SIM card

SD (Secure Digital) Card

FIGURE 37.5

Different types of SD cards

on the phone. With an iPhone, if you have the proper tools to analyze the backup file, you can actually see more information than you would from just the phone itself.

An iPhone backup can also contain both deleted and existing text messages and e-mails. The backup file even contains the voicemails from the iPhone. The amount of data stored in the backup files of many phones today can provide a significant amount of data relating to almost everything a user does with their phone.

37.5 ADVANCED CELL PHONE DATA ANALYTICS

Sometimes all you need in a case is the information contained on one phone. However, incidents involving cell phones usually do not happen in isolation. Since the purpose of cell phones is to communicate with others, it can be worthwhile to see how multiple phones interacted with one another as it relates to a particular case.

Cell phone forensic software has the capability of saving the collected cell phone data in a file that can be later imported into cell phone forensic analysis software. For instance, one of the tools used for this chapter, Susteen's svProbe, can import cell phone data files collected from multiple cell phone forensic software tools.

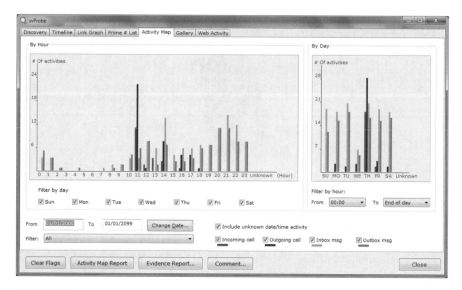

FIGURE 37.6

Susteen SecureView2 with svProbe showing call activity times at a certain date and time

This capability allows examiners to bring cell phone data from multiple users into a single case for advanced analysis of call traffic, timeline analysis, and call activity between two or more cell phones.

For example, imagine you had a client accused of running a drug ring because he was supposed to be the controller of the street dealers. Being able to visually see the call history activity between your client and the people he was communicating with could be very useful. Analysis of the cell phones in the case to show who was calling whom, and how frequently calls were made and for what duration, could support the argument that your client was not the controller at all. Figures 37.6 and 37.7 are example screenshots of advanced cell phone analysis using Susteen's svProbe software.

37.6 THE FUTURE OF CELL PHONE FORENSICS

Cell phone capability is expanding not only in response to consumer dependency for more powerful and multifunctional phones but also due to pressure placed on the market by Apple and Google with their iOS and Android operating systems.

Consumers have proven that they want a miniature computer in their pocket by voting with their pocketbooks.

As cell phones continue to progress in capability and complexity, the recoverable data from a cell phone is expanding almost on a monthly basis. Cell phones today contain not only the information you would expect to get such as call history,

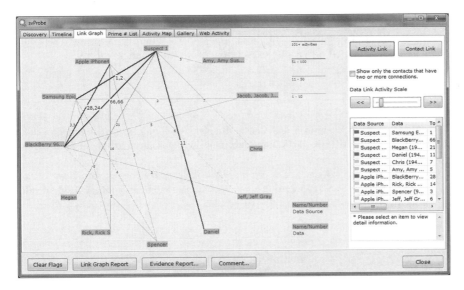

FIGURE 37.7

A diagram that depicts call activity between multiple phones

contact lists, and pictures, but also may contain office documents, social media data, voice mail, recorded conversations, recorded voice notes, and the list goes on.

The future of evidence recovery from cell phones will only grow as phones begin to replace computers. This will help the forensic examiner as the number of unique operating systems on phones today begins to consolidate into fewer standardized operating systems. Much like the computer industry, which has settled on three primary operating systems, Windows, Mac OS, and Linux/UNIX, the day is coming when cell phones will be in the same place and the vast majority of phones will be running the Apple iOS, Google Android, or Windows Mobile operating systems.

A smaller number of operating systems will allow forensic tool vendors to create ever more powerful extraction tools that can get more information from more phones on a consistent basis. The major cell phone forensic tools are covered in Chapter 5.

SUMMARY

In this chapter we looked at the methods for handling and preserving cell phone evidence and some of the issues with improper preservation of cell phones. We also discussed the types of evidence that can be recovered from a cell phone along with some of the different types of storage options available for cell phones that enhance the ability to recover deleted information. We looked at the advantages of getting cell phone backup files and the evidence those files can contain. We also looked at advanced cell phone analytics and learned how this technology can allow multiple phones to be connected into a single overview of multiple caller activity.

References

[1] P.M. Mackam, S.W. Wilson, US Census Bureau, *Population distribution and change: 2000 to 2010* (C2010BR-01). <http://www.census.gov/prod/cen2010/briefs/c2010br-01.pdf>, 2010.

[2] Central Intelligence Agency, *The World Factbook: Country comparison: Telephones – mobile cellular* (ISSN 1553-8133). <https://www.cia.gov/library/publications/the-world-factbook/rankorder/2151rank.html>, (n.d.).

Video and Photo Evidence 38

INFORMATION IN THIS CHAPTER:

- The most critical steps in the forensic examination of video and photo evidence
- Using video and photo evidence in cases

INTRODUCTION

The forensic examination of videos and images first requires that the evidence be collected properly, and requested properly. For information on how to get the evidence in the best possible way, and other supplemental information that can be critical in the examination of video and image evidence, refer to Chapter 18. Video and image evidence must be handled with great care, and any examinations or enhancements performed must be thoroughly documented. If the evidence is not received in the most viable format and preserved correctly, or if the examiner does not perform the forensic examination properly, it is possible to jeopardize the evidence.

38.1 THE MOST CRITICAL STEPS IN THE FORENSIC EXAMINATION OF VIDEO AND PHOTO EVIDENCE

It is critical that an examiner thoroughly document her work when performing video and photo examinations. One of the cornerstones of forensic methodology is that a process or examination method must be repeatable. If thorough documentation is not kept, it will hinder another examiner from being able to duplicate his work. An examiner should also understand how her video and photo enhancement tools work. If an examiner does not, then it is a plausible that the examiner could damage the evidence by adding visual information that is not in the original image when enhancing it.

38.1.1 Documentation

Documentation is paramount when examining video and photo evidence. The Law Enforcement/Emergency Services Video Association explains the necessity of proper and thorough documentation as follows:

> *The best way to ensure the reliability of the video evidence is to have standard operating procedures (SOPs) in place. SOPs assist the forensic video analyst in*

maintaining proper records of the processes used to examine the evidence and that the processes are performed in a scientifically appropriate and uniformed manner. Records should be complete enough that a similarly experienced and trained individual, working with the same technology, could reproduce similar results.[1]

Just as with computer evidence, examiners dealing with video and photo enhancement needs to document everything they do in the process of their examination so that another expert can duplicate the results. Without this documentation, it would be extremely difficult and inefficient for another examiner to duplicate the results, if it could be done at all. Improper documentation also calls into question the viability of what the examiner produces in forensic analysis or enhancement, as the improper handling of video and image evidence can create visual information that did not exist in the original video or image, known as artifacts.

An example of how the workflow of the enhancement of video or photo evidence should be documented is shown in sequential steps in Figs 38.1 through 38.7. With this information it would be possible for another examiner to duplicate the work exactly as the original examiner performed it.

38.1.2 Knowing how your tools work

An examiner who performs video or photo forensics should be able to explain what functions the tools they are using actually perform. If an examiner cannot do this, it calls into question whether or not he manipulated the image to show something that is not actually present in the original image. For example, many tools used in the enhancement of videos and photos allow for functions that increase the sharpness of the image, contrast, color correction, and so forth. If these enhancements are performed using a digital "brush" and painted on areas of the image, it can create detail that does not exist if applied incorrectly or too heavily. Figure 38.8 shows how an improperly enhanced image can distort the original and add additional information that was not present in the original.

Photoshop CS4 brush tools were used to enhance the picture of his face to try and pull out more detail. The brush tools were used in a manner that is not forensically sound, and as a result visual information has been created in the image that is not in the original. Notice that in the brushed image it looks as if Lars could have facial hair in this image, when in the original image he is actually clean shaven.

Similarly, if a filter performs functions such as sharpening to enhance an entire image or video at once, it can create artifacts and other detail in the image that does not exist in the original. This effect is shown in Fig. 38.9, which shows the same picture as seen in the previous figure. The image on the right was enhanced using filters in a method that is not forensically sound. If you look at his wrist, you can see that false visual information was created on the enhanced image. It now looks as if he could be wearing a watch or other item on his wrist. If this image was from a criminal incident, and a watch was of interest as an identifying item, this improper enhancement of the image could cause someone to believe that Lars was wearing that watch.

Enhancement Workflow
The exact workflow used to enhance the video images and individual frames is as follows:

Video Segments
The following workflow was used on all of the video segments which were enhanced.

1. The video segment was opened in Adobe Photoshop CS4 Extended and placed on a *Video Layer*.
2. The video was then cropped in dimension to include the viewable area of the screen containing the surveillance footage to be enhanced and analyzed.
3. The footage in the video segment was then enlarged using dimensional constraints in order to retain the fidelity of the image in height and width.
4. The adjustment layer *Vibrance And Saturation* was used with the following settings: Vibrance: +43, Saturation: +17.

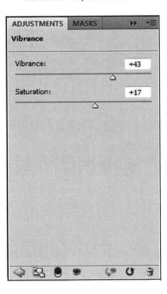

FIGURE 38.1

Video enhancement workflow sequence: overview

The necessity for examiners to understand how their tools work might seem like common sense, but it is often the case that they do not. If an expert cannot explain how his tools work, then in all probability he is not qualified to testify when it comes to the video or photo evidence.

38.2 USING VIDEO AND PHOTO EVIDENCE IN CASES

The most common usage of video and photo evidence in cases is either to attempt to identify a person or to capture a piece of evidence such as a license plate number

1. A *Curves* adjustment layer was used with the following output and input paths:

For the bottom value (box on the line closest to the bottom left) the values are Output: 67 and Input: 97. For the top value (box on the line closest to the top right) the values are Output: 186 and Input: 179.

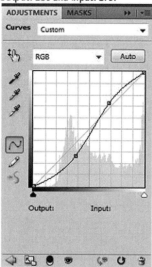

2. A *Brightness/Contrast* adjustment layer was used with the following settings:
   Brightness: 42 and Contrast: -12

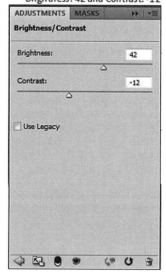

FIGURE 38.2

Video enhancement workflow sequence: curves adjustment

1. A *Color Balance* adjustment layer was used with the following settings: Shadows: no adjustment, highlights: no adjustment, and Midtones with the color adjustments as depicted below:

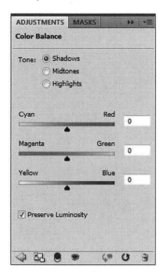

2. A *Photo Filter* adjustment layer was used with the following settings: Cooling Filter (80) with a density of 7% and luminosity preserved.

FIGURE 38.3

Video enhancement workflow sequence: color balance and photo filter

1. An *Unsharp Mask* Smart Filter was placed on the video layer. The *Unsharp Mask* smart filter was used with the following settings: Amount: 250%, Radius: 8.5 Pixels, and Threshold: 0.

2. The video files were then exported using the *Render Video* function in Adobe Photoshop CS4 Extended in .MOV file format.

The layer order for the video layer and adjustment layers is as follows:

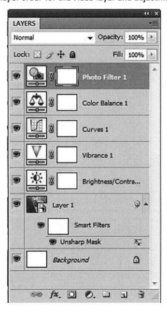

FIGURE 38.4

Video enhancement workflow sequence: unsharp mask with layers

Enhancement of Video Frame at Time 00:00:00 On Camera 3

The following workflow was used on the video frame, found at time 10:40:53 on Camera 5. This frame was copied from the video and opened in Photoshop CS4 Extended. The following workflow was used to enhance the image.

1. A *Photo Filter* adjustment layer was used with the following settings: *Warming Filter* (85) with a density of 25% and luminosity preserved.

FIGURE 38.5

Video enhancement workflow sequence: enhancement of video frame

or an object like a vehicle. In cases where there is surveillance video of a vehicle that may be suspected of being used in a robbery or murder, or a vehicle involved in a police pursuit, or traffic accident, identifying the vehicle's make, model, color, and other features can be a big help. Working with photographs as evidence when the photo has been edited poses many challenges, including how much of the photo may have been altered and in what manner. If the original is available, a comparison of the original unaltered photo to the allegedly altered photo is the best means of detecting changes. However, in many cases, the original is not available and the detection must rely on an expert who can spot artifacts created by altering a photo or other image. The following section shows some of the ways that photos or videos can be altered by a skilled graphics artist and how the changes can be detected.

38.2.1 Enhancing an image or video

The most obvious way to use video and photo evidence is in the enhancement of these forms of evidence to aid in the determination of whether or not the video or

1. A *Color Balance* adjustment layer was used. The adjustments made are depicted in the screenshots below.

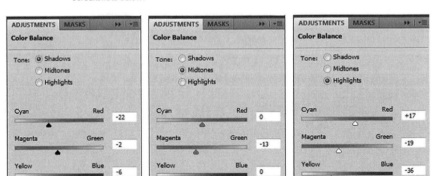

3. A *Curves* adjustment layer was used with the following output and input paths:

For the bottom value (box on the line closest to the bottom left) the values are Output: 72 and Input: 86. For the top value (box on the line closest to the top right) the values are Output: 171 and Input: 165.

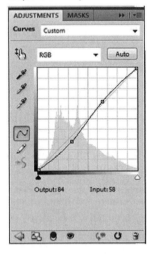

FIGURE 38.6

Video enhancement workflow sequence: color and curves adjustment

4. The adjustment layer *Vibrance And Saturation* was used with the following settings: Vibrance: +54, Saturation: +55.

5. A copy of the video frame was made. This layer was then inverted and lowered to 15% opacity. This layer was above the video frame layer in order.

6. An *Unsharp Mask* filter was used on the video frame layer with the following settings: Amount: 250%, Radius: 8.0 pixels, and Threshold: 3 Levels.

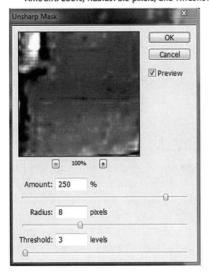

FIGURE 38.7

Video enhancement workflow sequence: adjusting vibrance and saturation, and using an unsharp mask filter

ORIGINAL IMAGE   **BRUSHED IMAGE**

FIGURE 38.8

A low-resolution picture of Lars carrying a toilet from a remodeling job for a church-related project

image evidence is of any interest. Enhancement can be performed to aid in the identification of a person of interest, and items of interest within the environment can be displayed in a video or photo. It is also possible to determine that the evidence cannot be enhanced enough to be relevant.

38.2.2 Determining the authenticity of a video or image

Many of the same tools that allow for videos and images to be enhanced or examined can also be used to create falsified images or videos. Programs such as Adobe Photoshop and Adobe Premier are available to the public and are powerful editing programs. A skilled operator of these types of image and video editing programs can create convincing fakes of images and videos. A faked image can come in the form of counterfeit money, documents, and pictures of persons who are not actually in the original picture. Usually, fakes are not created completely from scratch, but are instead composites and modifications of already existing videos or images. However, adding visual information to a video or image, or taking it away, makes it as much a fake as one intentionally made by a scam artist. Even the most convincing faked images and videos can display telltale signs of modification that a skilled examiner should be able to identify and explain in details the methods used

ORIGINAL IMAGE   **IMAGE AFTER FILTERS**

FIGURE 38.9

Image enhanced using filters

to create the fake. Adnan Hajj, a photographer, made the news in 2006 for modifying images he took for Reuters of an Israeli air raid on Beirut:

> *Mr. Hajj, a Lebanese photographer based in the Middle East, may not be familiar to many newspaper readers. But thanks to the swift justice of the Internet, he has been charged, tried and convicted of improperly altering photographs he took for Reuters. The pictures ran on the Reuters news service on Saturday, and were discovered almost instantly by bloggers to have been manipulated. Reuters then announced on Sunday that it had fired the freelancer. Executives said yesterday that they were still investigating why they had not discovered the manipulation before the pictures were disseminated to newspapers.[2]*

In Fig. 38.10 the photo on the left is the image Adnan Hajj modified to make the smoke plumes caused by the air raid look more dramatic. If you look closely, you can see that parts of the smoke plume look exactly the same, which is a clear sign of tampering with an image. This type of modification is called "rubber stamping." Look for the small circular artifacts in the smoke plumes.[2]

In Fig. 38.11 the photo of Lars toting a toilet is again used as an example, this time of creating a fake photo through image editing with Photoshop. In the photo, the toilet has magically become a cash register!

FIGURE 38.10

A photo that has been tampered with

FIGURE 38.11

An example of a faked image

If we zoom in on the image and look at some of the details, we can see telltale signs that this is a fake image. Figures 38.12, 38.13, and 38.14 show some ways to detect that something was added to a photo after the fact, in this case, the cash register. In Fig. 38.12, compare the edges of the cash register to the edges of Lars' arm. Notice that the register has much sharper edges, which indicate that the image of the register was added into this image from a higher quality image.

In Fig. 38.13, the shadow under Lars' arm on the cash register is unnatural given the location of the light source.

FIGURE 38.12

An image that has been modified after the fact

LIGHT SOURCE

SHADOW ON CASH REGISTER FROM ARM

FIGURE 38.13

Unnatural shadows in an image

In Fig. 38.14, if we zoom in very close to a portion of Lars' arm, and compare that with a portion of the cash register, we can see that there are more pixels present in the image of the cash register. This is indicative of a merging of two images to make a fake, since one image is higher resolution than the other.

ARM - LOWER RESOLUTION   CASH REGISTER - HIGHER RESOLUTION

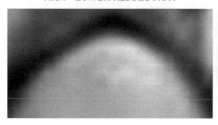 

FIGURE 38.14

Example of a merging of two images

38.2.3 Contesting unqualified claims to video or image evidence

A common scenario is that a person will claim, from video or photo evidence alone, that they can identify a person portrayed in an image or video. While this is possible if the video or image is of high enough quality and resolution, often in these situations the quality of the evidence is poor at best. An appropriate response to such claims is to have the images enhanced as much as they can be without damaging them, showing that the person depicted in the video or image evidence cannot be identified based solely upon those forms of evidence. Having a video and image expert write an affidavit or testify to this effect can be beneficial when it is applicable to a case.

SUMMARY

In this chapter we learned that video and photo evidence can be compromised if it is not handled properly in the process of being enhanced or analyzed by an examiner. We also learned that thorough documentation is critical when enhancing and examining video and image evidence so that another expert of similar training and experience can duplicate the work performed. We learned that a skilled examiner should know how his tools function so that he does not compromise evidence based upon inexperience or incompetence. We then learned how video and photo evidence can be used in cases.

References

[1] Law Enforcement/Emergency Services Video Association (LEVA), *Guidelines for the Best Practice in the Forensic Analysis of Video Evidence.* <http://www.leva.org/pdf/BestPractices forVideoEvidence.pdf>

[2] K.Q. Seeyle, J. Bosman, Bloggers Drive Inquiry on How Altered Images Saw Print. *The New York Times.* <http://www.nytimes.com/2006/08/09/technology/09photo.html>, 2006.

Databases

INFORMATION IN THIS CHAPTER:

- Databases in everyday life
- What is a database?
- Database files as evidence
- Database recovery
- Data as evidence

INTRODUCTION

Databases have been around as long as man has had a need to store and retrieve information. Beginning as simple lists of accounts and transactions to ledger books and finally to electronic form, databases are in many cases the number one data asset of a company or person. Databases are the underpinning for the financial, medical, securities, and commerce sections of the global economy. The ability to rapidly store and retrieve data as information is one of the greatest advances in computers in the modern age.

While businesses understand the value of databases, criminals also understand the value of the data stored in those databases. There is information about you in multiple databases in both the public sector and private sector, and probably many more databases than you might think possible. In this chapter we look at what databases are, a little about how they work, and finally, how they can contain evidence that can be a factor in criminal and civil cases.

39.1 DATABASES IN EVERYDAY LIFE

Basically every transaction or interaction with almost anything electronic in today's world results in a record being created. Even if the record does not contain any personal information about the individual, it will still be collected for analysis purposes.

However, that does not mean that anonymous data is without evidentiary value. It is just that data that contains personal data about people is of more immediate evidentiary value in many cases.

For instance, a hacker who breaks into a major online retailer is not going to be very interested in their analytical data, that is, their sales amounts or how many of which widget they sell. They will be going after the customer database to try to get credit card numbers and other personal information they can profit from either by using the data directly or by selling that data to someone else. Data theft is a lucrative business, and breaches of networks can result in some expensive litigation. While the biggest data compromises are typically via some form of online data breach where millions of records are stolen, the ways in which data can be compromised are as varied as the devices and methods used to store data; lost or stolen laptops, hard drives, and USB sticks account for lost data.

39.2 WHAT IS A DATABASE?

In its simplest form a database is a list of information that a person or entity would want to maintain. For instance, your checkbook register is a database of sorts. When you write a check, you make an entry in your check register to record the payee and the amount and date of the check. This would be the equivalent of adding a record in a database.

If you wanted to know where your money was going, you could then go and look in your check register and see that entry. That would be a very basic record retrieval, or query. In database terms, a query is nothing more than a question you ask to get information out of the database.

Finally, since you are very meticulous about your checking account, each time you make a new entry in your checkbook register, you add or subtract the amount of the transaction from your balance, giving you a new current balance. This is the equivalent in database terms of a summary report.

The sole purpose of database systems is to allow for fast and accurate storage and retrieval of records. With the introduction of computers, databases came into their own, allowing for massive storage of records, fast retrieval, and customized user interfaces for handling data input and output.

39.2.1 What is a database management system?

Our typical interaction with databases is through an end-user interface such as a website or an application that provides an interface or front end that allows a user to add, update, edit, and delete records in the database itself. It also provides tools for an application developer to write code to manipulate the data in the database. Database management systems include small desktop or workgroup database management systems like Microsoft Access, Alpha Five, or FileMaker, to name a few, where the software provides an easy-to-use program for handling all the functions of the database management including creating data entry forms, reports, and the table and record structure. The example checkbook database in this chapter was created using Microsoft Access 2010.

On a larger scale, enterprise-level database management systems are not fully integrated into a single application like a desktop Relational Database Management System (RDBMS). These include systems such as Oracle, Progress, Microsoft SQL Server, Sybase, MySQL, and the like. These systems are designed to handle extremely large data sets efficiently. To create an application using one of these RDBMS systems, the developer will typically use a third-party application development software program to create the part of the application the end user sees and uses.

39.2.2 **Modern databases**

This short discussion on modern databases is only for the purpose of giving a basic understanding of how modern database management systems look and work. Database management and design fills dozens or perhaps hundreds of books.

There are several types of database structures; however, computer-based database systems today primarily fall in the category of relational databases. A relational database system structure functions just as the name sounds. It is based on relationships between data.

Back to the checkbook register example. If you wanted to turn your checkbook register into a simple relational database, you would want to think about how it relates to you, the account holder, and how you relate to the transactions. Figure 39.1 is a simple relational diagram of a checkbook database. Each of the blocks is a table. Within each of the blocks are fields.

In Fig. 39.2 you see a screenshot of the checking account database with some data entered showing that Bob Smith has a checking account with Wells Fargo. Bob's Wells Fargo checking account has several transactions that look just like what he would have written into his check register.

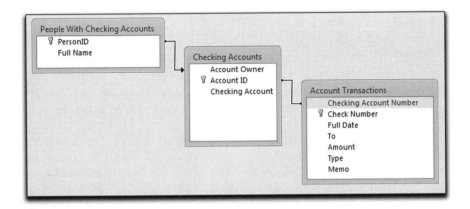

FIGURE 39.1

A relational diagram showing how people are related to accounts and accounts to transactions

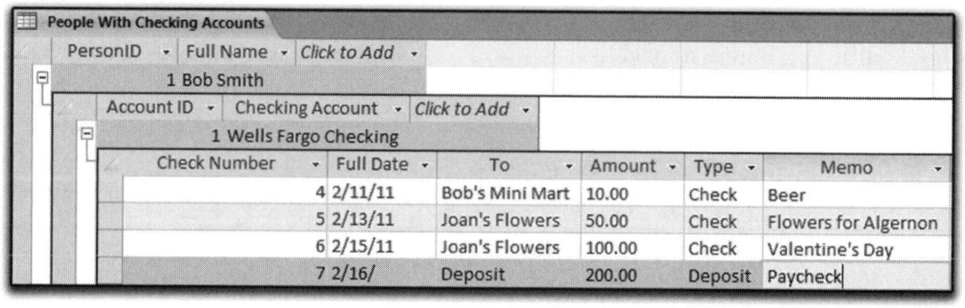

FIGURE 39.2

A simple database for a checking account without any frills

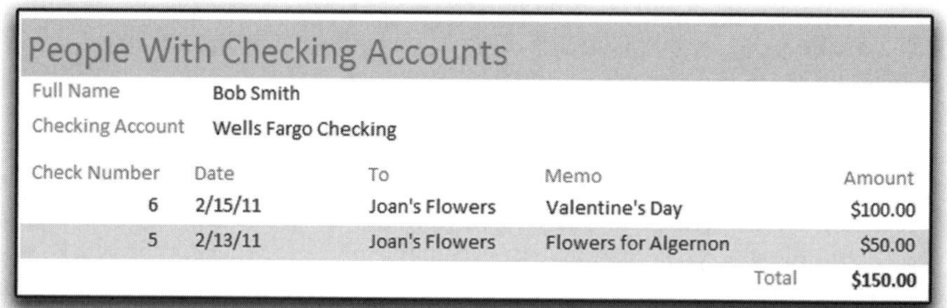

FIGURE 39.3

Report showing the amount spent on flowers extracted from the database

Here you have three tables:

- People with Checking Accounts
- Checking Accounts
- Account Transactions

Now that you are looking at the tables with data present, it is easy to see that these look a lot like spreadsheets with rows and columns where each row is a record and each column is a field. That is the basic structure of all databases: table, record, field.

What makes this a relational database is that instead of three spreadsheets that are all independent of each other, these spreadsheets are all related. That means getting data back out of the database for reporting is simple. If you want to know how much Bob spent on flowers, you can ask the database a question like, "Give me all checks where Bob spent money on flowers on the Wells Fargo account." The result of this question is shown in Fig. 39.3.

As you can see, relational databases are simple in concept. However, as they grow in complexity, they are far from simple. An enterprise-level database can contain thousands of tables and fields, and billions of records.

39.2.3 **Database formats**

Previously we looked at database structure. The database structure is the way the database handles data. Database formats are the actual file format of the database, the way it handles storage and retrieval of data internally.

There is a long list of database formats; some are very old in origin and are still in use today by various database management systems.

Each of the database formats has it own unique file structure, from some that split database tables into separate physical files and indexes, to those that maintain everything in a single large file.

39.3 **DATABASE FILES AS EVIDENCE**

Databases themselves pose some interesting problems from an evidence standpoint. If the data in the database can only be accessed by a proprietary system, then getting to the underlying data can be difficult.

There are still a great many database programs around that were designed for small-scale vertical market customers using older DOS (Disk Operating System) tools that also use older database formats such as Symantec's Q&A, Novell's Btrieve, or Ashton-Tate's Dbase II and III formats. These types of database formats can pose particular problems for an examiner if they are not familiar with the underlying format of the database and how it is organized and managed by an application.

One reason for this is that these particular database formats tend to be in separate files that are only connected by the application code of the program that is using them for storage. Unlike most modern database formats that encapsulate the data structure and relationships between tables internally in a single file, figuring out how to get data back out of these older formats can be a challenge.

One solution is to make sure you have access to the application that the user has on their computer for managing the database. Some examples of these types of applications are programs written for specialty contractors like landscapers, grading companies, jewelry stores, and pawn shops. These applications tend to be closely tied to the database in such a way that they cannot be separated and easily analyzed without the actual application, if at all.

In our simple example, even if all of the tables were in separate files, a database expert could probably figure out how to reconnect them and extract the data in a manner that is usable. In real situations, databases tend to be much more complex and have many more tables that would have to be reconnected to extract data.

It is rare that you would have the luxury of taking away someone's business computer to perform an analysis using their licensed software.

There are several reasons you may not be able to get the underlying structural information for a database application.

- The database structure documentation is lost or never existed in the first place.
- The documentation that can be found was several development generations ago.

- The database application is proprietary and the developer won't share the information.
- The company that developed the application is out of business.

In any case, if all you have is the database file or files, even if they are encapsulated in a single file like a SQL Server database or a Microsoft Access Database, the process of figuring out how the data is all related can be a daunting task.

The best solution in every case where the data is the evidence is to get it using the same application that the users have for generating reports and extracting data. Otherwise you are faced with what may be a long and expensive road for manually extracting and organizing the data into something you can use in a case. Even if you can use database design tools to reverse-engineer the database structure, the result will be incomplete to some degree. In order for a reverse-engineering tool to map the structure of a database, the database must be well designed, or the tool will fail when it cannot find the correct internal keys or connections in the database.

While using reverse-engineering tools may reduce the cost of figuring out the database structure, it will not be an easy process if the database application is very complex.

39.4 **DATABASE RECOVERY**

Depending on the database, there are various ways to get to evidence that may not be accessible via the user interface.

- Transaction Logs
  - These are logs that the database keeps in order to perform a rollback. A rollback can occur if a database detects an error condition and needs to roll back to a previous state to prevent data loss or corruption.
- Backups
  - Database backups can be a valuable source of historical evidence, especially if there is suspicion that someone has deleted records of interest from a database. By restoring the backups, it may be possible to locate the deleted data.
- Corrupted or Damaged Databases
  - If the only evidence available is a damaged or corrupted database file, all is not always lost. In many cases some or all of the data can be recovered. Database recovery becomes more likely as the type of database moves from the small desktop database to the large enterprise database. It stands to reason that enterprise databases tend to have better recovery tools because the cost of data corruption is so high compared to a small department database written in one of the desktop applications like Microsoft Access or FileMaker.

39.5 **DATA AS EVIDENCE**

In the majority of cases, the data is the evidence you are looking for; a patient record, a set of financial transactions, information about a person contained in a database, annual sales and profit information, a purchase made by someone—the list goes on.

This is the surface evidence. In other words, this is the evidence that may be the most important, but it is also the easiest to get if the only thing you need to do is to request that the data be produced and printed out as a report or screenshot.

The underlying data, or metadata, is also important. Metadata from a database standpoint is the information about the data records that may be of significant interest.

For instance, many database applications record information about changes to records in the database, but this information is not shown to the user as it is only saved for audit purposes and troubleshooting.

Metadata includes information about a record or transaction such as the date and time stamp when the record was changed and the name of the user who changed the record. Depending on the sophistication of the database application and regulatory and other requirements, these audit transactions may show historical record change information as well.

However, bear in mind that even if the audit trail contains this metadata for more than just the last change, it will probably not contain the contents of the changes as it creates a lot of overhead in the database to store the extra content.

Asking what metadata is saved as part of the database operation is very important in order to understand what, if any, transaction logs or audit logs can be obtained from the database administrator. In some cases, the database administrator will not be aware of exactly what the database application logs, as some of the logging is placed into the application to assist the programmers with debugging and troubleshooting.

Contact the person or company who programmed the database to find out what, if anything, they programmed into the application for their own maintenance and troubleshooting.

SUMMARY

In this chapter we learned about databases and database management systems. We examined a relational database and how the data is structured. We also looked at the methods and issues involved in getting evidence from databases and about the data itself in the form of database metadata. We also looked at the challenges presented by database applications and the need to use the same application the user has to get data out of a database system whenever possible.

Accounting Systems and Financial Software

40

INTRODUCTION

You have probably heard the phrase, "follow the money." This is true in all kinds of cases, from domestic disputes to Ponzi schemes and murder cases. Since so many people and businesses manage their money electronically today, there is a wealth of potential electronic evidence available residing anywhere from the Internet cache on a computer, to an e-mail attachment, inside an accounting program database, and even on a person's phone.

In this chapter we will look at some of the places and ways that financial information is stored, some of the analysis techniques, and some cases where financial information has played a factor.

40.1 ACCOUNTING AND MONEY MANAGEMENT PROGRAMS

Both individuals and businesses use accounting programs to track and manage their money. Accounting software ranges from packages designed for the home office business like QuickBooks, Peachtree, and DAC Easy, to mid-sized and enterprise-level business solutions like Microsoft Dynamics, SAP, and others.

Personal money management software is widely used by individuals to keep up with their home finances. Many of the major players in the small office/home office market for financial software also offer packages for personal money management that individuals and families use to record their expenses, track their credit card accounts, track their bank accounts, plan for their taxes, and plan for retirement.

There are even free services on the web for financial and personal money management like Mint.com (ww.mint.com).

40.2 PERSONAL MONEY MANAGEMENT SOFTWARE

Personal money management programs contain a lot of information about someone's personal financial habits. One of the things that make personal money management software very attractive from an evidence standpoint is the ability of the software to synchronize with the person's bank, downloading and storing all of the transactions made via the linked account to their online banking profile.

When this is the case, even if the records are no longer available via the bank, there is a chance these records can be retrieved from the individual's computer. Bear in mind that if the individual is using the account synchronization feature, these transactions can be obtained from the individual's computer without having to go through the process of obtaining the information from the third party via a subpoena.

The fact that personal money management software is an off-the-shelf type of application means that getting access to the software to analyze the data from a person's computer is normally easy to do.

40.3 BUSINESS ACCOUNTING SOFTWARE

One of the principles of good accounting practices in a business is to always have an audit trail that can be used to go back and see who did what in a transaction. This gives the accountant a way to check for transactions that are created by mistake, users who are making mistakes that have been corrected too many times, and also to look for potentially fraudulent transactions.

This is one of the most important features a software package can provide to forensic accountants. A forensic accountant is a specially trained person who performs an analysis of accounting transactions, processes, and procedures and audits the financial data to discover and document fraud or other potential issues. It is important to note that performing computer forensics on accounting software is not the same as the work of a forensic accountant. Where a computer forensic examiner who also knows accounting can be of assistance using transaction logs will be covered later in this chapter.

40.3.1 Small business accounting software

Depending on the version of the accounting software purchased, the audit trail feature may not be available.

For example, in Peachtree Accounting, the audit trail feature is only available in the Peachtree Complete Accounting versions and higher. If the user is not using one of the packages that support this feature, then the audit logs will not be available for analysis.

The other thing to bear in mind is that the audit-tracking feature in many of the programs can be turned off, rendering the feature useless.

40.3.2 Mid-level to enterprise accounting software

Accounting software packages used by larger companies and organizations will always have excellent auditing capabilities. This of course cannot account for whether or not an in-house developed solution would have such features. Unless the developer of an in-house or custom application is required to ensure compliance with regulatory requirements like Sarbanes-Oxley, it is possible that even a large company can be caught without proper safeguards in place. However, few businesses of any size would want to operate without such safeguards available to protect themselves against internal and external fraud.

40.4 GETTING THE EVIDENCE

As with any application that uses a database for storage—and all financial packages do—the simplest way to get the evidence is by using the software itself for the forensic analysis, not by digging it out via a forensic tool.

In many cases, making a copy of the databases for the accounting for financial software is an option, while getting the application that is used by the person or persons is not. One option in this case to make sure that the evidence is properly preserved is to either make a backup of the accounting database and forensically acquire the backup, or to forensically image the entire hard drive of the accounting computer or server that contains the database.

If this is the case and it is a commercially available package that is within a reasonable cost range, simply purchasing the exact product will allow the examiner to extract the data and provide it to a forensic accountant or to the person requesting the information.

However, if it is a large accounting package that would be prohibitive to reproduce by simply purchasing a copy of the software, then either the work may have to be done on site, or an examiner may have to extract data from the databases herself. Extracting financial information from databases where the examiner does not have the application is fraught with peril and can be extremely costly.

The peril in going forward with extracting data directly from the database for the accounting software is that the structure of the database may not be easy to plot out to make sure the correct tables and records are connected in the right way to accurately reflect the actual data.

In other words, if the examiner or expert cannot determine if the table of accounts is properly connected to the table of transactions, then it is possible to generate erroneous reports.

The good news is that electronic accounting systems operate in a manner very close to that of their paper predecessors. There will be a general ledger that has numbers for different types of account buckets and transactions, a general journal that keeps a record of the changes made, along with the typical information a book-keeper would enter into the system for accounting purposes.

So even if you do not have an audit trail, it is not impossible to reconstruct historical information from an accounting system database. It may be difficult and expensive, but it's possible.

Where such reconstruction starts to get weird, for lack of a better term, is when the database for the accounting software is written in one of the older formats that does not support a single file for the database. When this is the case, attempting to sort out how the data connects together can be a real challenge.

40.5 TYPES OF EVIDENCE FROM FINANCIAL SOFTWARE

Depending on the goal of the case, the evidence needed will vary. The type of evidence can be the database file itself, the file system metadata (the computer file system's recorded changes to the created, accessed, or modified times of the file itself), and even documents residing on the computer or server that holds printouts of reports in some other format.

The depth of the examination involves not only the accounting software, but other evidence, as we will discuss in the next section.

40.1 STOLEN ACCOUNT CASE

In this case, an employee was accused of stealing an account away from his employer when he left the company to work independently. A complete forensic image of the employee's personal computer was made for preservation and analysis. Also requested and received was a copy of the client's accounting software, in this case, QuickBooks Professional.

Since QuickBooks Professional has the audit log feature, it was used to extract the evidence needed. However, prior to viewing the audit logs in the company file (QuickBooks, like many small business packages, keeps a file for each company individually), an analysis of the hard drive was performed to make sure that previous copies of the company file were not present on the hard drive in other locations or that they hadn't been deleted to attempt to hide them from discovery.

Once it was determined that the company file present on the computer hard drive was the one in question based on the file system metadata, the company file was opened in the program and the audit log was reviewed.

The audit log completely supported the ex-employee's claim that he had received the new account after leaving the company and having been approached by the accounting client to contract with him for this service. The employee stated that he had gone back and manually entered historical transactions to bring the company file up to date, making the manual entries over a two-week period of work, after he had been contracted by the client.

This was simple to determine since the audit log keeps track of the transaction, the accounting date (the accounting date is the historical date for the transaction and is entered by the user), and the time stamp from the audit log. The time stamp in the audit log is entered automatically and cannot be changed by the user.

Further analysis to make sure that the dates and times on the computer had not been manipulated to distort the audit trail were performed to further authenticate the accuracy of the audit trail. The case was settled.

40.2 OLD BUSINESS—NEW BUSINESS CASE

In another case, the client suspected that the seller of the business (who immediately started a new business in the same line of work) was using the information from the business he sold to take employees and accounts away from the client's business.

In this case, the software being used was Peachtree Complete. Since Peachtree Complete also has the audit tracking feature, after getting forensic copies of the defendant's computers, the company file for the seller's current business was opened and reviewed.

The audit log contained entries showing the date and times when information from the business sold to the client was imported into the seller's company file. This was in direct contradiction to the seller's claims that he had not used any information from the business sold to the client.

40.6 BATCH FILES AS EVIDENCE

The good news about older accounting software that does not support audit trails, single-file databases, or some other features of more modern accounting software is that they typically keep batch files.

Much like its paper equivalents, accounting software may not permanently commit transactions to the general journal and various account buckets until the transactions are "posted." This allows bookkeepers and accountants to run a "trial balance" to make sure that everything is correct, prior to committing the transactions to the ledgers. Posting usually occurs at the end of an account day or at the end of an accounting period.

Depending on how the accounting software is constructed from a database standpoint, the batch files may be an internal table in the database, or stored on the hard drive as individual files.

One reason batch files can be important is that they contain transactions of what was to be posted to the permanent accounting ledgers. In a case where you have older software that does not have an audit trail, such as some vertical market accounting packages, the system may still have all of the batch files for the system going back to the very first time the business "posted" any transactions.

Even if you cannot read the batch files, they can provide a record of when the accounting system first went into use by the company, and the last time the user posted their transactions. This can be important when you are faced with a case where a company claims to have started using the software after a certain date of interest or they claim that they stopped using the software after a certain date of interest.

40.7 OTHER SOURCES OF FINANCIAL EVIDENCE

While accounting, personal money management, and financial systems all yield evidence in various forms, they are not all-inclusive when it comes to looking for evidence. Other forms of evidence that can be of interest in a case can be located in the Internet cache on the computer hard drive. This kind of evidence can contain bank transactions, purchases, payments, phone bills, money transfers, statements of money market accounts, and virtually anything you can do online to manage money.

Other items that can contain financial evidence are backup tapes, old floppy disks, USB sticks, online-only accounting systems, cell phones, and e-mail.

Finally, document types come into play as well. Electronic spreadsheets are an obvious choice for potential evidence. However, PDF documents, word processing documents, tax software data files, HTML files (web pages), and spreadsheets, stored on the hard drive, are all sources of evidence for cases.

There are a lot of software applications out in the marketplace for different purposes relating to money management, check writing, invoicing, and so forth. These types of programs can also produce data that can be recovered and used as evidence. Some of these programs are used only to write and print checks, to create invoices, to produce mailing and shipping labels, or other single-purpose uses.

40.3 A MURDER CASE

In a case where the client was accused of first-degree murder and was facing life imprisonment, his computer hard drives were sent in for analysis. The client along with another person was accused of plotting to kill the victim in this case. The client claimed that he never planned to kill the victim, but was only scamming him for money and that the evidence of the scam was on his personal computer in the program Versa Check.

When the police examined the computer, they were unable to locate any evidence of the Versa Check program. However, when the computer was examined by the defense expert, he found the Versa Check database. Based on his testing, the defense expert was able to determine that that version of Versa Check used the same database file as a Microsoft Access database. When he opened the database in Microsoft Access, he was able to produce all of the checks written by the defendant. The Versa Check evidence led to a plea bargain where the client pled to over one hundred counts of check fraud. The murder charge against the client was dropped.

SUMMARY

In this chapter we discussed accounting and financial software along with the various issues associated with them. We also looked at how the software works from the standpoint of evidence creation that can be recovered and analyzed in cases.

From single file–based systems to older vertical market applications using multiple file database storage, accounting and financial systems can be a challenge for an examiner.

We also looked at several cases where different kinds of evidence played a part in the case, both civil and criminal.

Multiplayer Online Games 41

INFORMATION IN THIS CHAPTER:

* The culture of Massively Multiplayer Online Role Playing Games (MMORPGs)
* MMORPG data as evidence

INTRODUCTION

Online multiplayer gaming started way back in the mid-1970s when people played games called Multi User Dungeons (MUDs) on the Advanced Research Projects Agency Network (ARPANET). The ARPANET was the first packet-switched network, which would eventually become what we know today as the Internet.

Online gaming today is now the most popular form of gaming in the world. With the advent of high-speed Internet, it became possible for online gaming to take off as a genre, and today tens of millions of people play games such as World of Warcraft, Everquest 2, The Sims Online, and Second Life. Console gaming units like the Xbox and PlayStation platforms now have online capability so that people can play together online. Where games like this exist, evidence also exists. These programs, especially Massively Multiplayer Online Role Playing Games (MMORPGs) such as World of Warcraft, store a significant amount of data that can be useful as evidence.

The first half of this chapter will introduce you to the world of online games, including the culture and the people who play. The second half will focus on the type of evidence these games create.

41.1 THE CULTURE OF MASSIVELY MULTIPLAYER ONLINE ROLE PLAYING GAMES (MMORPGS)

To understand MMORPG evidence, it is important to have a grasp of who plays these types of games and something about the strategies that game companies use to keep people playing over the long term.

The common stereotype of a MMORPG player is the jobless Mountain Dew–gulping nerd, living in his parent's basement with no aspirations for the future other than leveling up his Dark Elf Shadow Knight. While people do exist who meet this stereotype, they are the exception and not the rule. People from all walks of life play these games, from your most successful business people and professionals to housewives and retirees. In 2010, the average age of a game player was 34 years old, and the gender demographics report that the players were 60 percent male, and 40 percent female.[1]

In these virtual worlds, real friendships are developed. It is not uncommon for people to meet online in these games, get to know one another, move across the country to live together in romantic relationships, or to even get married. In a survey of 30,000 participants, it was reported that:

> *5.1% of men and 15.7% of women had physically dated someone who they first met in an MMORPG. Across these three sets of findings, a substantial portion of users across a broad age range have had meaningful social relationships in these virtual environments. What these three sets of findings make clear is that many users across all age ranges form meaningful relationships in MMORPGs.[2]*

This may seem odd to someone unfamiliar with MMORPGs, but when you see the structure of the communities developed in these games, and the amount of time people put into developing their characters and the relationships they have within these virtual worlds, it is not surprising.

> *Respondents were also asked to compare the quality of their MMORPG friendships with their real-life friendships. 39.4% of men and 53.3% of women felt that their MMORPG friends were comparable or better than their real-life friends.*

Almost all MMORPGs charge a monthly subscription to play. Because of this, it is in their best interest to keep people playing. The leveling up of your character, the quests, and the slaying of boss monsters is all developed to be as much of a time-sink as possible. In 2006, people spent on average 22.72 hours a week playing their MMORPG.[3] A significant number of MMORPG players spent even more time than this in the virtual world, regardless of age, career, family, or social commitments.

> *The distribution showed that about 8% of users spend 40 hours per week or more in these environments – the equivalent of a normal work week. The significant amount of time that users are willing to invest in these environments is further highlighted by the finding that 60.9% of respondents had spent at least 10 hours continuously in an MMORPG.[4]*

The prevalence of possible evidence coming from MMORPGs and gaming devices is likely to increase with time. In 2010, it was reported that 67 percent of American households were playing computer or video games.[5]

The most well-known MMORPG is World of Warcraft, and with good reason. As of October 2010, World of Warcraft reported having over 12 million subscribers.[6] With a user base reaching in the millions for only one of the many MMORPGs available today, it is no surprise that the data they create has become a potential source of evidence, and is appearing in cases with more and more frequency. The best way to illustrate this is to let the news stories speak for themselves:

A Houston mom is accused of luring a then 15-year-old Canadian boy into a sexual relationship after "meeting" him through the online game World of Warcraft, according to a report from Fox. Lauri Price, 42, apparently thought this through. She decided she'd fly to Canada to have relations with the boy when he turned 16 — as a way to sidestep U.S. statutory rape laws. (In Canada, the age of consent is 16.)[7]

A South Korean couple whose three-month-old daughter died of malnutrition while they were raising a virtual child in an online game pleaded guilty to negligent homicide on Friday.[8]

A Portland woman who met a 14-year-old Tennessee boy while playing the online game "World of Warcraft" is accused of engaging him in sexual chats and trading explicit photos.[9]

PORTLAND, Ore. – The Multnomah County Sheriff's Office has launched an investigation into allegations that a local corrections deputy bragged about using a Taser gun on people in an Internet chat room.

Lt. Jason Gates of the Multnomah County Sheriff's Office said he is appalled at the alleged online comments of the county corrections officer.

According to Gates, Thompson used a county work computer to play the online video game "City of Heroes" while on the job and then boasted about the joy he gets hurting people in jail in the chat room.

Budnick said that according to Trafalgar's [Thompson's] online chat, the deputy has posted more than 1,700 messages on the "City of Heroes" Web site since January. At one point, he allegedly posted 64 messages in 24 hours.[10]

On January 16, 2009, 29-year-old Andrew Warner's son, Brendin, died at his Kingsland home... He admitted that he had seen a pillow sitting on top of his son's head and didn't take the time to remove it. He also admitted that he'd heard the boy crying, but didn't turn away from World of Warcraft *until he had to go to the bathroom. On top of that, it turned out that records showed the man had been playing the game for much longer than he had told investigators.[11]*

Prosecutors in Canada hope to have two teens sentenced as adults after they admitted to planning the brutal rape and murder of 18-year-old Kimberly Proctor, and bragged about it on World of Warcraft, a sometimes violent online role-playing game. Some experts believe the killers' involvement with World of Warcraft, which has 12 million subscribers worldwide, may have been a contributing factor in the crime, and say the game provided key information to police, according to CTV. CTV reports that the teens planned the killing online, using code words to "initiate the attack, maps of where to dispose her body and what kind of fuel to buy to burn her body."[12]

Authorities said a 54-year-old Boston-area man traveled to Michigan to have sex with a 13-year-old girl who was his bride in an online role-playing game... Napoleon said the two had sex in Phillips' van, at a motel, and at the girl's home. Napoleon said Phillips met the girl online last year while playing RuneScape. Napoleon said the characters the pair assumed were married as part of the game, and Phillips gave the girl presents, including a cell phone, so that she could text him.[13]

41.2 MMORPG DATA AS EVIDENCE

Multiplayer games can potentially provide four types of evidence that could be used in a case:

1. Timeline
2. Content
3. General location
4. Game subscriber information

We will look at where to get each of these types of evidence and how to validate them as needed.

41.2.1 Timeline evidence

Multiplayer games can provide timeline evidence from two primary sources, client-side evidence and server-side evidence. Timeline evidence is both in the form of when someone was playing one of these games, but in some cases, equally important is how much a person was playing. In the following sections we will show how it can be determined when someone was playing and how much total time they spent online.

41.2.1.1 Client-side timeline evidence

Client-side timeline evidence is data that is collected and stored by the game on the local computer hard drive in various log files that the game stores without the player's knowledge. Client-side evidence can be located and analyzed by a computer forensic examiner.

Timeline evidence from these games can be used to establish when and how much someone has been connected to the game. However, to make sure that connection time is relevant and useful, analysis would need to be performed to make sure that you are looking at connection time and not just overall connection time. The reason for this is that these types of games do not typically have an auto-disconnection feature. In other words, you can log in to one of these games, leave for ten hours, and the log would reflect that you were connected to the game for that ten-hour period.

For this reason, reviewing the logs to ensure that some type of user activity is present throughout the course of those ten hours would be required to validate that a person was playing the game, rather than the game sitting there unattended.

In Fig. 41.1 you can see the overall timeline for play sessions. However, this will not give you any information as to whether or not the player was active at the keyboard.

In order to establish active connection time from historical logs stored on the user's computer, the examiner would need to locate the game logs that store not just the connection time, but also in-game activities such as chatting, fighting, crafting, and so forth, and view them in detail. These log files can become extremely large depending on the game and how the logging is done by either the game software or a third-party logging software.

Figure 41.2 is a screenshot of a player log from Everquest 2. The key words in the screenshot that indicate player activity are the words "you" and "your." These indicate

```
4/13 22:19:18.490  Login program=WoW platform=Win locale=enUS
4/13 22:19:18.526  Component WoW.Win.13623
4/13 22:19:18.545  Component WoW.base.13623
4/13 22:19:18.566  Component WoW.enUS.13623
4/13 22:19:18.587  Component Tool.Win.2210
4/13 22:19:18.662  GRUNT: state: LOGIN_STATE_CONNECTING result: LOGIN_OK
4/13 22:19:18.722  Connecting to 12.129.206.130:1119
4/13 22:19:19.350  GRUNT: state: LOGIN_STATE_AUTHENTICATED result: LOGIN_OK
4/13 22:19:20.403  ClientConnection Initiating: COP_CONNECT code=CSTATUS_CONNECTING
4/13 22:19:20.450  GRUNT: state: RESPONSE_CONNECTED result: LOGIN_OK
4/13 22:19:20.850  ClientConnection Completed: COP_CONNECT code=RESPONSE_CONNECTED result=TRUE
4/13 22:19:20.875  ClientConnection Initiating: COP_AUTHENTICATE code=CSTATUS_AUTHENTICATING
4/13 22:19:21.134  ClientConnection Completed: COP_AUTHENTICATE code=AUTH_OK result=TRUE
4/13 22:19:21.618  ClientConnection Initiating: COP_GET_CHARACTERS code=43
4/13 22:19:21.914  ClientConnection Completed: COP_GET_CHARACTERS code=44 result=TRUE
4/13 22:19:44.203  ClientConnection Initiating: COP_LOGIN_CHARACTER code=76
4/13 22:19:45.557  ClientConnection Completed: COP_LOGIN_CHARACTER code=77 result=TRUE
4/14 00:44:49.593  ClientConnection Completed: COP_LOGIN_CHARACTER code=77 result=TRUE
4/14 00:44:52.063  ClientConnection Completed: COP_LOGIN_CHARACTER code=77 result=TRUE
4/14 01:21:16.844  ClientConnection Completed: COP_LOGIN_CHARACTER code=77 result=TRUE
4/14 01:21:21.664  ClientConnection Completed: COP_LOGIN_CHARACTER code=77 result=TRUE
4/14 01:23:41.791  ClientConnection Completed: COP_LOGIN_CHARACTER code=77 result=TRUE
4/14 01:23:43.741  ClientConnection Initiating: COP_GET_CHARACTERS code=43
4/14 01:23:44.057  ClientConnection Completed: COP_GET_CHARACTERS code=44 result=TRUE
4/14 01:23:48.482  Client initiated Disconnect from 82ce810c
4/14 01:23:48.518  GRUNT: state: LOGIN_STATE_DISCONNECTED result: LOGIN_OK
```

FIGURE 41.1

A connection log from World of Warcraft showing the connection and disconnection times for play sessions

```
(1293251960)[Fri Dec 24 23:39:20 2010] YOUR Insidious Whisper hits a Sa
(1293251961)[Fri Dec 24 23:39:21 2010] YOU hit a Sablevein crumbler for
(1293251962)[Fri Dec 24 23:39:22 2010] YOUR Painbringer hits a Sablevei
(1293251962)[Fri Dec 24 23:39:22 2010] a Sablevein crumbler hits YOU bu
(1293251963)[Fri Dec 24 23:39:23 2010] YOUR Insidious Whisper increase
threat.
(1293251963)[Fri Dec 24 23:39:23 2010] YOUR Insidious Whisper hits a Sa
(1293251963)[Fri Dec 24 23:39:23 2010] YOU try to slash a Sablevein crun
(1293251965)[Fri Dec 24 23:39:25 2010] YOUR Painbringer hits a Sablevei
(1293251965)[Fri Dec 24 23:39:25 2010] a Sablevein crumbler tries to cru
(1293251965)[Fri Dec 24 23:39:25 2010] YOU try to slash a Sablevein crun
(1293251966)[Fri Dec 24 23:39:26 2010] YOUR Insidious Whisper increase
threat.
(1293251966)[Fri Dec 24 23:39:26 2010] YOUR Insidious Whisper hits a Sa
(1293251967)[Fri Dec 24 23:39:27 2010] YOU try to slash a Sablevein crun
(1293251967)[Fri Dec 24 23:39:27 2010] a Sablevein crumbler tries to cru
(1293251968)[Fri Dec 24 23:39:28 2010] YOUR Painbringer hits a Sablevei
(1293251969)[Fri Dec 24 23:39:29 2010] YOU try to slash a Sablevein crun
(1293251969)[Fri Dec 24 23:39:29 2010] \aPC -1 Malfoey:MalfoeyVa tells L
leveling guild is now looking for new members.  Come grow with us in a frie
more information or invite.  Happy Holidays and Happy New Year!"
(1293251969)[Fri Dec 24 23:39:29 2010] You have unread mail in your ma
(1293251970)[Fri Dec 24 23:39:30 2010] a Sablevein crumbler hits YOU bu
(1293251971)[Fri Dec 24 23:39:31 2010] YOU try to slash a Sablevein crun
(1293251973)[Fri Dec 24 23:39:33 2010] a Sablevein crumbler tries to cru
(1293251973)[Fri Dec 24 23:39:33 2010] YOU hit a Sablevein crumbler for
(1293251973)[Fri Dec 24 23:39:33 2010] You have killed a Sablevein crum
(1293251973)[Fri Dec 24 23:39:33 2010] You gain experience!
(1293251973)[Fri Dec 24 23:39:33 2010] Too little too late... Your target is
(1293251975)[Fri Dec 24 23:39:35 2010] There is no eligible target for this
(1293251979)[Fri Dec 24 23:39:39 2010] YOUR Insidious Whisper increase
threat.
```

FIGURE 41.2

A log from Everquest 2 showing player activity at the keyboard

that the player is causing something to happen, in this case by fighting a monster called a Sablevein crumbler. When these kinds of entries are seen in the log, the player is at the keyboard and this can help to verify that the game was not logged in and left idle.

41.2.1.2 Server-side timeline evidence

Server-side evidence would have to be provided to you from the company that hosts the game. Server-side timeline evidence should be able to provide even more detail if the logs have been preserved by the game company. The reason the server-side log may contain more information about the player's activity is that the server-side logs are used to respond to customer service requests from players. In order for the game company's customer service department to handle such issues as lost-in-game items, connection issues, player disputes, harassment issues, and so on, they must be able to see more information than what is displayed on the screen to the player. However, how long this information may be preserved on the server side is going to be game company–dependent and could be only a few days to several months.

41.2.2 Content evidence

The second type of evidence that can be gathered from multiplayer games is content evidence. Content evidence is going to consist of chat logs. Multiplayer games are designed specifically to have people interact with each other via their avatars or in-game characters. A multiplayer game without the ability to chat with other players online would be an abysmal failure. Most multiplayer games have the ability for the user to turn the chat logging on or off.

[Mon Sep 06 19:15:18 2010]	\aPC -1 Cogito:Cogito\/a tells you, "lol"
[Mon Sep 06 19:15:31 2010]	\aPC -1 Cogito:Cogito\/a tells you, "that was like a 1 100
[Mon Sep 06 19:15:34 2010]	\aPC -1 Cogito:Cogito\/a tells you, "duel me again"
[Mon Sep 06 19:15:45 2010]	You tell Cogito, "all my temps are down now"
[Mon Sep 06 19:15:50 2010]	\aPC -1 Cogito:Cogito\/a tells you, "mine are too"
[Mon Sep 06 19:16:11 2010]	\aPC -1 Cogito:Cogito\/a tells you, "??"
[Mon Sep 06 19:16:18 2010]	You tell Cogito, "same thing insta kill"
[Mon Sep 06 19:16:22 2010]	\aPC -1 Cogito:Cogito\/a tells you, "that doesnt make any s
[Mon Sep 06 19:16:36 2010]	\aPC -1 Cogito:Cogito\/a tells you, "your mentored LOL"
[Mon Sep 06 19:16:42 2010]	You tell Cogito, "lol no wonder"
[Mon Sep 06 19:16:48 2010]	\aPC -1 Cogito:Cogito\/a tells you, "unmentor and duel me n
[Mon Sep 06 19:17:10 2010]	\aPC -1 Cogito:Cogito\/a tells you, "lol to funny"
[Mon Sep 06 19:18:06 2010]	You tell Cogito, "lol"

FIGURE 41.3

A log from Everquest 2

Figure 41.3 shows a chat log from the game Everquest 2 showing a player-to-player conversation between the user at the keyboard and a player character named Cogito.

In Fig. 41.3 you can see a conversation between two players. Note that the player character name is only shown for the player the user is talking to and not for the user at the keyboard. The conversation in Fig. 41.3 has been parsed using a database program to exclude everything else in the log. In Fig. 41.3 you can also see the date and time stamp of the conversation, so you are getting both timeline and content evidence.

41.2.3 General location evidence

General location evidence can be obtained from the gaming company, provided they record the Internet Protocol (IP) address of the computer's Internet connection for each session. If you can get this information, an examiner can perform a *whois* lookup to determine who owns the IP address and where the IP address is located. With the IP address and the owner information gained from the *whois* lookup, you can then subpoena the Internet service provider for the subscriber information to get the actual physical address of the IP connection along with the name of the person who is financially responsible for the Internet access account.

41.2.4 Game subscriber information

The last piece of evidence these games can provide is the game subscriber information from the gaming company. The game subscriber account information can yield the real name, billing address for the payment method, the e-mail address for the account, and telephone contact numbers.

If you are performing an investigation into the activities of the person outside of the game, the e-mail address, phone numbers, and credit card information can potentially provide additional leads of value.

41.2.5 Getting server-side evidence

Server-side evidence is discussed in Chapter 23.

SUMMARY

In this chapter we discussed in some detail the world of multiplayer online games. We covered the culture of MMORPGs and who plays them, and also looked at a number of cases that have been in the news that have involved people who play these games. We also looked at the types of evidence these types of games can yield for the purpose of legal actions including timeline evidence, content evidence, subscriber information, and general location evidence.

References

[1] Entertainment Software Association, *Essential facts about the computer and video game industry.* <http://www.theESA.com>, 2010.

[2] NY. Yee, The demographics, motivations, and derived experiences of users of massively multi-user online graphical environments. Presence: *Teleoperators and Virtual Environments*. Retrieved from <http://www.mitpressjournals.org/doi/abs/10.1162/pres.15.3.309?journalCode=presdoi:10.1162>, 15(3), 2006.

[3] N. Yee, The Psychology of MMORPGs: Emotional Investment, Motivations, Relationship Formation, and Problematic Usage, in: R. Schroeder, A. Axelsson, (Eds.), Avatars at Work and Play: Collaboration and Interaction in Shared Virtual Environments, Springer-Verlag, London, 2006, pp. 187–207.

[4] N. Yee, The Psychology of MMORPGs: Emotional Investment, Motivations, Relationship Formation, and Problematic Usage, in: R. Schroeder, A. Axelsson, (Eds.), Avatars at Work and Play: Collaboration and Interaction in Shared Virtual Environments, Springer-Verlag, London, 2006, pp. 187–207.

[5] Entertainment Software Association, Essential facts about the computer and video game industry. <http://www.theESA.com>, 2010.

[6] "World of Warcraft® Subscriber Base Reaches 12 Million Worldwide." *Blizzard Entertainment.* <http://us.blizzard.com/en-us/company/press/pressreleases.html?101007>, 2010.

[7] "Houston Mom Accused of Luring Teen for Sex through Online Game: Moms at Work." Orlando Sentinel Blogs, *OrlandoSentinel.com.* 2010.

[8] A. Salmon, "Couple: Internet Gaming Addiction Led to Baby's Death." CNN.com International Edition. <http://www.cnn.com/2010/WORLD/asiapcf/04/01/korea.parents.starved.baby/index.html>, 15 May 2010.

[9] "Portland Woman Accused of 'World of Warcraft' Chat with Boy That Turned Sexual." *Oregon Local News*, OregonLive.com. <www.oregonlive.com/portland/index.ssf/2010/03/portland_woman_accused_of_worl.html/>, 15 May 2010.

[10] "Officer Accused of Bragging Online About Using Taser Gun." Portland News, KPTV FOX 12 News. <http://www.kptv.com/news/14065232/detail.html>, 15 May 2010.

[11] M. Thompson, "Man Let Son Suffocate Because He Was Playing WoW." The Escapist. <http://www.escapistmagazine.com/news/view/108907-Man-Let-Son-Suffocate-Because-He-Was-Playing-WoW>.

[12] "World of Warcraft" Played Role in Teens' Rape, Murder of Canadian Girl Kimberly Proctor, Experts Say." CBS News. <http://www.cbsnews.com/8301-504083_162-20021194-504083.html>.

[13] "Police: Man Had Sex with 13-Year-Old 'Bride.'" TheBostonChannel.com. <http://www.thebostonchannel.com/r/26793686/detail.html>.

Global Positioning Systems

42

INFORMATION IN THIS CHAPTER:

- An overview of global positioning systems
- An overview of the NAVSTAR Global Positioning System
- How GPS works
- Types of GPS evidence
- Collection of evidence from GPS devices
- Interpretation of GPS evidence

INTRODUCTION

Global positioning systems, or GPS units, have become commonplace in modern society. As is true with any device that can record and store data, these devices can become a source of evidence in civil and criminal cases. In using GPS data as evidence, it is important to understand what impacts the accuracy of the data these devices produce as well as the potential for errors in analyzing the data. The first part of this chapter provides some background on how global positioning systems work, and how what they store can become evidence in a case.

42.1 AN OVERVIEW OF GLOBAL POSITIONING SYSTEMS

While global positioning is best known for its use in navigation, it is also used to pinpoint and record precise locations in land surveying, and the GPS system is also used for time and frequency purposes in telecommunication systems because of its extremely accurate onboard clocks located in the satellites themselves. "GPS satellites have very precise clocks that tell time to within 40 nanoseconds or 40 billionths (0.000000040) of a second."[1]

GPS capability shows up in some unexpected places, and there are devices and programs that can perform GPS functionality without being a dedicated GPS unit. Companies use GPS devices to track their trucks and the employees driving them, and GPS units are in many rental cars both for navigation and for recovery of lost and stolen vehicles. The social media website Twitter can track your location, and applications for phones, such as Facebook Places, can send updates to your networking sites with information about where you are at the moment. Using your smart phone, you can also tag other's locations for posting to Facebook.[2]

42.2 AN OVERVIEW OF THE NAVSTAR GLOBAL POSITIONING SYSTEM

The Navigation Signal Timing and Ranging Global Positioning System, (NAVSTAR)[3] as it is known in the United States, is jointly operated by the Department of Defense and the United States Air Force.

The system consists of 31 satellites in geosynchronous orbit around the earth. This arrangement ensures that a minimum of 24 satellites are operational at all times, with seven satellites available as spares. The satellites are arranged around the globe in such a way that a minimum of four satellites are always visible from any point on earth. Each of the satellites continuously transmits data toward the earth that can be received and processed by GPS devices.

The purpose of the global positioning system is to provide Position, Navigation, and Timing (PNT) services worldwide.

- Positioning: The ability to accurately determine one's location and orientation two-dimensionally (latitude and longitude), or three-dimensionally (latitude, longitude, and altitude) as required.
- Navigation: The ability to determine current and desired position to apply corrections to course, orientation, and speed to attain a desired position anywhere in the world.
- Timing: The ability to acquire and maintain accurate and precise time from a standard coordinated universal time, anywhere in the world.

The GPS system consists of three parts or segments that can be broken down into the space segment, the ground segment, and the user segment.

- Space Segment: The space segment is the part of the system that is made up of the GPS satellites that are in geosynchronous orbit around the earth.
- Ground Segment: The ground segment is the part of the system that has the master control station operated by the Air Force, and both ground antennas and monitoring stations. The master control station is where the Air Force manages the satellite system. The ground antennas collect telemetry information from the satellites and also send commands and data up to the satellites for accuracy corrections.
- User Segment: The user segment consists of the devices that actually receive and use the data provided by the GPS satellites to perform navigation, such as handheld, marine, aviation, and automotive units.

Figure 42.1 shows the GPS system and its various segments.

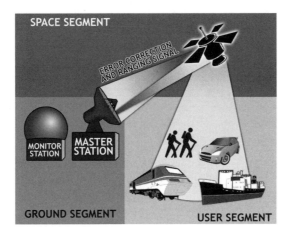

FIGURE 42.1

The three segments of the GPS system

42.3 HOW GPS WORKS

Each satellite in the system transmits navigation data toward the earth that contains the position of the satellite, a time stamp, and the health of the satellite. When a GPS device can receive signals from at least three satellites at once, the device can calculate its position in two dimensions, latitude and longitude. This process is called triangulation, and is illustrated in Fig. 42.2.

In order for a GPS device to calculate its position vertically for altitude, it must be able to receive signals from at least four satellites at the same time. This process is called trilateration, and it's illustrated in Fig. 42.3.

42.3.1 How geolocation works using GPS

In order for a GPS device to calculate its position, it needs to know the position of each of the satellites, the time it took for the signal to reach the device, and whether the satellite is healthy. Since the satellite signal travels at a known speed, the data provides enough information for the device to perform the calculations.

The data contained in the satellite signal is used by the GPS device to perform calculations not only for position, but also for direction (orientation) and speed. Bear in mind that direction and speed are derived values based on how the device is programmed to perform the calculations. Since device software is proprietary, the exact method and accuracy of the derived calculations can vary by manufacturer and model.

FIGURE 42.2

Triangulation can only locate an object in two dimensions

FIGURE 42.3

Trilateration can locate an object in three dimensions

42.4 TYPES OF GPS EVIDENCE

The most basic type of GPS evidence is made up of track points, track logs, way-points, and routes. This is data that can be saved to the device, depending on its make and model. When a device is on, it will periodically write the current location of the device in a log of track points. When a person is planning a trip or wants to return to a location, they can tell the device to record a waypoint.

42.4.1 Waypoints and routes

When you're using a GPS unit, the process of inputting an address and selecting it as your travel destination creates what is called a waypoint. With GPS units, it is possible to include multiple waypoints in one trip. For instance, if you were traveling across a state, but wanted to visit a park along the way, and then have lunch further down the road, the GPS unit allows you to include all of these waypoints and save them as a route. This set of waypoints makes up a route, exactly in the same way you might take a paper map and make notes of the places you want to visit along your route to a destination. And in the same way that you might decide not to stop at any of your planned waypoints on a paper map, the presence of a waypoint in the history of a GPS device is not an indication that the waypoint was ever visited.

The presence of a waypoint could show that the user intended to visit the location at some point in the future or that the user intended to return to the waypoint in the future.

In some cases, it may be possible to determine that someone was at a place where a waypoint was recorded, depending on how the waypoint itself was entered into the device. For instance, if a waypoint is set as a favorite using a feature that records the user's current location, then it could be possible to place them at that location.

For instance, if the user of the device sets a waypoint by selecting their current location, it is possible that the device will set the location along with the date and time the waypoint was set.

On the other hand, manually entering the latitude and longitude for a waypoint may not show a date and time. Whether or not the device has the ability to record waypoints is once again dependent on the device itself.

In automotive GPS units it is very common for someone to set a waypoint for their home, office, and other favorite destinations. While not definitive, this information can also present evidence about a user's habits, what they may have been searching for, and their recent destinations.

42.4.2 Track points and track logs

A track point is the record of a location that is recorded by the device. A series of track points is saved in a track log. Unlike waypoints, track points are recorded automatically by the device without user interaction, provided that the device supports the recording of track points. In some devices, the user can determine whether or not the device keeps any history of track points.

Also, some devices, such as certain marine units, by default do not record track points unless the function is turned on by the user.

Tracks logs are the most common type of evidence that can be obtained from a GPS device and are normally the most important. This is because the track log can give indication of a timeline as well as the locations visited by the GPS device. Note the distinction of "visited by the GPS device," since it is not possible to connect a particular person to the device from any evidence contained within the device itself. To do so would require a larger body of evidence linking a particular person to a vehicle or GPS unit, for instance.

If you have a good track log obtained from a GPS device, the locations and the dates and times can be an indication of where the GPS was and how long it remained in that particular location.

42.4.3 **Other GPS device evidence**

While the most basic GPS units only record waypoints and track points, GPS-enabled cellular phones and connected GPS units can contain a great deal more data that may be of evidentiary value.

A connected GPS unit is one that has a cellular radio built into the unit. Some examples of this are the navigation systems currently available in many vehicles that use the On-Star or Microsoft Sync systems. These units have the ability to make phone calls, receive real-time traffic alerts, search for local shopping deals, find movie times, and other functions. Since many of these units will also allow Bluetooth connections to smart phones, they can contain phone call logs and contact lists. And depending on the phone and unit, they can even receive text messages.

42.5 **COLLECTION OF EVIDENCE FROM GPS DEVICES**

The proper handling of GPS devices is a critical step to prevent the loss of potential evidence that may be present on the device. GPS devices are very similar to cellular phones in certain aspects: GPS devices are radios. Not all GPS devices can be examined using forensic software tools, and allowing data to be added to the device will destroy other data.

For these reasons, GPS devices should be handled with care to prevent any possible communication of the device and any accidental destruction of data through mishandling.

42.5.1 **Preservation of GPS data**

GPS units are radios that receive data from radio signals transmitted by GPS satellites. This means that in order to properly handle a GPS unit for evidence collection, the unit should be handled in a windowless room and inside a Faraday bag that will block any radio signals from reaching the unit. This is especially important in the case of units that have the Assisted GPS (AGPS) feature. The AGPS system allows the unit to receive information from the cellular phone system to help it more accurately determine its location in areas where a clear view of the sky is a problem.

42.5.2 **Challenges to data collection**

GPS devices are much like cell phones today. They have a wide variety of connection types, operating systems, and data storage methods and data structures.

This means that getting data from these units for preservation and analysis may require using several different forensic software tools. Forensic software tools that can collect data from cell phones in many cases can also collect data from GPS units. There is also software designed only for collecting data from GPS units. The forensic software available is covered in Chapter 5.

And in the case of in-dash vehicle navigation systems, at least for the present time, there is no simple way to retrieve data from them. In other words, the only method for collecting evidentiary data from some of the units would be the same as the manual examination of a cell phone (see Chapter 37). A video record would need to be made for preservation purposes as the unit was operated from the menu by an examiner. As with any device where a manual examination is performed, without a video recording of the entire examination, it would be difficult, if possible at all, to determine whether or not any data was deleted or created on the device in the process of the examination.

42.5.3 **Service-based data collection**

In addition to device-based GPS evidence, many companies used a service-based GPS collection process in which a GPS unit is located in a rental car and the data is collected by a service provider, and the location of the unit can be viewed on a map via the Internet. Also, in the case of a third-party provider for the GPS tracking, the user may have the ability to download the GPS records to his or her computer.

42.1 A DEATH PENALTY CASE EXAMPLE

In a death penalty case, one of the primary evidence items was the GPS records collected from a computer at a small rental car company for a car that was rented by the defendant. The records had been collected by law enforcement officers from the computer at the rental business in the form of printouts of HTML pages since the original electronic data was not preserved.

Upon review of the GPS records, numerous problems were noted regarding the GPS data contained in the records. There were instances where the GPS location would mysteriously jump from one location to another with no time difference, as if the vehicle had teleported from one spot to another, placing it conveniently in the area that the prosecution needed for the vehicle to be to support the case against the defendant. The defense attorney challenged the authenticity of the records. Since the computer from the rental company was no longer available and the hard drive had never been copied during the initial investigation, there was no way to authenticate the records. The client was allowed to plea to a minor felony and received credit for time served awaiting trial.

42.6 INTERPRETATION OF GPS EVIDENCE

Proper interpretation of GPS evidence is a critical step to make sure that the evidence is presented as correctly as possible. GPS units are not infallible, and errors in the data and in the interpretation can creep in, in subtle ways.

42.6.1 Data errors

GPS devices are radio receivers just like cell phones. And as such, they are subject to errors in reception due to multipath errors (radio signals bouncing off buildings) and data noise. While most units can and will correct this, the amount of correction is impossible to determine.

Additionally, data in GPS units can be either deliberately or accidentally deleted by persons attempting to retrieve data from the device, and through poor preservation practices.

Finally, data can be saved to a device in the form of a track point that is completely inaccurate due to the unit not having a view of enough satellites.

A good example of how GPS units can become confused is when you are driving in your car and pull into a parking garage. The GPS unit will continue to attempt to assist you with navigation, even though it no longer is receiving adequate signals from satellites. This is because some GPS units will operate by using historical data to "fill in" areas where satellite signal may be temporarily lost. The GPS unit will also attempt to make predictions based on loaded map data.

An illustration of this behavior is found in the parking garage example. You are in the parking garage and you start up your GPS. The GPS unit will alert you that you are not receiving satellite data and ask if you want to calculate your new route based on your last position. You input a new destination and the GPS starts attempting to assist you in navigating. However, you notice that the GPS unit keeps telling you to turn in the wrong direction and at the wrong place. This is because the unit is basically guessing based on its internal compass, the most recent historical data, and the map data in the unit. The longer you spend outside the view of satellites, the more inaccurate this data becomes.

When GPS devices are mounted on vehicles for the purpose of remote collection, that is, via a service that receives the GPS information from the remote units, the possibility of data errors is also present. This is because the remote unit may transmit to the service information that is inaccurate at the time, or the data may be corrupted by signal problems or noise and introducing inaccuracies during transmission.

42.6.2 Map errors

GPS satellites do not have any knowledge of anything on the ground. They do not contain map data or any other information except for what they "know" about themselves and the other satellites in the constellation.

Think of satellites like lighthouses. They are in a fixed location that they send to your GPS receiver. The receiver performs the calculations to determine your position and determines the raw coordinates for your current location.

For most people these raw coordinates don't mean anything in a human sense. If you wanted to figure out where you were in a way that you could actually use, you could take those raw coordinates and plot them on a map.

Modern GPS units provide that map plotting function for the user. However, what happens when you see a location on a map on the GPS unit and yet you know it isn't correct? Is the GPS unit wrong or is the map wrong?

And yet it is common in automotive GPS units for exactly this problem to occur. The map display does not match the actual road system due to new construction or traffic configuration changes that have occurred since the last map update.

Another issue in interpreting GPS data is using online maps for plotting purposes. Each of the major mapping services such as Google Maps, Bing Maps, and Yahoo Maps all collect and maintain their data individually.

When you are plotting a GPS coordinate on one of these maps and then look at the map in satellite or earth view, you can see the actual buildings and terrain. However, if you plot exactly the same coordinate using two of the mapping servers, there is a chance that the buildings and terrain will not match.

While Larry was in GPS certification training, one exercise he had to perform was to determine where a coordinate was and what the implications might be of a cluster of GPS track points. By viewing the coordinates in both Google Maps and Bing Maps, an interesting anomaly presented itself. In Google Maps the location showed a parking garage. However, in Bing Maps the location showed an empty lot where the parking garage should be. The Google map in Fig. 42.4 shows the presence of the parking garage. The Bing map in Fig. 42.5 shows an empty lot.

GOOGLE MAPS

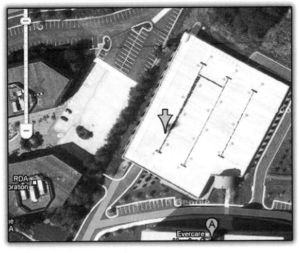

FIGURE 42.4

Google Maps view of a coordinate location showing the presence of a parking deck

BING MAPS

FIGURE 42.5

Bing Maps view of the same coordinate location showing an empty construction site where the parking deck should be

This underscores the importance of making sure that the map data being used is accurate for the date and time of any GPS track points that are being analyzed and presented as evidence in a case.

SUMMARY

In this chapter we learned about the global positioning system operated by the United States, and what makes up the global positioning system. We also looked at how GPS devices work in the system to provide geolocation information and navigation. Also discussed were the types of evidence that a GPS device can have, what impacts the accuracy of that data, and also some of the issues with interpreting GPS data. The importance of correct map data was illustrated using map images from the same location on the same date from two sources that differed significantly.

References

[1] NOAA National Ocean Service Education, Geodesy: Do you know where you are? The Global Positioning System. *NOAA National Ocean Service.* <http://oceanservice.noaa.gov/education/kits/geodesy/geo09_gps.html>, (n.d.) (accessed 11.05.07).

[2] P. Miller, How To Use Facebook Places. *Reviews and News on Tech Products, Software and Downloads | PCWorld.* <http://www.pcworld.com/article/203819/how_to_use_facebook_places.html>, 20 Aug 2010 (accessed 11.05.07).

[3] Andrews Space and Technology, NAVSTAR GPS – Summary. *Space and Tech.* <http://www.spaceandtech.com/spacedata/constellations/navstar-gps_consum.shtml> (n.d.). (accessed 11.05.07).

Index